"*The Definitive Drucker* brought back fond memories of
long discussions with Peter Drucker and my partners in the founding
of a new 'knowledge-based' Wall Street security firm in the
early 1960s. Peter's Delphi-like pronouncements were not always easy
to decipher. His insights were brilliant, an early glimpse as to how
Drucker became the single most influential observer of business in
the 20th century. Edersheim refreshes and updates Drucker's wisdom
through the lens of her own contemporary experience as a consultant,
a combination that is both exciting and provocative."

Richard Jenrette
Co-founder
Donaldson, Lufkin & Jenrette, Inc.

"One of the things that Drucker did very, very well was forcing
you to think, think away from traditional lines of thought.
This book forces the reader to think with Drucker's ideas today."

Dan Lufkin
Co-founder
Donaldson, Lufkin & Jenrette, Inc.

"A very accessible book on the thoughts and practices of the
greatest of all management gurus. It demonstrates, with its
numerous contemporary illustrations from around the world,
how Drucker's wisdom transcends geography as well as time."

Nikhil Prassad Ojha,
Director
The Monitor Group, Mumbai Office

"If you want the essence of Peter Drucker's thinking,
this book provides it in a superb way."

Hermann Simon
Chairman
Simon, Kucher & Partners

"A most impressive book full of practical advice.
We are most grateful to Edersheim."

Atsuo Ueda
author of "Introduction to Peter F. Drucker" (in Japanese),
representative of Drucker Workshop (Japan),
and Emeritus Professor of Institute of Technologists

THE
DEFINITIVE
DRUCKER

THE
DEFINITIVE
DRUCKER

ELIZABETH HAAS EDERSHEIM

McGraw-Hill

New York   Chicago   San Francisco   Lisbon   London   Madrid   Mexico City
Milan   New Delhi   San Juan   Seoul   Singapore   Sydney   Toronto

1 2 3 4 5 6 7 8 9 0   DOC/DOC   0 9 8 7 6

ISBN 10: 0-07-147233-9
ISBN 13: 978-0-07-147233-3

McGraw-Hill books are available at special quantity discounts to use as premiums and sales promotions, or for use in corporate training programs. For more information, please write to the Director of Special Sales, Professional Publishing, McGraw-Hill, Two Penn Plaza, New York, NY 10121-2298. Or contact your local bookstore.

Library of Congress Cataloging-in-Publication Data

Edersheim, Elizabeth Haas.
  The definitive Drucker / by Elizabeth Haas Edersheim.
      p. cm.
  Includes bibliographical references.
  ISBN 0-07-147233-9 (alk. paper)
1. Management. 2. Leadership. 3. Drucker, Peter F. (Peter Ferdinand), 1909-2005.
I. Drucker, Peter F. (Peter Ferdinand), 1909-2005. II. Title.
HD31.E356 2007
658—dc22
                        2006028011

This book is printed on acid free paper.

This book is dedicated to
Doris Drucker
and
Steven Gallen Edersheim

CONTENTS

FOREWORD

I did not realize it at the time, but I grew up with Peter Drucker. My father spent 25 years in management at GE, and another decade at Chase Manhattan. He met Peter at GE's Crotonville facility in the 1950s and always had Drucker's books on his bookshelf. Though I had no interest in business as a high school or undergraduate student, I flipped through my father's books—Drucker classics such as *The Effective Executive* and *The Practice of Management*. Later, when I was in the U.S. Navy, I grew more interested in business while running service and retail operations at a U.S. airbase in Japan, and returned to those and other classics. Slowly but surely, I was becoming a Drucker student.

Regrettably, I did not take the initiative to meet Peter until 1999. P&G was in the midst of major strategic change and arguably the biggest organizational transformation in its 162-year history. I was then responsible for P&G's North America region, the big home market, and for P&G's new global beauty business. I called Peter and asked if he would meet with me. He agreed, and four decades after he and my father had talked at Crotonville, I sat with Peter in his modest Claremont, California, home, talking about a world he had been thinking about for nearly a half-century.

I had hoped for one hour of his time. We talked for two. Then when my wife, Margaret, arrived to pick me up, she came in and we all sat and talked for another two hours. It was like drinking from a fire hose. For every question I posed, Peter had one or two more things to think about. Persistently, he urged me to choose, to focus on the few right strategies and decisions that would make the greatest difference. He challenged me to understand the unique leadership challenges of managing an organization of knowledge workers.

That exhilarating first conversation provided the themes Peter and I returned to for the next six years: how to unleash the creativity and productivity of knowledge workers; how to create free markets for ideas and innovation inside and outside a company such as P&G; how to build the organizational agility and flexibility to respond to and lead change. Later, we began a conversation about another subject on which he was focused in the last years of his life: the work of the CEO.

As I've looked back on these conversations and countless hours reading Peter's books and articles, I've thought about what made him so extraordinary. For me, it comes down to five things.

First and foremost, Peter's basic rule was the importance of serving consumers. As he liked to say, "The purpose of a business is to create and serve a customer." Plain and simple. At P&G, we have translated this principle into respect for the consumer as boss. Consumer-driven strategy, innovation, and leadership are cornerstones of P&G's success and a reflection of the influence Peter has had on our company.

Second, Peter insisted on the *practice* of management. He had little patience for detached theory or abstract plans. "Plans are only good intentions unless they immediately degenerate into hard work," he wrote. He and I readily agreed that execution is the only strategy customers or competitors ever see. I always came away from our conversations with clear, fresh insights that I could apply to P&G's business and organization almost immediately. But Peter was not a single-minded evangelist for the virtue of execution. He believed in the power of strategic ideas and making clear choices. He said, "From quiet reflection will come even more effective action." His ability to balance action and reflection is what makes his ideas so practical *and* so enduring.

The third characteristic that made Peter extraordinary was his gift for reducing complexity to simplicity. His curiosity was insatiable, and he never stopped asking questions. He called himself a "social ecologist" because he drew from history, art, literature, music, economics, anthropology, sociology, and psychology. From these many sources of inspiration came the clear questions and simple Drucker insights that lit the road to action: "Management is doing things right; leadership is doing the right things." "The only way you can manage change is to create it." "The marketer is the consumer's representative." His most enduring gift to future generations is that he taught so many others how to ask the right questions.

The fourth defining Drucker strength was his focus on the *responsibility* of leaders. Late in his life, he sharpened this focus on the responsibility of CEOs in particular. "The CEO," he said, "is the link between the inside, where there are only costs, and the outside, which is where the results are." For many reasons, business organizations become inwardly focused. Their business and financial measures are internal. Even if they have external metrics, those measures are often given lower priority because they don't drive short-term financial performance or because they are less precise and more qualitative. Peter argued that the CEO is in a unique position to balance this inward focus. The CEO has primary responsibility for bringing the outside in, for ensuring that the organization understands the views of the market, current and potential customers, and competitors.

The fifth and most important of Peter's many attributes was his humanity. He treated everyone with deep respect. "Management is about human beings," he wrote. "Its task is to make people capable of joint performance, to make their strengths effective and their weaknesses irrelevant." He noted that business and other institutions are "increasingly the means through which individual human beings find their livelihood and their access to social status, to community, and to individual achievement and satisfaction." While he did not suggest that businesses exist to supply jobs, he argued that managers have a fiscal, societal, and moral responsibility to ensure that jobs are fulfilling and individuals are able to contribute as fully as they can. I could not agree more. The most important thing I try to do as CEO is to inspire leaders and unleash the creativity and productivity of P&G's 135,000 knowledge workers.

Humanity infused everything Peter wrote and said. He was a force for good in the world. He received the U.S. Medal of Freedom because his management thought, beginning with *Concept of the Corporation,* helped develop free societies of organizations more productive than dictatorships of the left or right. This is his greatest contribution.

Peter Drucker was one of a kind. He was relentlessly focused on the promise of the future and the potential of individuals. It is entirely fitting that one of his final requests was for a biography of his *ideas* rather than of his life.

Liz Edersheim has fulfilled this request with *The Definitive Drucker.* She has captured not only the essence of Drucker's 39 books and seven decades of discovery and insight, but also the essence of Peter Drucker the man—the wise, funny, insightful, humble teacher who sat with so many of us in his living room asking questions and patiently giving us the time to catch up to where he had already leaped, the man who helped us see what he always described as "visible, but not yet seen."

Through his example and his ideas, Peter will continue to be a force for good in the world for generations to come.

A.G. Lafley
Chairman, President, and CEO
P&G
Cincinnati, Ohio
September 6, 2006

INTRODUCTION

Soon after I published a biography of my mentor Marvin Bower, the architect of McKinsey & Company, the phone rang at my home on a Friday night. "Hello." The caller paused and then added, "This is Peter Drucker." It took me a moment to grasp who it was on the other end of the phone, with his Viennese accent that sounded like my father's. I walked out of the kitchen, away from my family, to clear my head and be alone with this strangely familiar voice.

Peter Drucker? The man credited with inventing the discipline of management? The man who wrote 39 books which have been translated into countless languages? The man who single-handedly counseled the chairmen of GM and Ford, who advised the president of the World Bank and the CEO of GE, who reportedly told Margaret Thatcher to privatize the entire British mining industry? The man who had a formative influence on every company Jim Collins and Jerry Porras profiled in their book, *Built to Last*—legendary organizations like Hewlett Packard, Johnson & Johnson, Merck, and Motorola?[1]

In what I soon learned was Peter's usual no-nonsense way, he complimented me on my recent Marvin Bower book and asked if I might be interested in interviewing him. Drucker jokingly raised the idea of my writing a book about him, a book looking at how he had created the modern concept of management.

I was tempted, not to mention flattered, but commitments ricocheted through my head: In the next few weeks, I had to fly to Brussels for a global meeting at Avon Products, ride in a Starbucks delivery truck through downtown Manhattan at dawn observing the stores from a logistical perspective, and meet with senior pharmaceutical executives in New Jersey to discuss a new packaging format that could help patients remember to complete prescriptions. But this was Peter Drucker, and he was 94. It might be the last book he worked on. I told him I needed to think about it.

At the time, several ideas were coalescing in my mind about how management can best step up to the scary and exhilarating challenges of the twenty-first century. As a consultant, I work with clients in businesses ranging from chocolates to athletic gear, from diesel engines to computer chips. Much of what I do professionally is based on Drucker's take-home pointers about focusing on results and how to be effective. I am also the mother of two teenagers, and even in that realm his books offer good advice. My kids shrug their shoulders whenever I trot out my favorite expression, which comes right from Drucker: "Don't confuse motion with progress."

I have been working with managers in a dozen industries for over 25 years and have recently seen their struggles intensify as the traditions of the business world are being upended. Changing customers, changing technology, and changing ways of doing and even defining business are jolting these companies to the core—and often challenging their very survival.

When I started as a consultant at McKinsey & Company in the late 1970s, I worked with midwestern companies whose survival was being challenged by Japanese competitors with their lower-cost cars, televisions, and machine tools. By the mid-1980s, my clients were consumer goods companies that were struggling to meet the demanding requirements of an enterprise that my friends in New York had barely heard of—an Arkansas company by the name of Wal-Mart.

In the late 1980s, I started my own consulting firm and worked primarily with leveraged buyout companies (LBOs) that had paid too much for acquisitions and needed to drastically improve the economics of the companies in their portfolios. It was here I learned the expression, "The sins of omission are greater than the sins of commission." At my firm, we continually tried ideas to test their viability rather than be paralyzed by fear of failure. As I later learned, this was very much a Drucker thing to do. In the early 1990s, almost overnight my client list became crowded with electronics companies and medical equipment companies. They were losing out to Asian and other competitors that churned out cheaper and cheaper knockoffs.

Throughout all those years we didn't know how lucky we were. We could look inside a company, study the customers, and reinvent the business. We could often simply research other industries and top-flight companies to get ideas. For example, with Sealy Mattress, an overpriced LBO, we could pull $50 million out of cost and guarantee next-day delivery to retailers, fundamentally changing the retailers' need for inventory. With Motorola, we could connect with police stations and work with UPS to repair police mobile radios and return them within 24 hours.

But then the world got a lot more complicated. I began advising one company after another that it had to completely rethink its style and its core practices or else it would become uncompetitive and destroy tremendous shareholder value. There were no natural solutions or approaches to follow. Management had to take risks. Huge risks. Doing nothing was an even bigger risk.

At the time of Drucker's call, I was working with three clients, and all three needed a dose of Drucker. The first, a New England university hospital, was struggling with the decision to install a wireless network that would enable interns to swap patients' medical records on their laptop computers, speeding up the bureaucratic process and eliminating paper shuffling. The system had another benefit: It would qualify the university for more Medicare and Medicaid payments. But it contradicted everything hospital administrators held sacred about centralized information and patients' rights to privacy. Like many hospitals, this one was so bent on doing things the old way that it was heading toward bankruptcy.

My second client, a paper company mired in long-standing traditions, had taken a bold step by acquiring a dozen independent packaging companies. The companies served many diverse industries, from media to health care, and were based in many far-flung nations, including Brazil, the United States, Russia, and Europe. Senior managers wanted to seize the opportunity to help their clients use new packaging designs to grab customers' attention, but they used a painstakingly deliberate engineering approach to making decisions. The company had been through a slew of management consultants, from McKinsey to the Boston Consulting Group to Deloitte & Touche, and even management guru Ram Charan, a University of Michigan professor. I was working with the head of the packaging group to create a design center for customers, identifying potential partners in China and India. But after three critical years, executives were no closer to uniting their various acquisitions to provide designs for clients than when they had begun.

My third client was a cosmetic company with a household name that had too many ideas and way too little discipline. At the same time, it was uniquely positioned to touch customers around the world, but, like many consumer-goods companies, it was being slowly asphyxiated by the complexity of its offerings. The sales reps were so overwhelmed that they had become more like clerks processing orders than salespeople proactively describing a product. Manufacturing facilities produced one item, then the next, and the next, unable to capture economies of scale and often discarding unused inventory. This company was an ace at customizing orders and delivering them quickly to all reaches of the globe, yet it was missing great opportunities.

And it wasn't just my clients that were being overwhelmed. Something has gone wrong with business in the twenty-first century. Consider this: Since 2000, the management at 18 different public companies—*18 companies!*—has each destroyed more than $50 billion in shareholder value. That's more than Enron did, 18 times over. Why? Because, in most cases, the CEOs, boards of directors, and other well-paid managers held on to yesterday—to doing business the way they always had—and didn't know how to free their organizations to embrace tomorrow.

Management in the twenty-first century faces fundamental changes in the size and scope of opportunities. Businesses have historically defined "opportunity" as a chance to capture market share and rake in higher profits through greater productivity, a new and improved product or service, the acquisition of a competitor, or expansion into a new territory. But increasingly, opportunity is all about seeing, or even creating, white space— uncharted markets that can be identified only by looking hard at both the external environment and the numerous unsatisfied demands of increasingly informed customers. What is fascinating is that often the customers aren't even conscious of what they want until someone comes up with a product and a marketing campaign that makes people say, "I need that cell phone that shows the Comedy Channel." In a very real sense, truly innovative products and services *create* their own markets.

As I traveled to Brussels and bumped around the streets of New York in a Starbucks truck, I couldn't get Drucker out of my mind. All these companies—all the CEOs, all the CFOs, all the COOs, all the Chief-You-Name-Its I was dealing with—were trying to cope with this bewildering 24/7 world of outsourcing, changing demographics, sharpened competition, and new customer requirements. They were dealing with the very challenges

Drucker had anticipated for decades, before anyone truly understood what he was talking about.

As I began to reread Drucker's books and articles, several things quickly became clear. No one has understood the implications of social trends and transformed them into opportunities the way Drucker has (see sidebar on page 13). No one has done a better job of helping organizations capitalize on opportunities. Despite the vast numbers of business books, no book clearly and powerfully explains the implications of the transitions that are underway and how to effectively manage in this new world. Something told me that this man, who had been the first to emphasize the human element of management, had some of the answers. I promised Peter I'd think about doing a book and would visit him on my next trip west.

Three months later I flew to Claremont, California, to see the man who had defined the field in which I'd spent a quarter-century of my life. Peter was a sagacious nonagenarian with thick glasses, an even thicker Austrian accent, an ineffective hearing aid, but a surprisingly warm smile and hearty handshake.

We went to a dimly lit Italian restaurant where everyone knew him. They knew the wine he wanted, and no one had to tell them to bring him his double espresso after lunch. He was a fastidious eater, but he had an insatiable appetite for discussions of art, music, and world affairs. We talked about Vienna and Claremont College, where he was still advising the dean on the management of the Drucker business school. We discussed Trollope, the great English novelist. He talked about Doris, his wife for almost 70 years.

He helped me think through how to move the university hospital management beyond its traditional mindset. Peter was fascinated by the way information technology was changing everything about medicine, from costs to privacy concerns. He spent some time discussing the extent of technology's impact on health care, and he proudly discussed his nephew's scanning and diagnostics business.

Peter suggested that I focus on how much revenue the university hospital was losing by doing things the old way. Were there, he asked me, instances where patient health was jeopardized by doing things the old way? What was important to hospital administrators, and how could we help them understand the need to adopt the alternative ways of operating that we were suggesting? Drucker also happened to have information from two California hospitals facing the same quandary as the university hospital.

As we made our way back to my rental car, I watched Peter take large strides with his walker, his frailty dwarfed by his determination. And I thought: this is going to be fun. In that first visit, Peter was very clear about his aims. He didn't want me to write a traditional biography, nor did he want an authorized biography so he could dictate what would be included. "Do not hide things," he insisted. "Do not be biased. This is your book. I want to see it. I am happy to discuss the ideas with you. This is your interpretation."

In interpreting Peter, I stayed focused on today. This is a crazy time. Opportunities are significant and often more difficult to identify than they were in the past, the time frame for capitalizing on them is much shorter than it ever was, and the cost of mistakes is much greater. Nobody knew how to capitalize on the past and make way for the future like Peter Drucker. His writings are all about business as an innovative agent of change; he provided solid, practical advice on how to succeed with start-ups as well as with established companies. Should a business stick to what it knows best, or should it take a risk and make a foray into a different area? More than seven decades as an observer and adviser to businesses gave Drucker a unique perspective on finding a healthy balance between preservation and change. The amazing thing is that this man, who was born in pre-World War I Vienna, had the vision to come up with theories that are still revolutionizing management in the age of the Internet, changing demographics, and the knowledge worker (a term Peter coined).

I began testing Drucker's ideas with my clients. For example, Starbucks was pushing a paper-goods distributor to find a way to distribute cups and napkins to urban stores with limited storage space and little time for receiving packages daily, in order to save money. Rather than simply minimize cost, we asked a Drucker question: What would be of greatest value to the customer? Using Peter's question, I came up with some very different answers. The solution was to make everything easy for the Starbucks store so managers and associates could focus on their customers—providing everything from automatic replenishment to cup dispensers with presleeved cups. And, for some rural stores, the answer was to use the same distribution channel for both the cups and the coffee.

My colleagues couldn't believe I had the good fortune to make Drucker my personal mentor. Michael Hammer, a classmate of mine from MIT's Sloan School of Management and author of an insightful business book, *Reengineering the Corporation*, said that Drucker was one of his heroes: "It is with some trepidation that I open his early books, because I am afraid that I will discover that he has anticipated my latest ideas by a matter of several decades. It is all there." Michael reminded me of what I was coming to know firsthand: that Drucker is the original outside-the-box thinker.

So, three months after we first met, I told Peter that he was right not to want a conventional biography as the "father of modern management." I didn't want to write about his favorite childhood board games or his testy relationship with his autocratic father. I wanted to use Drucker's life and ideas to help companies navigate the treacherous waters of the twenty-first century. I wanted to distill his ideas into a practical book about how to help organizations thrive as their traditional ways of doing business are overturned. It seemed like the best way to honor someone who has guided scores, if not hundreds, of careers in corporations and nonprofits. Peter immediately agreed. He said, "We need a new theory of management. The assumptions built into business today are not accurate." And with that, this book and an unlikely partnership began.

Peter Drucker taught me more than I learned in MIT's doctoral program in operations research. We talked while driving around in rental cars. We talked in his den, surrounded by his collection of simple Japanese paintings with his pool glistening beyond glass doors. We talked as we sat in the Drucker archives at Claremont University. We talked on the phone late at night but never before 12 noon California time—I don't think he liked mornings. Whenever I sent him a fax, I would receive a scribbled response the next morning.

His wife Doris was very protective. She rebuked me for bringing him doughnuts one day; that was the end of *that* ritual. I had to limit my visits to two hours. Invariably, at the end of those two hours Doris would come over to where we were sitting; she carefully watched Peter's time and energy. Peter would say, "Just a couple more minutes." I would want to listen to Peter for those couple more minutes but knew that if I didn't start packing up my tape recorder, it would upset Doris. It went on like this for 16 magical months. After Peter died in November 2005, I continued to touch base with Doris, who was a repository for even more of his great stories culled from a whirlwind life of changing the world of business.

During that time, I read and reread Drucker. There were plenty of moments when my head was spinning. I interviewed and visited more than 50 of his clients and students, and a dozen of his academic colleagues, as well as senior executives who had never met Drucker but who were influenced by his work. While interviewing former students and clients, I noticed a pattern. Virtually everyone I interviewed said, at some time in the interview, one version or another of essentially the same thing: "Peter liberated me.

He elevated my expectations." I never really understood the power of liberation until I started hearing stories about it from so many people.

Peter's ideas were the catalyst that freed people to pursue opportunities they had never expected to have. He liberated people by asking them questions and eliciting a vision that just felt right. He liberated people by getting them to challenge their own assumptions. He liberated people by raising their awareness of, and their faith in, things they knew intuitively. He liberated people by forcing them to think. He liberated people by talking to them. He liberated people by getting them to ask the right questions.

When I played this theme back to Warren Bennis, a longtime friend of Peter's and one of today's leading thinkers on organizational effectiveness, he responded, "Yes, I had never thought of it that way, but Peter Drucker does liberate." Warren sat back in his living room chair and smiled. When I checked it with Richard Cavanagh, president of the Conference Board, he smiled and said, "Yes, I've seen him do that a lot. I've even seen him liberate whole audiences as he spoke."

A particularly poignant moment came when I was interviewing Tony Bonaparte, special assistant to the president at St. John's University in New York. With tears in his eyes, he looked at me and told me how Drucker had changed his career and his life. Bonaparte had always wanted to teach at a community college. He had a chance to attend the Executive MBA program at NYU. There he met Drucker, who was a professor and teaching an evening class. Drucker took an interest in him, and Peter and Doris started taking him out to dinner every few weeks. Drucker would ask questions and implore Bonaparte to push, push, push—to liberate himself. "He made sure I always was stretching just a little further, liberating me from my constraints," Bonaparte remembered. "Each time I went back, my expectations of myself were higher. He would not let me do anything but succeed. And if it weren't for him I wouldn't be where I am today. He looks at things as they are with a very realistic sense of how they could be and helped me do the same. It changed my life."

Drucker worked with great leaders for over 75 years and liberated them, too. Churchill went so far as to say that the amazing thing about Peter F. Drucker was his ability to start our minds along a stimulating line of thought. Mexican President Vicente Fox commented that Peter's insights on societies were second to none. Peter F. Drucker so increased the credibility of the concept of "management" that the U.S. Bureau of the Budget was renamed the Office of Management and Budget in 1970. And, of course, Drucker liberated and inspired great corporate leaders, among them Akito Morita, founder of Sony; Andy Grove, one of the founders of Intel; Bill Gates of Microsoft; and Jack Welch, former chairman and chief executive of General Electric.

DRUCKER IDEAS

As I began to write about Peter's ideas and share my own perspectives on them, he opened up. I would pick one topic from my list of Drucker ideas and discuss with him how it applied to the challenges of this century. He generally liked me to send him my questions in advance of my visit. I would write down his responses and study them, reread something he wrote, call a client or two, and test the thinking.

For example, when we were discussing the knowledge worker, Peter said, "Today the corporation needs them more than they need the corporation. That balance has shifted." I called my friend Alan Kantrow, head of the knowledge effort at Monitor, the Boston-based consulting firm. Without missing a beat, Alan said, "We are constantly asking ourselves—what are we providing to the knowledge worker to keep him or her here, rather than go off and be an independent contractor. We believe it is the opportunities they get and the people they have a chance to work with that keeps them here. It is not the money." I then called David Thurm, head of operations at the *New York Times*. In this era of job-hopping executives, David is as much of a company lifer as I know. I asked him why he worked for the *Times*, rather than as an independent contractor. He replied, "I'm proud to be associated with such a great institution."

Drucker had told me that there is no such thing as unquestioning loyalty: An organization has to earn the loyalty of its employees every day. David agreed and said that the *Times* was still earning it. I called three other high-level executives and asked them what keeps them at their corporations. They said they stayed on because of job security. I guess asking this Druckerian question prodded them to think. Since then, two have left their corporations.

While I continued consulting with companies large and small, I kept on thinking about how management could navigate this difficult new landscape and what lessons from Drucker's 70 years of observations could help them. I questioned executives whom I admired, added my own ideas, and shared the results with Peter as we discussed the book.

On a warm August day in 2004, during an intense conversation about what makes a good leader, Peter looked at me and said, "The most important thing anybody in a leadership position can do is ask what needs to be done. And make sure that what needs to be done is understood." At the time, the newspapers were full of headlines about once-thriving businesses that were faltering badly and about scandals at Tyco, Enron, Adelphi, and WorldCom. He continued, "You ask me why do so many people in leadership fail. There are two reasons. One is that they go by what they want, rather than what needs to be done. And the second is the enormous amount of time and effort to make oneself understood—to communicate." I asked how leaders can be

Efficiency is doing things right.
Effectiveness is doing the right things.

On Money

Money follows knowledge. Money is not a problem. The problem
is leadership and direction.

Profitability is not the purpose of, but a limiting factor on, business
enterprise and business activity.

We need a measure, not a count.

On Management

Management has mostly to do with people, not techniques and
procedures. Their engagement is what matters.

The effective decision maker actually makes very few decisions.

The three most important questions are:

- What is our business?
- Who is the customer?
- What does the customer consider value?

Management by objectives works if you first think through your
objectives. Ninety percent of the time you haven't.

On Knowledge

We now accept the fact that learning is a lifelong process of keeping
abreast of change. And the most pressing task is to teach people
how to learn.

The essence of management is to make knowledge productive.
Knowledge exists only in application. (Actionable knowledge as
opposed to just information.)

We will not be limited by the information we have. We will be
limited by our ability to process that information.

On the Individual

Know your strengths.

The first question to ask is what needs to be done.

Every six months, ask yourself, what do I want to be remembered for?

certain they know what needs to be done. He emphasized two things: asking and listening.

Drucker was known for his Socratic style—asking questions and asking the right ones. I once asked Dan Lufkin, a founder of Donaldson, Lufkin, & Jenrette, to describe working with Drucker back when the firm was starting in the 1960s. First, he said, Drucker made sure everyone was focused on the questions that needed to be asked. "I can't tell you how important he was to the development of the firm. He forced three young and ambitious guys doing well to step back and think, and on occasion make decisions."

I have used Drucker's most insightful questions to structure every chapter in this book. As Peter often said, the right questions don't change as often as the answers do. As you read, think how you might answer the key questions in each chapter if you were asked them by your CEO or your customer.

The book also reflects Drucker's passion for making organizations and management work well in the present and to create tomorrow. The importance of and need for great management are reflected in virtually all his writing. Peter's passion was the direct outgrowth of having witnessed Europe's economic free fall in 1930. The failures and collapse that he wrote about in the 1930s were, to his mind, directly connected to poor business and government management. He was convinced that the lack of a viable economic engine in Europe is what brought Hitler to power.

The rise of Fascism and Communism only confirmed Drucker's view of the critical need for vibrant businesses in any society. Without economic opportunity, he wrote in 1933, "The European masses realized for the first time that existence in this society is governed not by what is rational and sensible, but by blind, irrational, and demonic forces." He then went on to say that the lack of an economic engine isolates individuals and they become destructive.[2]

Drucker's understanding of the fragility and interdependency of our economic systems and the enormous human cost of failure is even more relevant in our global economy. And, as Drucker emphasized, we all must step up to the responsibility to manage our way to an optimal tomorrow. "Human values, capabilities, and tenacity comprise the engine that keeps the world going. In short, we are all charged with influencing and managing the changes that will define our future."

Peter and I saw this as a book for a wide assortment of people: A CEO leading an organization, a recent recipient of an MBA or a graduate of an executive education program who wants to think about the challenges and possible solutions that academics don't dwell on, a midlevel manager worried about declining sales, a vice president who is dealing with dilemmas of outsourcing, a CFO who is keeping a wary eye on competition from a company in another country, probably another continent. These people have some common traits: They want the best for their businesses. They are leery of short-term profit making at the expense of long-term growth. And they want their careers to make a mark.

The book begins—as Peter and I agreed it should—looking outside. Chapter 1 describes the revolutionary changes that have created the business environment of the twenty-first century and the challenges of this new world.

The remaining chapters reflect a logic Peter used often. I call it his vehicle for creating tomorrow and charting a course for the future.

The windshield is what enables you see where you're going (with the help of mirrors that reflect where you've been). The first step in creating tomorrow is to build a picture that reflects your understanding of the environment. I call it *Peter's Marauder's Map*; it keeps changing and being updated. As things, situations, and people move, the map reflects those changes. Chapter 1 covers this part of the vehicle; it outlines the role of management and

Vehicle for Creating Tomorrow and Charting a Course for the Future

strategy in this new business world, where strategy is more important than ownership.

Chapter 2 deals with the customer—the steering wheel on the vehicle. A close connection with the customer helps the enterprise look at the world from the outside in—from the external world, where customer needs develop and business results are achieved, inside to the organization, which must mobilize to identify and meet the needs and to achieve the results.

Chapters 3 through 5 deal with the fundamentals needed on the journey—the wheels on the vehicle, if you will: Innovation and abandonment, collaboration, people, and knowledge. Chapter 6 addresses the decision mechanisms, discipline, and values that connect the fundamentals—the chassis of the vehicle.

The last chapter of the book is about the role of the CEO. It is a chapter that recognizes that each of us is his or her own CEO, as Drucker liked to say. We can, and must, be passionate about creating our tomorrow.

Peter Drucker's insights, as incisive as ever, have much to offer the twenty-first century organization seeking to liberate itself in our fast-moving, borderless world—to create tomorrow. That is what this book is about. As you read it, I hope some of the Drucker magic rubs off, helping you to free yourself of constraints, to think creatively, and to act. I think that is the legacy he would want.

Drucker's declarations have withstood the test of time. He objected to being characterized as a visionary or a seer. Yet he painted uncannily accurate pictures of the future thanks to his ability to anticipate the consequence of things that had already happened. Consider a few examples from among many:

- In 1927, while attending the Editorial Conference of the Central European Economic and Social Weekly, when asked what he feared the most, Peter Drucker responded, "I am afraid of Hitler." Others laughed at him, because Hitler had just suffered a resounding defeat.
- In 1942, Drucker wrote that institutions (not nations, states, or other geographically defined entities) were the most important communities and that market stakeholders would become as critical as nation stakeholders.[3] (Today, market stakeholders may have even superseded nation stakeholders. Of the hundred largest economic entities in the world, as measured by GDP and revenue, 44 are countries and 56 are companies.[4])
- In 1947, Drucker wrote, "Management is leadership."[5] For the past 15 years, no single topic has received more attention in the management world than leadership. Frances Hesselbein is a frequent

speaker in her role as chairperson of the Board of Governors of the Leader to Leader Institute. "I always include a quote from Peter Drucker," she notes. "Inevitably, that is the high point of my speech. When I leave, it is the Drucker quote that people remember."[6]

- In 1954, Peter told his publisher, "Management needs strategy." His publisher responded that "strategy" was a term for war, not business—and it would repel readers. By 1975, the topic of strategy dominated the top management writings in journals and books.[7]

- In 1985, Peter told Walter Wriston, chairman of Citigroup, that the Berlin Wall would fall. Wriston said that he would have dismissed the prediction if it came from anyone but Peter Drucker. In 1989, when the Berlin Wall came down, Drucker smiled and said, "I didn't know it would happen so soon."[8]

- In a conversation in 1986, Drucker said that the Soviet Union would collapse. Henry Kissinger responded, "You are wrong." When Gorbachev delivered the speech dissolving the Soviet Union in 1991, Drucker was once more prescient when he warned, "Now we have to be concerned about their resources and economics."[9]

- In 1990, when most of business was still figuring out the implications of that Berlin Wall crumbling, Drucker wrote that communities of companies would be critical to business survival in the transnational world.[10] We are now clearly, and sometimes painfully, in a globally networked world.

- In 1992, Drucker wrote, there is no longer a "Western" history or a "Western" civilization. There is only world history and world civilization.[11]

- In 1999, Drucker commented on the Internet boom, "It is not the access to information that is important. It is how organizations, business, and every horizon will change as a consequence that will matter."[12]

ONE | Doing Business in the Lego World

The assumptions on which most businesses are being run no longer fit reality.[1]

—Peter F. Drucker

As I crisscrossed the country over the past couple of years, interviewing Peter Drucker and working with clients, something struck me. The staid world of business—the world I'd studied, the world I felt I'd mastered during 20 years at McKinsey & Co. and as head of my own consulting firm—had been turned upside down by a silent revolution. In this chapter, I describe that revolution, tell you how Peter helped me understand this radical transformation, and explain what it means for you right now.

THE SILENT REVOLUTION

Change came gradually, predictably, to businesses in the period following World War II through the early 1990s. But then, *boom!* A silent revolution took place on five fronts:

1. Information flew.
2. The geographic reach of companies and customers exploded.
3. The most basic demographic assumptions were upended.
4. Customers stepped up and took control of companies.
5. Walls defining the inside and outside of a company fell.

Developments on these five fronts played off one another, further accelerating the revolution.

First, *information flew*. Since the expansion of the Internet, information travels instantaneously, without regard for distance, and its widespread availability is unprecedented. In the globally integrated economy, management must make decisions at all hours of the day and night. Purchasing managers in Plano and distributors in Dubuque can now distinguish between good suppliers and bad ones instantaneously. The greater velocity of information has accelerated the pace of everything in business. Success is measured not by the quarter or the month, but by the minute or second. Every industry, from manufacturing to movies, has had to adjust to this fast-forward world. As Lynda Obst, a producer at Paramount, recently noted, "We used to have a weekend to get our money out of a movie like *Stealth* or *Doom*. Now we get one night, tops."[2]

The greater velocity of information has accelerated the pace of everything in business.

For decades, information was power. But today, with the unprecedented availability of instant information to anyone with a laptop, true power comes from screening, interpreting, and translating vast quantities of information into action.

Second, the *geographic reach of companies and customers exploded*. Remember that cartoon of the kid scraping a hole in the ground and saying, "Hi, Mom, I'm digging to China"? Today that same 11-year-old gets on his Mac and connects to a peer in Guangzhou for a game of war, and his 13-year-old sister goes to sweetandpowerful.com to buy a fleece pullover made in Sri Lanka. Companies and their customers now have an astounding geographical reach. Even mom-and-pop firms can scour the world for resources. And in this global marketplace, brands are created and gain widespread recognition in weeks or months rather than years, cutting down the advantage of the big-brand players who used to be the select members of an exclusive club.

Companies and their customers now have an astounding geographical reach.

Third, *basic demographic assumption were upended.* Populations in the developed world have been jolted by an aging group of workers and a declining birth rate. The migration from industrial to knowledge workers and the increasing success of women in the workforce have changed customers' needs and forever changed the relationships of corporations with both customers and employees. Until quite recently, only customers in affluent countries reached the apex of Maslow's pyramid of self-actualization, which starts with the basics of food and shelter. Now, millions more people in all social strata have been freed from worrying about the basics; they seek service and fulfillment.

With longer life spans, later retirements, and a record number of women in the workplace, convenience matters more than ever. I noticed recently that my supermarket was touting premade peanut butter and jelly sandwiches for parents who don't have an extra 60 seconds to slather two spreads on bread. With changes in how customers are distributing their income, companies are offering more useful information and more service. The three fastest-growing consumer purchases today are not traditional consumer goods; they are activities (such as sporting events and health club memberships), health care, and education. Health care and education make up almost a third of America's gross national product (GNP).

To managers, the biggest effect of these demographic changes is that societies, markets, and workplaces are driven by new populations with new demands. Once-dependable workers over age 50 do not necessarily keep on toiling as full-time, 9-to-5 employees. Instead, many dive into the labor force as temporaries, part-timers, consultants on special assignment, or knowledge workers. Some of these older workers will be pushed into free agent status because of layoffs and buyouts.

> ## Societies, markets, and workplaces are driven by new populations with new demands.

Fourth, *customers stepped up and took control.* Never before have customers been so clearly in the driver's seat. They are engaged with companies in ways that would have astounded Henry Ford or Thomas Watson. Customers are no longer simply passive recipients of goods and services; they are active participants from the product inception, whether as groups evaluating the product or as individuals working with software programs and design engineers to custom-build everything from Levi's jeans to light fixtures. Consumers can access virtual shelves for almost any product, and they want customized products delivered with the click of a mouse.

Customers create their own weblogs with their own online content. Hachette closed its *Elle Girl Teen* magazine while its competitor, Condé Nast, is launching a Web site with all its content created by teen readers rather than by Condé Nast staffers. We read each other's blogs and socialize at virtual meeting places such as MySpace.com and the online dating site Match.com. Shopping for a mate has become almost as easy as shopping for a book on Amazon.com ("Add this man or woman to My Cart!").[3]

Savvy customers have become part of the process that used to exclude and dismiss them with condescending remarks like,

"You'll have that dining room table delivered in eight weeks. And, no, we cannot make it three inches taller just because you have a relative in a wheelchair—you'll have to find a carpenter to do that." Today you design it with one of several manufacturers such as Thomas Moser—often online—exactly the way you want it.

Finally, defining *walls fell*. These days, a company draws on capabilities outside its own walls in ways that would have been unheard of just a few years ago. To test ideas, companies now use expertise drawn from completely different industries and form alliances with other companies with overlapping missions. Since Home Depot recognized that its strength was internal to its stores, it has passed all its logistics issues off to UPS; now UPS manages everything at Home Depot connected with shipping. This partnership allows the two companies collectively to serve Home Depot customers more efficiently.

Sometimes companies even team up with direct competitors. Last year, two global rivals, China National Petroleum Corp. and India's Oil & Natural Gas Corp., teamed up to buy a Syrian oil field, and this year they jointly bid for another one in Colombia.[4] Walls have fallen to bring the best people and divisions within companies together rapidly and to enable organizations to adapt without huge write-offs. Whereas independence was once key to speed and a barrier to the entry of competitors, it has come to signify isolation. And isolation is corporate death.

Isolation is corporate death.

The impact of this silent revolution hit me one day in 2005. Although I had studied the company carefully twice before, I was making my first visit to Procter & Gamble (P&G) in Cincinnati as a writer. Everyone welcomed me, from sales reps to the chairman, president, and CEO, A.G. Lafley. They wanted my thoughts, and they were eager to give me every bit of information I requested.

What a vast change this warm reception was from my two prior dealings with the firm in 1990 and again a decade later in 2000. I wasn't working for P&G on either occasion; I was studying it for a competitor. Back then, the Cincinnati behemoth was so secretive that the chairman of my client company told me not to even so much as mention P&G's name in any report. He felt that if P&G found out I was analyzing it, there would be "repercussions." I dubbed it Company S for "secret"—as if any executive couldn't figure out who was making all those soaps, detergents, and diapers I was writing about.

Now here I was in Cincinnati in 2005—feeling a certain amount of dread mixed with excitement—interviewing Lafley over a lunch of chicken and green beans in his office. At the conclusion of our meeting, he told me to call with any questions. And it wasn't just Lafley who was forthcoming. Rather than a hermetically sealed conglomerate, I found a company so open that it invited me, an outsider, to visit one of its product testing centers. The company is intent on tapping outside sources and retirees for research and development (R&D) and is even testing a program with DuPont to link the two firms' technology centers. P&G had changed its attitude so radically that it was letting employees write articles about how they were managing. Drucker's influence was apparent. He had been working with P&G since about 1990, and he had constantly pushed executives to see beyond the borders of Ohio. And they had listened.

On my way home, I reflected on my day. What impressed me was not just that P&G was more open; what was really striking was that it was rethinking the way it did everything. I had seen the same ability to rethink the present and embrace the future at GE's corporate headquarters in Connecticut, and then across the country at a completely different place—the Myelin Repair Foundation, a little-known start-up foundation in northern California.

EMBRACING THE FUTURE

My GE experience began as I prepared to interview its former chairman, Jack Welch, a long-time Drucker client. Before seeing this legendary executive, I wanted to know what GE insiders thought and what tips they could offer for drawing Welch out. I called Dave Stevenson, a friend who used to run GE's major appliances marketing group. He told me that he had created his own company, doing research on major consumer expenditures. Seven companies, including GE, were buying his research and market planning. That was unusual for GE, which used to distrust outside researchers. But Dave said that Welch had forced the major appliance group to ask not only what others could do better, but what activities should be spun off and which department heads could work independently. When Dave had volunteered to take marketing outside, the bosses surprised him by agreeing to it. Dave gave me his tip: Listen to Jack Welch and don't be offended by his rough style. Another thing: Jack likes specific questions that demand specific answers.

When I called Welch at the appointed time, I grabbed his attention by asking what he was doing for his birthday. He asked me how I knew, and I told him it was the same as Peter Drucker's—a bit of trivia that surprised him. My second question was how Peter had influenced him. He said that Peter had made him conscious of GE's ability to work with another organization that was excited about something that GE found boring. "If it's not your front room," Peter had asked Welch, "can you make it someone else's front room?" Peter had expressions that everyone seemed to remember. His point was that if you don't have passion for a particular activity, then find an ally who has expertise and passion for that activity *and* can do it better. Harness GE's clout and the ally's passion and move forward. "GE recognized that they were never going to be the best in the world at programming and found a company that was passionate about it in India 20 years before anyone else," Welch told me. This wasn't what the press calls *outsourcing*. Outsourcing is meant to save money or make things easier for the manufacturer. Instead, GE wanted to put the best teams together, even if some members were external and including them added to logistical demands. It sought partnerships that would deliver the best value to the customer. Jack termed this shift "boundarylessness" and indicated that it is a continual challenge for most companies.

Over the years GE executives continued to ask themselves that question and go outside its walls more and more. This effort began in earnest with Peter exhorting Welch to focus on strengths and find somebody else to do the rest.

Focus on strengths and find somebody else
to do the rest.

Big, profit-hungry companies aren't the only ones breaking boundaries. After talking to Welch, I visited the Myelin Repair Foundation, an innovative group in northern California that is trying to find a cure for multiple sclerosis (MS). (This organization is discussed in detail in Chapter 4.) Its approach challenges two long-standing practices that create barriers in research. First, the foundation is connecting separate, competing research groups that used to share findings only after their papers were published. A group of five leading neuroscientists from different universities are piloting a new, collaborative approach to medical research with a shared research plan right from the start.

Second, the foundation is collaborating with patients at every step—something even the best researchers don't do. Their meetings include not just researchers and fundraisers but also patients, the people most affected by MS. The patients' presence creates a new sense of focus and urgency in the researchers. This isn't an academic exercise that will culminate in articles for specialized journals. This is about life and death and about finding a breakthrough in a few years, not in a future someone's lifetime. The scientists are looking for take-home solutions to the deterioration of myelin, the protective insulation surrounding nerve fibers of the central nervous system, which is destroyed by MS. This relatively small foundation is pioneering the twenty-first-century way of doing business.

Embracing the new requires abandoning the past.

Industrial mainstays like P&G and GE and newcomers like the Myelin Repair Foundation are reshaping where and how companies work with customers, other stakeholders, and even potential rivals. These innovators are accelerating the pace at which companies connect, disconnect, and reconnect. P&G and GE recognize that the financial market values soft assets, such as customer relationships, international access and agility, and intellectual capital, and that's where they put their investments. We'll learn from their successes—and some of their mistakes—throughout this book.

To paraphrase Drucker, embracing the new requires abandoning the past. In our conversations, he often said that we are at a moment of transition where businesses and organizations will be redefined. If they don't, they'll go the way of pterodactyls.

THE PRIMACY OF KNOWLEDGE

I was eager to test my observations about the silent revolution with Peter Drucker the visionary who had an astounding track record in predicting and shaping the future. The companies I advised were reeling from the changes around them, and I knew his counsel would make my advice better. It was a lucky coincidence that several of the companies I worked with had consulted with him decades earlier.

When I drove to Drucker's house in a middle-class enclave of Claremont, California, in February 2005, a lone Toyota sedan was parked in the driveway. I remembered my first visit the previous summer when we began to talk about the possibility of my writing a book. On that day, I drove by the house three times, checking the address. It was a nice house, but not ostentatious—an average ranch house in an average neighborhood. It did have distinctive landscaping. The lawn resembled one of those British creations where someone manages to cram in twice as many plants as you'd think possible and make it look wonderful nonetheless.

This time, with the book under way, I rang the bell and heard Peter's usual, "Just a moment!" Then I heard a thumping noise through the house. Peter opened the door and commented, "I'm not as fast as I used to be." The thought flashed through my mind, maybe not physically. He continued, "Pleased to see you." He grabbed my hands and said, "Well, come in." We walked past Doris's office and a shelf stacked with mail. We walked through the living room, which was always immaculate. The *Financial Times* was spread on a long table.

We sat down in the den, next to a round coffee table, with me on his right, by his better ear. Peter enjoyed small talk, but today we plunged right into a business discussion. I wondered if he had noticed the phenomenon of the outside world becoming part of companies. I began by asking his thoughts about the most important challenge for managers today. I used the classic B-school question: What should be keeping managers up at night? He laughed and said, "I don't know."

By now, I understood him well enough to realize that he did know. This was his way of prodding a questioner to dig for the answer. Then he'd go into his "I'll-tell-you-something-else; we'll-get-back-to-that-question-shortly" routine.

We did get back to it, and this chapter does too, in a moment. Peter often talked in circles—beginning with something that might appear totally unrelated and ending with an insight into a question. Somehow it connected to his initial observation.

Peter observed that we are now in another
critical moment: the transition from
the industrial to the knowledge economy . . .
We should expect radical changes in society
as well as in business.

In this case he didn't start by discussing managers, or even science. He talked about World War II. It was, he said, the first war won on industrial power, not military depth. It was the first time in which industry was not an auxiliary but the main fighting force itself. In fact, in the first six months, the United States manufactured more aircraft, tanks, and artillery than Hitler and his advisers thought the Americans could make in five years. They did it by applying the discipline of management from operations research and quality control to rapidly convert factories from making cars to producing tanks. Peter then mentioned my friends from the Sloan School and the role they had played. That led him to a soliloquy about peace. He said that any peace following such a war must be an industrial peace—a peace in which industry is not just on the periphery but at the center. He was on a roll, tracing the transition from a mercantile economy to an industrial economy . . . and the concomitant tension between policy and reality.

Peter observed that we are now in another critical moment: the transition from the industrial to the knowledge-based economy . . . We should expect radical changes in society as well as in business. "We haven't seen all those changes yet," he added. Even the very products we buy will change drastically.

I asked how the Americans won the Gulf War in 1991. He didn't take his usual moment to collect his thoughts. "Technology," he shot back. When I asked how the war on terrorism will be won, he took a moment and said, "Knowledge." He then explained the difference to me: "Technology is the application of yesterday's knowledge. The war on terrorism will be won based on our ability to apply knowledge to knowledge—or someone else's ability." He meant the ability to integrate the pieces and add to what we know individually.

And that brought us to management, or what he called "knowledge-based management." He spent the better part of the next two hours defining and pulling this idea apart: the importance of accessing, interpreting, connecting, and translating knowledge. He spoke about how critical it is to find and manage knowledge in new places like pharmaceutical companies as they move beyond chemistry to nanotechnology and software. Knowledge-based management is also critical to old multinationals like GE as they begin to build infrastructure for the developing countries, with the caveat that they first need to fully understand those countries. Essentially, GE has to access information about the developing world and its infrastructure, interpret this information, and connect it with the rest of GE. Drucker commented that information will be infinite; the only limiting factor will be our ability to process and interpret that information. That is what he meant when he emphasized the importance of the productivity of the knowledge worker.

Peter had a way of looking at something and teasing out both the positive and the negative. "On the one hand, it's important to specialize," he said. "On the other hand, it's dangerous to over-specialize and be isolated."[5] The ability to access specializations while cutting across them—that's what I'd seen at the headquarters of the Myelin Repair Foundation only a few hundred miles away. Finally, Peter was answering my questions—finding a way to specialize enough, but not too much, and without isolation. "That," he said, "is what should keep managers up at night."

Doris appeared. All too quickly my morning session with Peter had ended. That afternoon, when I went back, our topic was Thomas Friedman's bestseller *The World Is Flat*. Friedman argues persuasively that it doesn't matter where work gets done—it makes no difference whether a computer company produces a part in India or Indiana.

Everywhere I went, executives seemed to agree: The world is flat. I asked Peter if he thought the world was flat.

"From whose perspective?" he asked.

"Yours," I said.

"I have trouble walking around my living room," he joked. "It doesn't seem flat to me."

His mind was so spry that sometimes I forgot he was 95 years old. "All right," I said, "then from the manager's perspective."

He paused and said, "Their landscape is flat only if there is an opportunity from it being flat. But if there is an opportunity, it will not be flat for long."

THE LEGO WORLD

After several more discussions with Peter, I came to understand what he was telling me. The management world is flat only if you take an industrial perspective. If you just want the lowest cost, the capabilities exist virtually every place in the world to get the low-est cost. But if cost is not your only concern and you recognize that the industrial world has given way to an information and knowledge-driven world, you will see that the world is not flat and that Indiana and India are not interchangeable. Indeed, the ability to put together and connect the pieces in different ways and with the customer all the time defines an enterprise's performance. Many more than two dimensions of place and time matter all the time. Even country geography is not flat. Silicon Valley is different from Silicon Alley which is different from Wall Street.

> The ability to put together and connect the pieces in different ways and with the customer all the time defines an enterprise's performance.

In the twenty-first century, businesses exist in a Lego world. Companies are built out of Legos: People Legos, Product Legos, Idea Legos, and Real Estate Legos. And these aren't just ordinary Legos; they pass through walls and geographic boundaries, and they are transparent. Everything is visible to everyone all the time. Designing and connecting the pieces is at least as important as providing them. It's crucial to remember that these aren't simply pieces of plastic or metal—they are not just factories or warehouses. They are also humans who program computers, train newcomers, and think about innovation as they prowl malls, libraries, and parks, coming up with new products. These pieces are constantly being put together, pulled apart, and reassembled.

My company's Legos—manufacturing, distribution, skills, and services—cannot be unique unto themselves; they have to connect with your company's Legos. I can build my company, but in a year or two, my CEO and I might have to tear down and rebuild part of it in a totally different configuration, perhaps with fewer

American People Legos and more of your company's People Legos in Sweden or South Africa. Leading visionaries in business are expressing the same notion. Ray Ozzie, Microsoft's chief software architect, recently explained: "What's more important than any one individual Lego is that you know how to build with all the Legos. With everything out there, all those programs and applications and accessories, what's important is the ability to find a way to *connect* fragmented software pieces rather than simply finding the next piece of software."[6]

In the twenty-first century, businesses exist in a Lego world.

That's the idea that Peter embraced, but it was larger than software and components. He thought in terms of people, with a tremendous sense of humanity and compassion for the individual. That's the beauty of it. We are not talking about commodities. We are talking about individuals and their ability to create. As these Legos connect and interconnect in ways we could never have imagined a decade ago, when the Internet was in its infancy, we find a powerful, human structure. In an organization, we can connect individuals' strengths, minimizing their weaknesses. And across organizational boundaries, we can connect the strengths of each corporation and provide the customer with far greater value than can any single enterprise.

Dell is a classic example of a Lego manufacturer. It has configured its offering so that customers can custom-build computers to meet their individual needs. Michael Dell claims that the firm's important capabilities are the management and integration of information and the ability to quickly build a computer to a customer's specifications. Dell's Product Legos include anything from processor and memory capacity to screen size. Its internal network includes vendors, shipping locations, and the location of the customer service center (depending on the time of day, customers can be helped by someone in South Africa, India, or Texas). Connecting pieces include Dell's systems, user interface, assembly centers, and customer support service. Although Dell recognizes customer service as its weakest link, Dell can deliver a customer-tailored product to anyplace in the world at an incredible speed, largely because of the interchangeability of its components, which is at the heart of Dell's "Lego-like" operations. Dell's challenge will be to disconnect and reconnet in a new way as the PC moves from a worktool to the entertainment and communication center.

Amazon exemplifies the Lego approach in the retailing arena; it connects with other vendors who have expertise in making everything from textbooks to toys. Its Web site links you to book publishers, third-party used bookstores, individuals reselling books, and vendors for any product you can dream of—from televisions to telephones to T-shirts. Amazon knows you, and, when you log on, it welcomes you by name and offers you purchase suggestions at lightning speed. It often knows what I want before I do. It's the high-tech version of the old grocer who not only knows you by name but also has a hunch you need sugar before you run out. The company is connected to you, your mind, and your credit card. It is the connection that is important. Dell took its expertise and understanding of the electronics world and connected that capability with each consumer to greatly increase its impact. Amazon linked one Lego to another, from baby clothes to DVDs, and created a simple interface offering the consumer scores of products and incredible ease of use—one-click checkout. Jeff Bezos had the patience and foresight to build a company around connections, and, after a decade of testing, learning, and growing, he made a profitable business. He also had the insight that told him that building an initial customer base around books would ensure that his core customer would be literate, savvy, relatively affluent, and likely to return to purchase more.

A NEW SOLUTION SPACE

The most significant trends affecting business transcend all companies and all industries. They cross borders and touch all areas of civil society. Business as we know it is disappearing. Companies aren't selling products; they're selling experience. Relationships have gone far beyond the roles of buyer and seller. There are no competitors. Let me repeat that, because it's something that Peter Drucker loved to say: *There are no longer competitors,* just better solutions and more choices that can be put together in more ways. In other words, companies focused on competitors are focused on the past, not a future full of technological and demographic opportunities.

Business as we know it is disappearing. Companies aren't selling products; they're selling experience. There are no longer competitors, just better solutions and more choices that can be put together in more ways.

The evolution of cellular phones into instruments capable of doing much more than handling voice communication offers a striking example. The obvious convergence of functions to give a customer a product that does many things—capturing and transmitting still and moving digitalized images, connecting with the Internet, even functioning as a TV—not only means serving a wide range of consumer needs but also guarantees that customers will upgrade to a new device frequently because they want the latest version with new and enhanced capabilities. And the carriers will constantly have to upgrade infrastructure and systems in order to not only constantly improve service, coverage, and signal quality but also to be prepared to offer new forms of service functions. Sprint "competes" with Verizon in recruiting and retaining subscribers by focusing on constant innovation, which is the primary engine of growth and sustainability. By constantly innovating in both technology and range of services offered, what was once an enterprise offering a commodity—cellular phone service—becomes one offering a rapidly increasing range of value-added services. The winner is the organization that offers the most varied menu from which a customer can pick, choose, and customize. And this trend is driving change not just in electronics generally, but in a variety of goods and services unimaginable even 10 years ago.

IMPLICATIONS FOR MANAGERS

One of Drucker's talents was his ability not just to see trends but also to shed light on their implications so that managers could act on them. In our conversations, we discussed three consequences of the silent revolution:

1. Financial markets now value knowledge more highly than they value hard assets, underlining the emergence of the knowledge economy.
2. The U.S. economic engine is facing the gravest threat of the past 100 years: the need for corporations to be strategic collaborators rather than unilateral superstars.
3. Strategy has become a crucial ongoing activity for management, not simply an annual planning exercise.

Financial markets value companies based on what they think they can earn over time. For decades—since the Industrial Revolution, really—what mattered was hard assets: factories, inventory, and accounts receivable, or the ability to build products. Reflecting the preeminence of the knowledge economy, the silent revolution has prodded the financial markets to value the intangibles, such as relationships, intellectual property, and knowledge, and to quantify the value they might generate in the future. We are buying services more than products—health care, education, personal trainers. The market reflects this shift in value. In the last five years, soft assets—intellectual property, patents, and connections—have doubled in value compared to traditional assets, such as plant and equipment.[7]

Drucker noted two developments that drove this shift to soft assets. Old companies, like Boeing, were being revalued as their physical assets took a back seat to their knowledge, relationships, and ability to connect. At the same time, innovative companies, like Google, Yahoo!, and Craigslist, were launched in cyberspace with very little in the way of physical assets, providing services that had never existed before. Unlike a traditional newspaper that relies on classified ads, Monster.com is a forum, a truly interactive business. At first it sounded like just an electronic version of the classified ad—hardly a big advance. But browsers can see what is happening in the labor market, how jobs are being described, and which industries are prospering. It offers a much more comprehensive view of the job market than does a stack of the Sunday *New York Times*, or even nytimes.com.

Consider Craigslist, which, though not a newspaper, has had an even more profound effect on the print media, because it does not charge for classified ads. In just one day, I sold my car on Craigslist to someone who lives just outside the circulation area of my hometown newspaper—and rather than paying $50 for agate type that might or might not lure a buyer, I didn't pay a cent. And then I was hooked. I started buying garden equipment from people in my suburb who posted ads on Craigslist. In just one week, I gave up my lifetime habit of scanning the classifieds in my hometown paper. Monster.com and Craigslist are more than mere services; they are locations—virtual Starbucks. You join a crowd. It's comfortable.

The second challenge is one that Peter and I talked about frequently and one that keeps me up at night: U.S. companies' ability to cooperate in the global marketplace. America's institutions—even our economy and our mindset—are designed for the individualism of an industrial economy, not a Lego world. The game has changed. Peter agreed. He kept saying, "The theory of business has changed." He saw a warning in England's behavior at the time of the later stages of the Industrial Revolution. By holding on to the past, England survived as a nation but lost its world leadership. Peter foresaw a time when many countries would be as strong economically as the United States. The booms in India, China, and even Brazil have created world-class competitors.

Americans will have to play as equals, something that's not easy when you've spent a good part of a century as the undisputed Number One. We have to retool our schools so that students don't simply learn how to answer multiple-choice questions. They need to synthesize information and think critically. If we want our children to thrive in this new world, we should immerse them in Mandarin or another language by the age of five so they learn to connect to other cultures and languages.

> The most significant business implication of the silent revolution is the new role and importance of a good business strategy.

The most significant business implication of the silent revolution is the new role and importance of a good business strategy. Simply put, a strategy focuses critical resources on tasks aimed at producing results. I used to assume that business strategy was like strategy in chess. You had a quantifiable number of moves to choose from. Everyone played on the same basic board from year to year, from decade to decade, learning a few new moves and facing new competitors. The best strategist won the game.

But, today, it's as if chess is played in four dimensions, on multiple boards, simultaneously by experts on five continents. And in business you don't have to worry about competitors so much as ever-changing rules and unidentified customers.

From 1950 to 1990, the boundaries of strategy were well defined, as were the customers, markets, competitors, suppliers, and potential threats. Enemies—regulators or rivals—were clear. Companies spent three to six months every year crafting their strategies, which were then translated into budgets, capital requests and approvals, and personnel changes.

But not in the Lego world where strategy arises from proactive and innovative moves that create opportunities. The boundaries may be global; the markets may not even fit into any convenient categories, such as 13-year-old girls with $50-a-week allowances who like fleece pullovers. The resources will likely extend outside your own company, and the direction of your business will have to align with other strategies. Even if you own the right physical assets and employ the best minds, you are no longer guaranteed control over the right-of-way to the customer; too many filters influence a customer's purchase decisions. For example, when influential teenagers with a presence on MySpace.com decide that teens must buy their pullovers from a hot new place, it's bad news for the old place. In the Internet age, the classic value delivery chain makes about as much sense as a chain letter.

Strategy has to move and be refined at a speed comparable to what used to be called *tactics*; it has to be in real time. You don't have six months, or even three months, to create a master plan. Opportunities disappear as rapidly as they can be captured.

Strategy is not a goal; it is a direction, a blueprint for putting the pieces together and building. It must have continuous feedback to translate real-time results into refinements and changes as appropriate. In a Lego world, fluid design and the ability to connect and reconnect provide a new agility that is a central element of the twenty-first-century enterprise.

> In a Lego world, fluid design and the ability to connect and reconnect provide a new agility that is a central element of the enterprise.

As Drucker often pointed out, companies face unparalleled demands. They must craft and communicate a strategy that invigorates their employees and collaborators and that gives them a shared purpose and direction. They must be ready to adopt almost anything that will give them an edge in innovation and enhanced productivity. A company that builds on each individual's potential is far more likely to succeed than one that inches people forward in dull tasks. Creating tomorrow—by taking

Drucker identified himself with a character in Goethe's *Faust* (1831). In the last act, in a contract with the devil, Mephistopheles, Faust utters the taboo words, "Stop! Time is so beautiful." Just before the climax, Lynceus, the lookout on the top of the watchtower, introduces himself loudly, "Born to see, meant to look," and starts to report what is happening there and what is coming here. To observe and report what the world faces and what looms—that was Drucker's job. It should also be the job of every CEO who wants to survive the next decade.

advantage of opportunity and human talent and capability, in a manner which enhances society—is the challenge of management in the twenty-first century.

CONCLUSION

As Drucker maintained for over 70 years, businesses are the critical engine of a thriving and sustainable society that values individuals and reward achievement, with management effectiveness the determining factor in keeping the engine running. Let's be clear: Business isn't just business. It's the economic engine of democracy.

Business isn't just business.
It's the economic engine of democracy

Drucker believed that with the right questions, the right judgment, and the right mindset, the manager who "walks outside" and thus liberates himself or herself and others from the confines of "what you think you know" is more than capable of rising to the occasion. We will not all be the genius Peter was, but we can all learn from his approach, beginning with asking the right questions.

TWO | The Customer: Joined at the Hip

An enterprise's purpose begins on the outside with the customer . . . it is the customer who determines what a business is, what it produces, and whether it will prosper.[1]

—Peter F. Drucker

On paper, it seems like the most obvious notion: The customer is in the driver's seat, at the control panel. What could be more fundamental? And yet few organizations, busy with all they are doing inside their own walls, are truly focused on the outside world of the customer.

If you are in business, beware. The silent revolution of technology and demography described in the last chapter has given each customer his or her own handy remote control. Everything has changed about your customers and your relationships. You've never had as many people around the globe to reach. And they reach you, too, one by one, not as a homogeneous group. Dozens, maybe hundreds of factors influence the way these individuals around the world see value. Customers aren't just in the driver's seat these days; they are also gassing up the vehicle, doing some of the service, and controlling a fair amount of the traffic on the road.

Peter Drucker's conviction that the customer is at the center of it all shaped his thought from the very start. As a young journalist in the 1930s, Peter credited Time-Life's success to Henry Luce's understanding of the customer rather than his journalistic savvy. In Peter's first management book, *Concept of the Corporation*, he attributed General Motors' success to Chief Executive Alfred Sloan's unique understanding of the customer, not Sloan's scientific approach. As recently as 2004, in his last *Wall Street Journal* editorial piece, "The Role of the CEO," Peter again said that everything begins with understanding the customer. In today's world, where customers are standing up and taking control, understanding your customers and the value you provide to them is more critical than ever.

> Drucker's conviction that the customer is at the center of it all shaped his thought from the very start.

In this chapter, we look briefly at what customer focus is all about since the silent revolution: We examine Peter's classic questions about the customer, tuned to the twenty-first century, and look at how customer focus (or the lack thereof) drove day-to-day corporate life and strategy at Procter & Gamble. As you read, think about how getting inside the mind of your customer could redefine your business from front to back.

Peter Drucker credited the great journalist Henry Luce with opening his eyes to the truism that all successes start with the customer: "Most people hated to work for Luce. He was not an easy man to work with. I loved it because I always learned . . . I saw that mind of his, seeing an enormous amount of material, and seeing the one central issue, which I think is the mark of the really great editor."[2]

With little more than his own vision, Henry Luce founded *Fortune* magazine, the first true business magazine, in 1930, at the beginning of the Great Depression. In launching his first venture, *Time*, Luce had met numerous businessmen whom he felt should and would want to know how their work related to and affected the society around them.[3] Most business magazines of the time were little more than trade journals, and Luce believed that there was a glaring need for a magazine to help businessmen examine their values, goals, and biases, noting on *Fortune*'s debut that to "accurately, vividly, and concretely . . . describe modern business is the greatest journalistic assignment in history."

Fortune hit newsstands in 1930 at the then-exorbitant price of one dollar per issue. It provided value for the dollar—an 11- by 14-inch magazine printed on the highest-quality paper with cardboard covers and countless photographs, not to mention articles written by a notable list of ambitious and talented young writers, including Peter Drucker and Archibald MacLeish, who later won three Pulitzer prizes for poetry and drama. By the end of 1930, *Fortune* had a circulation of 30,000, which more than quadrupled in the next decade.[4] Simply put, Luce had anticipated his customers' needs.

"*Life* was another Luce idea. He saw it as an attempt to see the world as the viewer of a movie sees it, not the maker."[5] Two decades later, Drucker heard a photographer describe working with Luce. "'You know, every time I walked out of those conferences, I swore I would never do another assignment, and every time after three days I reached the conclusion that Luce had been right. He did not have a photographer's eye; he had a viewer's eye. I have a photographer's eye. They're very different.' *Life* he edited himself, and those sessions when he picked the . . . photos that went into *Life* were absolutely fascinating. Because Luce would look at 18, 20, or 40 photos, 3 of which would get into the book. In most cases it would take him absolutely no time to pick those 3, [which] were always very well received."[6]

The lessons Drucker drew from his association with Henry Luce grew into a conviction that an outside-in perspective is essential to business success. What gives life to and sustains the corporation resides on the "outside," not within its direct control, and the customer is the primary mover of these external realities and forces. It is the prospect of providing a customer with value that gives the corporation purpose, and it is the satisfaction of the customer's requirements that gives it results.

MEDTRONIC

Medtronic is a company that personifies Peter's ideal of customer focus. Founded in 1949, it is the world's leading medical technology company, with $11 billion in annual revenues and an average annual growth of 18 percent for the past 20 years. At the core of this financial success is Medtronic's customer orientation, which is embedded in its mission: to alleviate pain, restore health, and extend life. Each year, 6 million patients benefit from Medtronic's technology for treating chronic conditions such as heart disease, neurological disorders, and vascular illnesses.

One of my high-school friends, Stephen Oesterle, M.D., is Medtronic's senior vice president for medicine and technology. He explained that the company considers physicians its all-important partners and shares their passion for improving the quality of patients' lives. The doctors help Medtronic decide what products to invent by understanding patients' problems and the devices needed to address them. "At least 99 out of our top 100 products were conceptualized in the field by physicians who were struggling at the bedside to try to correct something," says Oesterle.

Connecting to the customer—
being joined at the hip—is the beginning
of defining your tomorrow.

Partnering with physicians has resulted in a cornucopia of life-saving inventions; Medtronic has developed new ways to rewire our bodies, restoring cardiac rhythms with pacemakers and defibrillators, and devising more effective approaches to managing diabetes. It is also using neurostimulation (electrical stimulation of the spinal cord or a targeted nerve) for depression, incontinence, deafness, Parkinson's disease, epilepsy, migraines, and spinal cord injuries—the possibilities seem endless.

The growth opportunities for the company are spectacular. In the next 25 years, the number of Americans, Europeans, and Japanese over age 60 will double. At the same time, the number of people in developing countries who can afford high-end medical devices is increasing exponentially. Many of them will likely have the degenerative diseases that Medtronic products address.

With an unprecedented responsiveness to customer needs, Medtronic came up with a vision for disease management. Devices, implanted in patients, will be remotely programmed and use wireless networks to transmit vital signs such as blood pressure, glucose levels, and pulmonary pressure, thus saving face-to-face visits for instances when serious problems occur. So a heart patient from Manhattan can go on vacation to Puerto Rico knowing that the staff at his doctor's office will alert him if they spot a build-up of fluid in his chest—a primary indication of heart failure. His doctor will urge him to go to a hospital—and even tell him which one in San Juan is best—where a local doctor who never heard of him before can access all his key data. The San Juan doctor can confer with the patient's own doctor back home, who will look at a computer screen and double-check the treatment. This is happening already, thanks to the implanted monitor. Years ago, when Peter Drucker started consulting for medical suppliers, this sounded like science fiction. Now it's science—*customer-driven* science.

Connecting to the customer—being joined at the hip—is the beginning of defining your tomorrow.

CONNECTING WITH YOUR CUSTOMER: FOUR DRUCKER QUESTIONS

When Peter talked about the customer, he had four classic themes that he came back to over and over again. These themes ran through 70 years of his work. Peter asked every one of his clients:

1. Who is your *customer*?
2. What does your customer consider *value*?

After long discussions answering those two questions, he would then ask:

3. What are your *results* with customers?
4. Does your customer *strategy* work well with your business strategy?

Virtually every one of Peter's clients I spoke with had a story about the tremendous impact of these questions. Rethinking the answers with Peter changed how the clients thought about the business they were in. Southern Pipe, a regional plumbing company, redefined its customer; instead of serving contractors alone, its branches began serving local communities and homeowners as well as contractors. Herman Miller, the design-centered furniture company, changed its customer focus from midwesterners with an eye for a striking look to large city dwellers and lovers of modern art.

When I interviewed John Bachmann, the retired managing partner of the financial service firm Edward Jones, he described his moment of truth about the customer. Peter got into a disagreement with Ted Jones, the managing partner at the time, about who the firm's customers were. It began when Peter asked Ted, "How do you decide where you put your offices?"

Being clever, Ted said, "Well, you do it like the baseball player, Wee Willie Keeler. We hit 'em where they ain't." Ted explained that they targeted cities where there were no competitors, where Edward Jones was the only stockbroker in town. Peter, pushing him, asked, "Why would you do that?" Ted responded, "Because we do better." Peter asked how much better and suggested that they look at the facts. When they lined up all their offices, they found that Edward Jones did 25 percent better where there were competitors. Ted had seen the market geographically and had defined the customer as the rural American with no alternative access to the stock market. In fact, their customers were people who wanted personal service and relatively low-risk investments. Peter's questions fundamentally changed their understanding of their customer and their value proposition. When I drive by their office near my home in Westchester, New York, I smile, thanking Peter for putting them there.

The question, "Who is your customer?" seems awfully simple. But don't be deceived. The customer is no longer a passive receiver of products but is engaged in designing and refining them.

The question, "Who is your customer?" seems awfully simple. Mission statements and quarterly reports suggest that most companies and nonprofit organizations know the customer as intimately as a favorite neighbor. But don't be deceived. In this complex, ever-changing Lego world, identifying the customer is not the straightforward task many assume it to be. For one thing, the real customer is not necessarily the one who pays for the product or service, but the one who makes the buying decision. Every marketing analysis needs to start by assuming that the business doesn't know its customers and needs to find out who they are. The customer is no longer a passive receiver of products but is engaged in designing and refining them. Consider health care. It is now standard procedure for patients to investigate symptoms on the Internet, learning about diseases and treatments and tracking records of doctors and hospitals. Patients assess the latest clinical drug trials and experimental procedures. Consumers are now actively directing their own medical treatments. The specialist or

MD doesn't make the decision; he or she advises and is an influencer. It's a clear example of the customer taking charge in the new world.

WHO SHOULD BE CONSIDERED A CUSTOMER?

In this interconnected environment, there's an entire team behind every customer. The user, the buyer, and the influencer are linked together as never before, and they sway other buyers. We need to do more than understand them; we need to engage with them, alone and in groups, and understand how they want to be engaged. This is a whole new type of relationship, with the customer influencing other customers.

WHO IS YOUR CUSTOMER?

1. Who should be included in your definition of the customer?
   a. The end consumer?
   b. The buyer or decision maker?
   c. Critical influencers such as communities and sources of information?

2. Who in the interlocking world of alliances and partnerships should you view as customers versus competitors?

3. Who is not your customer?

4. Which of your current "noncustomers" should you be doing business with?

Companies spend a lot of time trying to reach the women—and yes, it is usually women—who fill supermarket carts. But they have a supporting cast of decision makers: kids and doctors and nutritionists and Pilates instructors and friends who proselytize about the various supplements and diets. Drucker went so far as to say that there is never only one consumer. He believed that at least two people usually stand behind a buying decision. Now companies have to keep tabs on intermediate customers and "filters," such as Web sites that rate products. All these influence end-users' buying decisions—even if the customer doesn't realize it.

There is never only one consumer.

Drucker identified the phenomenon of the customer team when he was advising the Girl Scouts of America more than 20 years ago. He found that the mothers were as much the organization's customers as the girls were. And mothers from different backgrounds required different kinds of connections. By emphasizing family values, the Girl Scouts were able to woo Latina mothers and thus recruit new members among their daughters. Capturing this rapidly growing population helped make the Girl Scouts the fastest growing not-for-profit organization in the 1980s.

At Avon the customer is as much the sales rep as the end-user. The sales rep needs to understand the differences between products and help the buyer decide. Intermediaries, like sales reps, work in unexpected ways which can give consumers more power than ever. Peter told me about one doctor whose patients dictated where she took a job. I recently talked to a surgeon who switched to a new hospital because it had gotten a better rating in *U.S. News & World Report* based on surveys of patients. The patient is not only the hospital's customer but also its evaluator and a major influence on its staff.

IDEAS IN ACTION: SHADOW CUSTOMERS

One of Peter's clients, a hospital equipment company, asked him to conduct a study to identify its customers and ended up redesigning its entire product line. Management had always assumed that the customer it needed to satisfy was the doctor. The company spent a good deal of time and money promoting itself and its products to those all-powerful doctors. It designed its products to provide the value, utility, and excellence the doctors wanted. But sales to hospitals tanked.

Peter had a customer analysis done that shocked the company. Unlike the Medtronic example where physicians made the purchase decision, hospital doctors are not the ones who buy. They don't even have much say in the purchase. Equipment is bought by administrators—many of whom don't even have an M.D. degree. They have to run complex institutions with poorly paid and not particularly skilled personnel. Their definition of "excellent" equipment is based on what the equipment does *not* do. It's excellent if it does not tie down scarce, highly skilled nurses and technicians. It's even better if it does not require a lot of training to operate and if it does not harm the patient or the staff. That was a revelation to the hospital equipment company: "We found out that our equipment has to be end-user focused rather than 'doctor-focused' and sophisticated."[7]

CUSTOMER VERSUS COMPETITOR?

In this networked world, your customer often turns out to be a competitor as well. In some cases your product may be packaged with others and sold as an integrated unit. Those sales may increase your revenue but decrease your brand identity, because the final product may not carry your brand.

I recently worked with a company that does graphics for software, games, movies, and music releases. Not long ago Sony or Disney would buy the company's graphic work and packaging and have it sent to a replicator to box with the disk. Now, replicators have begun to handle the purchase of graphics printing for the studios. The replicator is both a customer and a competitor of the graphics company. As this shift was occurring, my client was building its in-house graphics management and structural design capabilities. It is now managing all the artwork for several products—and the replicator is a complementor, a customer, and a competitor, combined into one. As the CEO put it: "Our customers and competitors have become all wrapped up into one—and we have to work with them all."

It is becoming increasingly difficult to tell friend from foe. In the online business world, the line between competition and cooperation is especially blurred and constantly changing. For several years Google has had a close, mutually profitable customer relationship with eBay, the online auction company. eBay spends twice as many advertising dollars on Google as it spends on other search engines and gets about three times the traffic.[8] And yet this symbiotic relationship is complicated. In its quest to become a one-stop information shop for the world, Google has launched a classified-advertising business called Google Base, which is free to users. Google is rumored to be ready to launch an online payment business code-named Google Wallet. Both are in direct competition with eBay.

In response, eBay has sought out alliances with two other technology leaders, Yahoo! and Microsoft, which are also under attack from Google. Yahoo and Microsoft could potentially become eBay customers using its online payment business, PayPal, and eBay's Internet phone service, Skype. Simultaneously, syndicating their clients' ads on eBay's auction pages is a huge opportunity for Yahoo! and Microsoft, and Google would like to do it, too.

Will Google's technological advantage enable it to walk all over its competitors? Or will it overreach from hubris, as so many other companies have? Keep your eye on this young company to see the answer.

In our new world, where relationships have proliferated, the customer you are ultimately serving can change from transaction to transaction. "When is our customer a competitor?" is a question that needs to be asked again and again.

WHO IS NOT YOUR CUSTOMER?

In my many conversations with Peter, he frequently asked the "not" question. He would sit back in his den, smile, and say, "It is also important to ask the other side of the question. Make sure you know the bounds you are assuming and that they are the bounds you want and that you want everyone in your organization to understand."

Bill Donaldson, of Donaldson, Lufkin & Jenrette (DLJ), told me that Drucker's "not" question made a big contribution to DLJ's success: "I think one of the greatest things that Peter left with me was [the understanding that] one of the most important decisions you're going to make in building this firm is the decision about whom you're not going to do business with. That can be credited with a large part of the success of DLJ in the heyday of the 1960s, and again in the 1980s and 1990s. We didn't do business with customers when we had questions about their ethics in the growing market. We didn't have to, and putting the question on the table made the decision that much easier."[9] Donaldson further credited the firm's internal identity for facing up to the issue. Often in the hallway, he would hear associates discuss and debate who was and who was not a DLJ customer.

Identifying noncustomers includes asking, "Who among our existing customers should not have customer status, and why?" In 1993, Colgate North America was struggling with the complexity of its products and customer base. After carefully reviewing its customers, Colgate realized that it needed to transition smaller customers to distributors so that it could focus its efforts on the larger customers who accounted for the bulk of its sales. This decision helped the management team regain the number one position in oral care two years later.[10]

Having explicitly defined its customer groups, management has the foundations of a robust outside-in perspective.

Drucker frequently said, "It is good to do one thing right. Don't do too much." Asking who is not the customer helps keep an organization focused and encourages transitions at the right moments. Having explicitly defined its customer groups, management has the foundations of a robust outside-in perspective. The work then needs to center on setting the business up to resonate with each customer's current and anticipated realities, needs, and value placement.

WHICH OF YOUR CURRENT NONCUSTOMERS SHOULD YOU BE DOING BUSINESS WITH?

In a changing world, this inquiry, which Peter used so often, forces managers to think a little harder. Andy Grove, Intel's former chairman, says, "Peter Drucker is a guiding light to a whole lot of us." Over time, Intel has grown by converting noncustomers to customers. In the early 1990s, Intel began to understand the needs of a key noncustomer—the wireless phone companies. To serve this fast-growing market, Intel dropped its historical third-party connection to players like Motorola and Nokia in favor of direct relationships. Intel thus focused on the wireless phone companies and began selling them chips and capabilities to support their emerging needs.

Today, Intel is crossing into another new area, selling laptops to the developing world—an Intel PC, not a PC with Intel inside. Laptop companies were Intel's customers. Now they are competitors. Intel is making customers out of noncustomers in vast, overlooked regions of the world. It recently announced several regional PC design initiatives, including a desktop computer for the Indian market and another for Mexico. The Mexican machine, offered in partnership with Telmex, the Mexican communications company, offers a subsidy for a broadband Internet connection and is priced at about 20 percent below similar machines.

Teachers are another newly discovered customer for Intel. CEO Paul S. Otellini announced a five-year, one billion dollar program to train teachers and to extend wireless digital Internet access worldwide. The goal is to train 10 million teachers around the world and give them and their students access to a low-cost, Microsoft-compatible machine to be called Edu-wise. "It doesn't need exotic technology and it runs real applications," Otellini explained.[11]

When I asked Peter to tell me the action items here, he said to just keep asking the question and to make sure that the answers are really thought about, not just reflex responses.

The essence of a business's identity lies in the value the business provides to its customers. What that value is remains the most important question a company can ask itself. Yet the question is rarely asked, because people often assume they know the answer. That assumption has killed many companies.

When I cut my teeth as a young McKinsey consultant in 1980, AT&T was a company I admired immensely—as did most of the business world. Drucker wrote with much praise about its iconic leader, Theodore Vail, and its legendary customer focus. In the 1990s, however, AT&T lost touch with what its customers valued, which was low cost and convenience. Instead it focused on leveraging its expanding network and became mired in a monopolistic culture of bureaucracy and complacency. When Michael Armstrong took the helm in 1997, the market had great hopes that he would overhaul the company and stem erosion in its core long-distance business while positioning AT&T as a telecom leader. Instead, the focus was on trying to fight the local Bell companies by acquiring cable companies to gain access to their local customers. At the same time, customers were gradually moving away from traditional long-distance calling in favor of wireless phones, e-mail, and instant messaging. They were not interested in making telephone calls through cable, and AT&T's move fueled customer defections to the Internet. Thanks to the vastly increased number of high-speed, broadband Internet connections made available in recent years, however, and driven by such firms as Vonage and Skype, a significant number of customers now use their Internet service suppliers for multiple services, including telephone.

WHAT DOES YOUR CUSTOMER CONSIDER VALUE?

1. How does your customer's perception of value align with your own?

2. How do connectivity and relationship influence value?

3. What is the value of the connecting whole that is different from the sum of its parts?

4. Which of your customer's wants or demands remain unsatisfied in your target markets, and can you or should you step up to fill those gaps?

It didn't help that senior management spent valuable time thinking of ways to placate its increasingly angry shareholders by creating complex schemes to split the company into separately traded units. During Armstrong's reign, AT&T's customer base plummeted from 90 million to 54 million, and it lost about $60 billion, or 75 percent of shareholder value. While AT&T was busy talking to investment bankers and upgrading its technologically deficient cable networks, two young Scandinavian entrepreneurs were forming alliances and launching the Internet telephone company Skype (acquired by eBay on October 14, 2005),[12] which offers its users free calls to other Skype users online. Today, Skype has 61 million customers in 225 countries and is adding 170,000 new ones every day;[13] AT&T is down to about 22 million.[14] In early 2005, AT&T—once the world's largest company—agreed to be taken over by one of its former children, SBC Communications. Although SBC renamed itself AT&T, it's safe to say that AT&T as I knew it in 1981 no longer exists.

Whether companies like it or not, the customer is the boss.

With the silent revolution, what the customer values and what influences that value are shifting dramatically. Whether companies like it or not, the customer is the boss. In the developed world, most customers have moved up on Abraham Maslow's "hierarchy of needs" and are seeking fulfillment and service rather than another material product.[15] With time increasingly valued, convenience commands a greater premium. And, of course, the customer's increasing role in tailoring the product influences perceived value. These fundamental shifts in customer values must be recognized.

Explicitly making the customer the boss does not place the company at a disadvantage as some fear. By embracing the notion of the customer as boss, management can make the relationship a win for both parties—by asking the questions that force the organization to "walk in the customer's shoes" and understand what the customer values.

DOES YOUR CUSTOMER'S PERCEPTION OF VALUE ALIGN WITH YOUR OWN?

Over the years, consultants and internal marketing groups have performed countless customer value analyses. We have interviewed customers, identified major attributes that they value, and carefully assessed their relative importance—all excellent work. The problem is that everyone from the board of directors to the CEO on down needs to be out there talking directly to the customers themselves and finding out what is going on. Direct, personal contact carries an emotional intelligence not readily reported on paper. Value has to be understood from the customer's perspective, and the only way to do it is to ask the customer directly. This task cannot be delegated. In this data-rich world, first-hand emotional intelligence still matters.

In this data-rich world, firsthand emotional intelligence still matters.

That is why, on any given day, you may find Procter & Gamble chairman, president, and CEO A.G. Lafley in the kitchen of a Venezuelan housewife or walking around in the most dangerous parts of São Paolo and Rio de Janeiro to see firsthand how consumers are buying and using P&G products. The analysis can be delegated, but not the customer contact.

I spoke with Robert Gwyn, former executive vice president and board member of Jacobs Engineering, a $6 billion company that designs and builds facilities and installs equipment for industries with very precise requirements, such as aerospace and defense, chemicals, and pharmaceutical companies. He explained that Jacobs's value proposition is targeted at CEOs, even though COOs and heads of engineering make the purchasing decisions. Jacobs maintains relationships with the full executive committees. It does not claim to provide the lowest cost or best quality buildings, but the company does promise to minimize business risks by addressing the customer's strategic tradeoffs (such as spending more time on developing a particular drug versus starting to build the production facility needed to get the drug to market). Jacobs Engineering doesn't ignore cost; it brings a cost discipline to everything it does. But its top-level value proposition has to do with strategic tradeoffs. Its customers are not in commodity businesses but in dynamic industries where the bets are high.

I asked Gwyn how Peter Drucker had influenced the company. He told me that Jacobs had begun as a family-owned company focused on process equipment and the chemical industry. In the 1980s, Peter's writings had helped the members of the management team think through the value they provided and articulate their value proposition. They realized that they were more than an industry service company, and their target customers rapidly expanded beyond chemical and energy companies to include defense, pharmaceutical, and infrastructure businesses, fundamentally changing the scale and scope of the firm. The company is now about 10 times the size it was 17 years ago. As to how the silent revolution is affecting Jacobs's value proposition, Gwyn said that the value proposition hasn't changed but delivering on it has. Many more people at each company are now customers and have their fingers in the pie. Each person adds value but also costs time, and threatens to unsynchronize the whole. It has become far more difficult for Jacobs to have the discipline and ability to integrate ideas rapidly and to further enhance the value being provided than it used to be.

HOW DO CONNECTIVITY AND RELATIONSHIPS INFLUENCE VALUE?

Beyond the significance of the product itself, the value perceived by a customer increasingly depends on his or her relationship with the company and control of the end result. This has remained true even as face-to-face interactions have given way to cyberspace transactions. Sumerset Houseboats boosted online sales dramatically by more directly engaging the customer in the process of building a boat. In the 1970s, Sumerset was a neighborhood company, and the locals would wander in daily to see their boats taking shape. They knew the boatbuilders and were involved every step of the way. When Sumerset's online business took off, it wanted its online customers to have the same opportunity as neighborhood folks. Today, Sumerset customers go online to customize the plans for their boats and to view photos of their boats being built. This is far more than a gimmick. It is a way to empower customers and create a sense of community.

On the industrial side, the value of deep, close association with the customer has been demonstrated over and over again, with suppliers placing staff or whole departments at customer sites to handle logistics, or assigning systems engineers to the customer site long term to assist with complex equipment. And yet this kind of connectivity can be slow in coming. For every company that will use Jacobs Engineering to help it make strategic tradeoffs in planning a new facility, there are others unwilling to entrust aspects of their operations to a third party. A senior executive at Cincinnati Milacron estimates that when it works with customers on the full system design, equipment productivity is 20 percent higher. Yet a number of its customers feel that system design must remain in house. Despite the explosion in connectivity, companies still encounter pockets of resistance and need to find ways to provide value while respecting the customer's desire for autonomy.

Part of the connection is a holistic understanding of customer needs, which drives many marketing decisions. Motorola found that at Wal-Mart new mothers often bought cell phones in the same purchase "decision window" as disposable diapers. Apparently new mothers were very conscious of their need to stay in touch with their families, hence the odd juxtaposition of diapers and dialing. Motorola bought end-aisle displays near the diapers to prompt increased purchases.

A very different approach to understanding and meeting customer needs is in bundling capabilities, products, and services to meet those needs. The master bundler—or, as competitors might argue, the master bully—is of course Bill Gates. Microsoft's cofounder and former chairman explicitly looked at the bundles consumers buy when defining Microsoft's strategy of integrating previously stand-alone products and technologies into its Windows operating system. From a customer perspective bundling provides tremendous value. It saves not only money but also time and aggravation as the bundled software works well together and is compatible with a variety of computers.

Competitors have successfully argued that the bundling is predatory, and in 2001 a U.S. court ruled Microsoft's own Internet Explorer browser bundle was illegal. This doesn't seem to have stopped Microsoft, however. Since then Windows Media Player, Outlook Express, Windows Messenger, and Windows Movie Maker, among others, have been bundled. There are rumors that the next operating system, Vista, will include antispyware and security software, threatening to kill Symantec and MacAfee just as bundling Internet Explorer killed Netscape. In the computing landscape, the terrain is always changing. Google has started to offer free, downloadable software bundles called Google Pack, consisting of software from Google and other companies. None of these programs is from Microsoft.

WHICH CUSTOMER WANTS REMAIN UNSATISFIED?

Managers must determine which customer wants in their target markets are unsatisfied and then further determine whether they can or should step up to provide value. By regularly challenging the organization to give fresh answers to these issues and by promoting a culture of respect for the customer, management stays current on the dynamic circumstances that determine the customer's wants and buying decisions. Such knowledge and culture give logic to what otherwise might be viewed as irrational or inexplicable behavior on the part of the customer.

Consider the Apple research team which regularly scrolls through chat rooms searching for customer comments about unsatisfied needs. The need for a car charger for the iPod was found in one such chat room two years ago.[16]

In a very real way, nothing mattered to Peter if you couldn't talk about the results. He often asked his clients to write down the results they expected from a particular decision and check them six months later. Results have to be measured carefully and understood and interpreted properly; they are not absolute and can be understood only in context.

By the late 1980s, Peter felt that many companies were so focused on shareholders that they had lost sight of the customer. He'd thought a lot about this, and he wondered why CEOs weren't listening. Although he believed that profits are a company's ability to invest in tomorrow's opportunities, he liked to remind me that profits follow customer satisfaction, not the other way around. Peter often reminded executives that the person buying a pair of shoes is not paying for the shoemaker's profit. She or he is paying for a nice, comfortable pair of shoes. The purpose of a business is to provide value to the customer—to provide something that an independent and knowledgeable outsider who can choose whether or not to buy is willing to get in exchange for his or her purchasing power. The profits that flow from this value reflect the company's effectiveness in aggregate, but those results do not necessarily show the company where it is meeting customer expectations and where it is falling short. And the company needs to know this, especially now. According to the New York branch of the Federal Reserve Bank, the number of products offered to a consumer in New York State increased fourfold from 2000 to 2005.[17]

WHAT ARE YOUR RESULTS WITH CUSTOMERS?

1. How are you measuring your outside results?

2. How are outsiders measuring and sharing results about your products and services?

3. Are you fully leveraging the information your results provide?

4. Are you honest and socially responsible in presenting your results?

HOW ARE YOU MEASURING YOUR OUTSIDE RESULTS?

What key pieces of intelligence are you missing, and how do you calibrate your antennae to capture this intelligence? Do you employ a manageable set of the most telling metrics? At an Ogilvy & Mather board meeting, one member asked, "Are we a financial company? When you look at what we are measuring, we look like a bank, not like a creative company." The company changed its tracking measures to capture information more relevant to its culture and mission—advertising effectiveness, the percentage of repeat clients, the lifespan of ads, and creative awards and investments.

In 2001, when Colgate switched its customer service measure from "orders on time and complete" to "product available on the shelf," its revenue jumped by 3 percent.[18] I had the opportunity to watch how that simple shift fundamentally changed the company's orientation. A conventional service metric, on-time and complete delivery, is an internal measure that is more responsive to the retailer than to the consumer. Availability, on the other hand, is a prerequisite for customer purchases and satisfaction. Although the store is a customer of sorts, it is only part of the chain that supplies the end-user; it is not the end-user. It is not enough to focus on the right customer; the results must be quantified and tracked to keep the customer focus clear.

HOW ARE OUTSIDERS MEASURING AND SHARING RESULTS AND INFORMATION ABOUT YOUR PRODUCTS AND SERVICES?

The wealth of information available on the Internet very likely includes more about your business than just what's contained in your company Web site. The "customer team" that Drucker talked about has moved beyond the consumer's friends and family to include product-specific, Web-based information sources such as blogs, bulletin boards, and chat rooms—many of which provide detailed descriptions, critiques, and ratings as well as contact information. These sites are often very influential, more so than are friends and family. They are also vehicles for exchanging information. It only makes sense to monitor these sites to ensure that your information is accurate and up to date, that you are not being overlooked, and that you take advantage of every opportunity to create a positive Internet buzz.

But you can use the Internet for more than promoting your products and services. It offers a wealth of information on how customers experience and perceive your products, what features they are looking for, and what they value. Responding to information on the customer experience—by improving your product offering or refining your sales approach, for example—is one more way of building your company's outside-in perspective.

ARE YOU FULLY LEVERAGING THE INFORMATION YOUR RESULTS PROVIDE?

Where do gaps exist between targeted and actual results—and what causes them? What comparative information are we using to interpret our results (e.g., market trends, competitive performance), and what does that tell us about our performance? For example, a 30 percent growth rate looks good but loses some of its luster and signals missed opportunity when direct competitors are achieving 40 percent growth rates. Or strong performance in a declining market might suggest, "It's time to reassess our purpose and identity," rather than, "We are on the right path."

To get the maximum impact from results, the business must communicate those results throughout the organization as well as to external partners. Even more critical is to link results to strategy decisions and then translate them into actions that produce better results. I helped Frank Weise do this at Cott when he took over as CEO in 1999. We worked together to translate every measure reported and link it clearly with the relevant organization inside the company. To link production-line performance with customer shelf availability, we rewarded Cott employees when every Wal-Mart shelf had 100 percent stock availability every day for a week (there were a lot of pizza parties in the plants). And when there were issues at the shelf, SWAT teams from the plant and logistics organizations went out to the customer to discover the underlying causes of those problems and to communicate and solve them. This program changed Cott, now the leading private label provider of carbonated beverages, from a second-rank supplier to a leading partner with many of its customers.

ARE YOU HONEST AND SOCIALLY RESPONSIBLE IN PRESENTING YOUR RESULTS?

An enterprise needs to examine the ethical dimension. As Enron and so many other corporate frauds have made monumentally clear, social responsibility is inextricably linked to sustainability. Corporations flout this reality at their peril.

The "outside-in" perspective:
An organization's point of reference should
always be what is going on in the marketplace,
not in the company's boardroom.

While fraud still occurs, it is not only outright fraud that engenders misreporting. Many companies just can't stand to look in the mirror. They fool themselves into thinking they are doing better than they really are. A glaring example is the myth, widely held during the high-tech bubble, of "Internet traffic doubling every 100 days."[19] Companies must monitor their results 24 hours a day, 7 days a week. Managers need to use their intuition and judgment to capture a rich understanding of the large and growing landscape "outside" the corporation. Running the business from the outside-in also ensures that management doesn't fall prey to the insularity that dooms many institutions.

Peter believed that all opportunities were evaluated and all resources allocated in the context of management's understanding of the "outside" marketplace. Peter called it the "outside-in" perspective: An organization's point of reference should always be what is going on in the marketplace, not in the company's boardroom. This brutally honest perspective has a huge impact on everything a company does, from its overall strategy and direction to its continued progress.

Within the business, an outside-in perspective is based on the business's systematic capability to gather external information and interpret it honestly in order to build an organization that truly listens to the customer, and to devise and implement customer-tailored strategies in response to customer needs.

DOES YOUR CUSTOMER STRATEGY AND YOUR BUSINESS STRATEGY WORK TOGETHER?

1. What is your level of integration with customers and your scope of offering?

2. How are outsiders measuring and sharing results about your products and services?

3. How do these relationships all fit together in a portfolio that fits with the business strategy?

4. Are you allocating resources where you want to be investing in relationships?

Individualized strategies are a new approach to serving the customer. They require a degree of bonding and a solutions-oriented approach that has been made possible by standards, the new ease of data management, and people becoming comfortable with having their own shopper cards at A&P. Targeting and serving large customer segments have given way to creating a value chain (and, often, a delivery system) for each customer. Constructive, enduring bonds result from an up-to-date, outside-in perspective and from relationships based on mutual trust. Outside-in intelligence becomes a wealth-producing strategy when it is translated into unique and meaningfully differentiated value that is delivered to the customer. And this strategy cannot be monolithic—it is designed and executed customer by customer to reflect the unique configuration of value sought by each customer. Customer-tailored strategies fall into four broad categories reflecting the level of the firm's integration with its customer and the scope of its product offerings, from a one-product shop to a one-stop shop (see Figure 2.1).

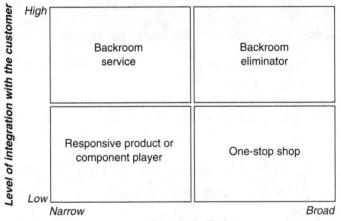

Figure 2.1 Types of Customer Strategies Reflecting Level of Integration and Scope of Offering

The vertical axis captures the extent to which the capabilities of different entities that provide value to a given customer—the company, its customer, and its other outside partners—are integrated with the customer's operations. The silent revolution makes it massively easier for independent firms to collaborate in solving a customer's problem and to function as part of the customer's organization without actually having to merge or be acquired. Consequently, integration has become a fundamental element of customer strategy.

Today's flow of information and standardization enable the high level of integration targeted by Infosys Technologies, the India-based firm that is competing with giants like IBM and Accenture to manage its clients' entire global IT needs. By assuming full responsibility for clients' IT, Infosys acts as a *backroom eliminator*. Founded in 1981, Infosys cut its teeth providing nuts-and-bolts IT solutions (from devising the business plan for a new online community to designing the portal to writing the software it runs on). It is rapidly adding high-end IT strategy and business process consulting in transforming one of the largest global players in independent software development and maintenance.

The *backroom service* provider is highly integrated with the customer. It assumes discrete responsibilities that lessen but do not eliminate the customer's backroom operations. For example, Doane, the private-label pet food manufacturer, manages the store and delivery functions for Wal-Mart's private label dog food, Ol'Roy. Doane's services do not eliminate Wal-Mart's backroom, but it does take on part of the burden by providing a pet food specialist that ensures that the product is where it needs to be all the time.

At the lower end of the integration spectrum is the *responsive product* or *component player*, typically with a unique brand or capability offering, which is continually being updated. Also at the lower end of the integration scale is the *one-stop shop* or bundler, which fully meets a range of customer needs but does not integrate itself into the customer's operations. No longer limited to the department store, one-stop shops include Expedia and Orbitz. These web sites allow travelers to compare prices and schedules on flights, cruises, hotels, rental cars, vacation packages, and vacation activities, and to customize and plan every aspect of their trip, even to the point of receiving e-mails with flight status information, weather forecasts, and packing suggestions in the days preceding departure.

Exceptional companies generally participate in all four categories. UPS is one such organization. UPS manages the full logistics and delivery function for Home Depot, effectively eliminating this retailer's backroom. For other customers, UPS locates a pickup and sometimes an operator at the customer's site to facilitate backroom operations. And customers such as Wal-Mart use UPS as a one-stop shop for all shipping services. Finally, there are those, like Amazon, which use UPS's service for a discrete piece of their delivery needs, such as cost-effective home deliveries to and returns from individual customers.[20]

PROCTER & GAMBLE

From its humble beginnings as a soap and candle maker, P&G became one of the world's best known and most admired consumer goods companies, with sales close to $57 billion in 2005. Fully 17 of its brands have at least $1 billion in sales, including such well-known names as Tide, Pantene, and Pampers. Although it went global later than Colgate-Palmolive and Unilever, P&G today derives about 48 percent of its sales from outside North America, operating in over 80 countries and marketing its products in more than 160.

In June 2000, P&G was faltering. The board of directors had decided to replace CEO Durk Jager after only 17 months, following several profit warnings and a more than 50 percent drop in market value in the previous six months. However, problems had been in the making for many years.

Until the mid-1990s, P&G was a reliable growth machine. It doubled sales every 10 years and grew its earnings by 10 percent through the acquisition of higher-margin health and beauty companies and by reducing costs through economies of scale. With the emergence of Wal-Mart, P&G became known as a leader in collaborative partnering. The company simplified product lines and formulations, and it introduced global brand names to reduce costs and speed up product launches.

But its relentless focus on distributors' needs to the exclusion of the consumer eventually made P&G a victim of its own success. It became a very powerful, successful, almost arrogant bureaucracy that gradually lost sight of the outside world—most notably the all-important consumer. As A.G. Lafley notes, "I think there is something about bureaucracies that turn inward, especially successful bureaucracies. They . . . get a lot more fascinated by the operation of the bureaucracy than what's going on in the world around them."[21]

By 1995, growth in sales dropped to below 4 percent, and international sales grew by less than 3 percent during 1995–2000. While earnings held up initially, huge restructuring costs depressed net earnings between 1998 and 2000. Global market shares were stagnant or dropping in 70 percent of P&G's businesses, and, adding insult to injury, Colgate Total overtook Crest as the leading toothpaste.

In January 1999, Durk Jager replaced John Pepper as CEO. Jager strongly believed that the only way for P&G to emerge from its slump was to rapidly create new products by speeding up innovation and to break up the bureaucracy through massive organizational changes—in effect, to create a cultural revolution. "A measure of our business vitality is the vitality of our organization—the degree to which people are breaking barriers, challenging conventional wisdom, stretching to achieve the unachievable, redefining the marketplace."[22] To make his point, Jager was reportedly fond of saying, "If it's not broken, break it." This initiative, called *Organization 2005*, was to be a six-year, $1.9 billion effort. P&G's identity as a preeminent marketer had been challenged, and an intense effort to change old beliefs, reporting structures, and incentives ensued.

In 1999, during an informal brainstorming meeting with a few P&G senior managers, Drucker was asked his opinion on Organization 2005. He said:

> It's a very impressive document, but it left me very dissatisfied. I felt I had gotten only the appetizer of the meal because it focused on products and technology. There is a dimension in there that's lacking . . . I call it attitude. The greatest opportunities, and the greatest threats to a company like P&G in the next 10 or 15 years, are changes in demographics, in consumer segmentation, in distribution channels, which always need a totally new consumer, and I did not get any of that. You're still looking from the inside out, and the landscape you see is yesterday's landscape. And when you look from the outside in, it isn't P&G that has changed. It's the landscape that has changed. And I missed that. I [also] don't like the way you talk about changing the culture. My question is, how do you utilize your culture? When I look at your company, it represents enormous achievements. Your job is not to repudiate them, but to build them. And to be proud of them. Otherwise you

alienate far too many [of your] people and tell them you are no longer worth anything. And for the next 10 years at least, your bread and butter will come from what these people produce. And so I don't like changing the culture. I like how we build on it for a changed world.[23]

Jager's gamble was that introducing many new, innovative products would prevent commoditization and maintain P&G's premium prices around the globe. Huge investments in R&D followed, increasing that investment from a historical average 3.8 percent of sales to 4.8 percent in 2000. Meanwhile, advertising fell from 10.2 percent in 1998 to 9.2 percent of sales in 2001. The innovation process was driven by internal scientific and engineering perspectives rather than by consumer needs and ideas from outside partners. As a result, only about 20 percent of the new products were successful.

The premium-pricing concept also was unsuccessful in the low-income, high-growth developing world. Thinking that every consumer would appreciate the value of a higher-quality product, P&G offered the same global brand names, formulations, and gross profit margins in every market. Since most low-income consumers could not afford P&G products, sales growth was slow, and countries representing over 80 percent of the world's population accounted for no more than 15–20 percent of P&G sales. In its efforts to find the next killer brand, P&G had neglected its bread and butter business.

In June 2000, A.G. Lafley replaced Jager as CEO of P&G. Lafley agreed with many of the strategies set forth in Organization 2005 but recognized that P&G "tried to do too much too fast,"[24] and as a result "the wheels were coming off in a lot of places."[25] His first order of business was to get back to basics: that in a consumer goods company, the consumer is the boss:

I would say that still one of the biggest opportunities of my company is what [Peter Drucker] calls "outside-in," what we call "externally connected and focused." I am pushing really hard for us to stay connected to the messiness and the unpredictability and the volatility of the external environment, some of which is customer, some of which is competitor, some of which is innovation and technology, that's coming at you in all directions, a lot of times from outside your industry. Economic and political happenings. It's big and messy and complicated, and I'm just paranoid that we're going to miss important things that are going on out there that are going to impact our customer and our enterprise's interaction with that customer. I think it sounds too simple to believe, but the first thing we did is elevate our consumer to the boss. And it was way more than words because it meant we really needed to understand who she is.[26]

I think it sounds too simple to believe, but the first thing we did is elevate our consumer to the boss.

This strategy fit P&G's strengths and culture as a marketer and restored the confidence of the workforce. It also helped challenge the insular mentality. "We don't exist in silos anymore,"[29] says Susan Arnold, P&G's beauty-care and feminine-care boss.

Lafley immediately set out to rebuild the old major brands—Tide, Pantene, and Pampers. The renewed focus on consumer needs drove the marketing push. "When A.G. first came onboard, we were struggling. We were trying to get new brands out there and do everything at the same time," recalls Martin Nuechtern,

A.G. Lafley, chairman, president, and CEO of Procter & Gamble, said in 2005: "The CEO must create the conditions that are necessary for an organization to attack problems and seize opportunities. Most importantly, he/she has to get people to see things as they are, not as they'd like them to be. The CEO is the link between the reality of the outside and the insularity of the inside—CEOs are in a unique position to bring outside reality in. As CEO, you have to remind yourself of that every day. I mean, really, when you walk into the office, who's the boss? The consumer's the boss. What are our core assets? At Procter & Gamble, our core assets are our brands, and our knowledge workers."[27] R. R. Deupree was chairman of the Procter & Gamble Company in the 1930s and 1940s. He said something to the effect that you could take away everything at P&G—take away the office buildings, take away the manufacturing plants, take away all the physical assets—leave the company its brands and its people, and in a decade we'd build it all back again. "I think that's very much Peter Drucker."[28]

head of global hair care. "A.G. made things very clear: Make sure you focus on Pantene."[30] The Pantene line was revamped from a primarily features-driven product (e.g., shampoo for fine hair) to a consumer-benefit product (e.g., greater volume).

With Pampers, the outside-in perspective resulted in an almost counterintuitive change—the painful realization that a pull-on diaper more completely satisfied consumer needs. P&G had the largest installed base of taped-diaper converters, which drove the engineering group know-how and R&D formulation expertise. Letting go of the taped diaper and embracing the pull-on was difficult. "In too many of our businesses, the technology or the machine had become the boss."[31]

P&G's new approach radically changed how it prioritized R&D, and a relentless, disciplined weeding resulted. The company killed 75 percent of corporate innovation projects because they could not pass the litmus test of delighting consumers more than competitors' products could. Similarly, P&G is revamping its approach to global advertising.[32] Carpet bombing television audiences with traditional 30-second commercials is, much to the horror of the advertising industry, a thing of the past. In the developed world, technology has enabled viewers to avoid commercials altogether. In response, P&G is trying to figure out what information is relevant to the consumer, even when the consumer can't articulate it. To improve its two-way communication with consumers, P&G launched the interactive Web site Pampers.com, offering mothers advice on everything from breastfeeding to temper tantrums in over 20 different languages. To woo consumers in the developing world, P&G is embracing a new cultural diversity, reaching out to Jews (by publicly washing donated clothes during Passover in an Orthodox Jewish community) and Muslims (by launching Tide White Musk for Ramadan, when Muslims carry small bottles of white musk essence).

To reach its growth targets, P&G had to expand its definition of the customer to include low-income customers who could not afford any of P&G's products. This required a complete change in mindset. Rather than ask, "What is the best way to market our global product line in this country," the company had to ask, "How much can a consumer reasonably be expected to pay," and then develop the formulation and supply-chain strategy to meet that customer need—fundamentally building the company from the outside in. That often meant reformulating the product to its bare minimum elements, giving up previous sacrosanct minimum margin requirements, and using local contract manufacturers.[33] In 2005, 8 of P&G's top 16 countries in terms of sales were developing markets—countries that are expected to add about a percentage point of growth each year.

THE GRANDFATHER OF MARKETING

According to Harvard professor and business writer Theodore Levitt, "Peter Drucker created and publicized the marketing concept." In an essay on Drucker's importance to marketing, Arnold Corbin, former professor of marketing at New York University, states that despite being essentially a management writer, Drucker "has probably contributed more to the development and understanding of marketing than any 'marketing man.'"[34] And in the Wharton School's farewell tribute to Peter Drucker,[35] Stephen J. Hoch, chairperson of the marketing department, describes Drucker as "the Warren Buffett of management gurus. His analysis of management and marketing issues always was pithy and to the point. No pandering to buzzwords and fads, but a constancy of message, with straightforward reasoning and clearly articulated ideas. The following statement attributed to Drucker is today still the essence of marketing: 'The aim of marketing is to make selling superfluous. [It] . . . is to know and understand the customer so well that the product or service fits him and sells itself. Ideally, marketing should result in a customer who is ready to buy.'"

Wharton marketing professor David J. Reibstein remembered as one of the most memorable days of his life, "The day I spent with Drucker in his home nearly seven years ago. A man of such enormous impact on business and society was a very modest man, surrounded in a humble yet very comfortable home in Claremont, California. He had such tremendous insight into every facet of business and its role in society. Drucker considered a business's most valuable asset to be its people. Generally, he is considered the father of marketing. He said the role of business is to create a customer. He always emphasized focusing on customers and understanding what they valued. I assume many fields want to claim him as their 'father.' While he contributed to the literature for more than 65 years, his thoughts are way ahead of our time."[36]

As marketing writer and Kellogg Business School professor Philip Kotler stated, "Peter Drucker is the Father of Management. . . . I regard it as a compliment when some people call me the Father of Marketing. I tell them that if this is the case, then Peter Drucker is the Grandfather of Marketing."[37]

CONCLUSION

In a world where the customer has become a key controlling force, the importance of knowing and working with your customer has never been greater. In answering the four questions about customer identity, value, results, and integration, we must keep in mind:

1. The customer is no longer merely a receiver of goods and services. He or she is your partner, and your roles are evolving all the time. The relationships are not simple, and they often include whole communities.

2. Value is based on your ability to connect with the customer and know more about his or her needs and desires than he or she can articulate. This connection requires openness and integrity. It benefits from being personalized—there are no bundles of customers. The vertically integrated brand is being replaced by the multiparty, networked value chain that coherently integrates parts, products, and services into a bundle.

3. Results happen customer by customer. The customers know the results—good and bad—as soon as you do, if not sooner.

4. Customer strategy depends as much on the level of integration with the customer as on the product and service itself. The strategy needs to be built on the bundle of capabilities and strengths within and accessed by your company.

These realities and the corporation's need to operate effectively in the Lego world only underscore the importance of beginning and ending with the customer. When I asked Peter what managers should do about this new customer, he said, "Ask yourself every day, which customers did I touch today, and what did I learn?"

Delivering value depends on your listening and translating, and innovating accordingly. As we discuss in Chapter 3, it is only with an outside-in view that businesses can change customers' expectations and begin to provide products and services that customers did not know they wanted—the truest measure of an innovative product.

THREE | Innovation and Abandonment

The best way to predict the future
is to create it.[1]

—Peter F. Drucker

Nobody was better at defining and helping companies capture opportunities than Peter Drucker. When I think back on our conversations, one phrase that sticks in my head because Peter said it so often is, "Tomorrow is an opportunity." Peter's first view of the United States was in 1937, and he was forever influenced by a country striving to create tomorrow. Drucker believed that the most important measure of a company is its ability to anticipate and invest in tomorrow's opportunities. This view is why innovation was so central to Peter's thinking. It was fundamental to everything he wrote. To Peter, the conventional view of innovation, focused solely on product development or brand extension, missed the point. To truly innovate, Peter believed you had to radically change customers' expectations.

Tomorrow is an opportunity.

For Peter it was simple: If you don't understand innovation, you don't understand business. Starbucks exemplifies what Peter considered to be true innovation. Beginning with a single store in 1971, Starbucks grew to over 12,000 locations in 37 countries in 2006. While visiting Starbucks, I spoke to Dorothy Kim, a

Starbucks executive vice president, who told me that Starbucks didn't set out merely to make a better cup of coffee. That was the old way of looking at the coffee retail business. Instead, the executives had a much bigger idea: to make Starbucks a destination between your home and office—a place where people can find a respite.

Starbucks didn't just offer a better cup of coffee than the average restaurant; it delivered an instant community—a shared experience. The company made it easy to relax with a comfortable, "stay as long as you like" setting that now includes wireless Internet access. Starbucks became the extended living room, the familiar meeting place in a strange city, the funky (but not too funky) way station to escape from the corporate cubicle, the place to stop between classes to surf the Net. It did much more than simply crush, boil, and filter a sack of coffee beans; it *changed our expectations*.

If you don't understand innovation, you don't understand business.

Much of Starbucks' innovation has to do with marketing, not product. This isn't just about coffee served one cup at a time. Starbucks came up with an insider mystique by inventing a new language for size—tall, grande, and venti, instead of small, medium, and large—along with endless variations on what's essentially the humdrum old theme of coffee and milk. Think about it: tall, grande, and venti have become part of your vocabulary, especially if you earn more than $50,000 and you're under age 60. Starbucks makes you feel like a savvier consumer by telling you the flavor difference between Ethiopian and Guatemalan coffees. And the third time you visit the shop, the barista generally knows your preference.

Apple is another company with a high innovation IQ that changed our expectations with the introduction of the iPod.

Before the iPod, people didn't sit around thinking, "I wish I had a little jukebox with 1,500 songs that I selected, and I could carry it in my pocket." Apple introduced the iPod in 2001, and within four years more than half the people in the United States owned or used iPods. Apple changed people's expectations and their definition of value. It was no longer fine to have a Sony Walkman with 20 songs on a CD. Anything less than an iPod was unacceptable. Today Apple appears to be taking this to video with ambitions of linking everyone wirelessly.

Innovation is about shaking loose from yesterday's world so that we gain the freedom to create tomorrow.

Peter Drucker liked to talk about what was and what was not an innovation. On one of my business trips, I overheard two airline travelers debate the merits of the new Apple PowerBook with an Intel chip. They decided it was not an innovation. Customers are sure that every new model will have more computing power and capabilities; simply meeting their expectations is not true innovation. When I replayed the conversation and posed the question to Peter, he seemed to agree with the travelers, but added there may still be an innovation lurking that does change our expectations, but it is not there yet. Peter believed that innovation is about shaking loose from yesterday's world so that we gain the freedom to create tomorrow.

CREATING YOUR TOMORROW: FOUR DRUCKER QUESTIONS

Peter wrote about innovation for decades—long before anyone heard of iPods and Starbucks, or even the Internet; it fascinated him. By the Vietnam War years he was predicting that technology would change everything about the way we do business. He liked to discuss the delicate balance between innovation and change on the one hand, and preservation of the status quo on the other. He first described this fundamental tension between the new and the old 70 years ago, shortly before World War II. During one of our last conversations in 2005, he told me that finding this balance was still critical to business survival. "You can't throw everything out, or you'll have anarchy," he said. "You can't hold onto everything, or you'll die."

"You can't throw everything out,
or you'll have anarchy."
"You can't hold on to everything, or you'll die."

Peter understood the difficulty of innovating for the future while hanging on to the past from personal experience. In 1935, he left London to make his first trip to the United States. He'd decided then and there to leave Europe. "America," he wrote, "was starkly different from Europe. In America, people were looking to tomorrow. In Europe they were trying to re-create yesterday. That is why we moved to America."[2]

Half a century later he wrote one of his best books, *Innovation and Entrepreneurship*. In it Peter focused on innovation as a discipline rather than a serendipitous flash of brilliance. The book, written in 1985, is remarkably practical. It is based on the executive courses on innovation he taught at New York University, where he had one of the best business laboratories around—evening students working at all sorts of jobs in New York. After trying his ideas out on his students, he tested them with his clients. More than 20 years later, the book is still astoundingly relevant. In fact, when I listened in on the 2005 Fortune conference on innovation, more than half the speakers alluded to Drucker's ideas. All of them were leaders of highly innovative organizations, from the Toyota Hybrid Car Division to Cisco Systems.

This chapter explores Peter's four basic questions about innovation:

1. What do you have to *abandon* to create room for innovation?
2. Do you systematically seek *opportunities*?
3. Do you use a *disciplined process* for converting ideas into practical solutions?
4. Does your innovation *strategy* work well with your business strategy?

Included as well is the best proof I've seen that Peter's approach to innovation actually works in the real world, a case story about GE. GE is successful because it embraced innovation as Peter defines it, while its competitor, Siemens, struggled. As you think about these questions, you will likely come up with some interesting answers. Then you'll be faced with an even harder task: acting on your answers.

In many organizations, innovation is stymied by excessive loyalty to the old products and to the old ways of doing things. Drucker put it this way: Most companies hang on to the business they have and are hugely reluctant to loosen their grip. This prevents them from innovating and determining their own destiny.

Kodak built a legendary film business, but it finally had to abandon this mainstay in order to invest talent and resources in the digital imaging business. Xerox is another innovative company that had to embrace abandonment. Xerox chairman and CEO Anne Mulcahy said, "I don't think any company gets to restore or preserve what made them great in the first place. I have

WHAT DO YOU HAVE TO ABANDON TO CREATE ROOM FOR INNOVATION?

1. If you weren't in this business today, would you invest the resources to enter it?

2. What unconscious assumptions might constrain your business practices and limit your innovative thinking?

3. Are your highest-achieving people assigned to innovative opportunities? Or are they merely working on yesterday's problems and yesterday's products?

no illusions we're going to be the Xerox we once were. We're in a very competitive marketplace. We're not a monopoly. We have to fight to be best in class." Mulcahy adds, "I believe by not hanging onto the past, we have a much better chance to redefine a future of excellence."[3]

IF YOU WEREN'T IN THIS BUSINESS TODAY, WOULD YOU INVEST THE RESOURCES TO ENTER IT?

I spoke with Jack Welch while I was writing this book. He said that by far the most important lesson he learned from Drucker was to ask the above question. It led him to issue an edict early in his tenure as CEO: Each of GE's businesses had to be number one or number two in its market, or the manager would have to sell it or close it. Welch said that Drucker's questions raised the bar for every business unit in GE and freed up resources, thereby greatly strengthening the whole company.

GE is one of the best-known examples of Drucker's principle of abandonment in action. Another is Kimberly-Clark, the giant paper company. For one hundred years, Kimberly-Clark was mainly a coated-paper manufacturer with mills in the United States and overseas. In 1972, Darwin Smith took over as CEO. Despite the company's large historical investment in paper mills, he believed that making paper was a mediocre business, and he decided to sell most of Kimberly-Clark's mills and put its muscle behind two brands, Kleenex and Huggies. Both product lines had shown promise but lacked corporate support. Darwin Smith took an enormous risk by abandoning everything Kimberly-Clark had done successfully until then. He planned to market what were essentially afterthoughts, going head to head against the globally recognized leader Procter & Gamble and Scott Paper, a strong American rival.

Without the will to take risks, to venture into the unknown and let go of the familiar past, a corporation cannot thrive in the twenty-first century.

One board member described Smith's decision as "the gutsiest move I've ever seen a CEO make." Critics inside and outside of Kimberly-Clark were less diplomatic, calling the idea stupid and Smith a fool. Wall Street analysts downgraded the stock.[4] *Forbes* magazine lambasted the move. Thirty-three years later, Kimberly-Clark's revenues had jumped from less than $1 billion to over $15 billion, and *Forbes* recanted its criticism. By 2006, Kimberly-Clark owned Scott Paper, its former rival, and was outselling Procter & Gamble in six of its eight categories.

Darwin Smith exemplifies the courage it takes to innovate. Without the will to take risks, to venture into the unknown and let go of the familiar past, a corporation cannot thrive in the twenty-first century.

Yet courage isn't enough when it comes to breaking from the past. Companies that want to innovate must adopt what Drucker called *systematic abandonment*, the deliberate process of letting go of familiar products in favor of the new or as yet unknown. Peter went further than almost anyone: "Even when a product is being launched, its target abandonment date should be set."[5] As part of routine operations, you need to constantly evaluate which of your existing businesses should be jettisoned, and revisit these decisions annually, quarterly, or even monthly. Peter went so far as to advocate regular abandonment meetings. Of course, unprofitable businesses are clear candidates for abandonment, but so are businesses reaching the end of their useful lives whose growth has slowed or stopped. The same goes for those where it is becoming more difficult to compete—often because the rules of the game have changed unfavorably.[6]

Drucker put it this way: "Putting all programs and activities regularly on trial for their lives and getting rid of those that cannot prove their productivity works wonders in stimulating creativity in even the most hidebound bureaucracy."[7]

WHAT UNCONSCIOUS ASSUMPTIONS LIMIT YOUR INNOVATIVE THINKING?

Managers can't stop at abandoning just a business unit or product line. They need to leave behind their assumptions as well; they need to challenge all beliefs and make room for new ideas. Hansjorg Wyss, chairman and CEO of Synthes, recently shared a story about challenging his company's assumptions. Synthes is the world's leading provider of implants and biomaterials for rebuilding joints and bones. The company had always assumed that having the highest-quality products was the only thing that mattered, so executives were surprised to discover that competitors' products were being used when Synthes products were not immediately available. Looking into the distribution problem, they learned that hospital ordering systems made it difficult to have enough Synthes implants on hand.

"We didn't sit still," Hansjorg told me as we sat in a conference room at MIT. "We stepped back and reevaluated how we were serving hospitals." The company developed an inventory management service for hospitals so that Synthes products would always be available. These changes required innovating how business was done, rethinking customer relationships, and seeing hospital managers as well as doctors as customers to be served. The company now also provides a counseling service for doctors to discuss which of its product fits best.

Systematic abandonment is both the
most important and most difficult step
in innovation.

Challenging assumptions often leads to changes in the basic operations and economics of a business. As a pioneer in grocery home delivery, Peapod assumed that the economics of its business would require large volume (which it did not have). Mark Van Gelder, Peapod's president, told me about his eureka moment: Rather than build the company around the ability to move a lot of product, Peapod challenged this assumption and partnered with Stop & Shop, using its warehouses and size as the foundation for Peapod's operations. By partnering with an established megastore, Peapod didn't need to spend a fortune on infrastructure, and it could turn a profit on more modest volume.

This all sounds logical enough, but it is tough to break free from the relentless hold of past and present. Sometimes the constraints are so subtle that they are hard to recognize. In many ways, systematic abandonment is both the most important and most difficult step in innovation. It requires real discipline to regularly challenge the organization's assumptions and encourage the outrageous. But as Peter said, "If you don't abandon, you can't innovate. The effective organizations learn systematically to abandon or at least to build systematic abandonment into their ordinary life cycle. Extra weight is a burden on the heart and the brain. And volume by itself is no great benefit."[8]

ARE YOUR HIGHEST-ACHIEVING PEOPLE ASSIGNED TO INNOVATIVE OPPORTUNITIES?

"There's an old medical proverb," Drucker once explained. "There's [probably] nothing more expensive, nothing more difficult, than to keep a corpse from stinking!"[9] Most corporations waste time, energy, and precious resources on keeping their corpses—their old products—from stinking. Because these old products are still generating large revenues, most executives don't even recognize that they have stinking corpses. And so the bosses assign smart people to tackle serious problems in old businesses. This is a misallocation of precious, creative resources.

In an interconnected world, trying to generate high-impact innovation, despite the high failure rate, is actually much less risky than sticking with the old standby. The innovative organization uses incentives, employment guarantees, performance measures,

DO YOU SYSTEMATICALLY SEEK OPPORTUNITIES?

1. Do you continually look for opportunities as if your survival depended upon it?

2. Are you looking at the seven key sources of opportunities?
   a. The unexpected
   b. Industry and market disparities
   c. Process vulnerabilities
   d. Incongruities
   e. Demographic shifts
   f. Changes in perceptions
   g. New knowledge

and active engagement by leadership to help people embrace change rather than fear it.

Peter Drucker viewed innovation as a discipline, a skill that can be learned and practiced like playing the piano. To innovate, you must devise a systematic method of identifying opportunities that provide new value for your customers. Many people think that the discovery of new ideas is random and unpredictable. Far from it; such discoveries come from scouring the landscape and translating sightings into "what we don't know that might matter."

The organization needs to be continually on the offensive. It must watch for potential new frontiers instead of just playing defense against intruding competitors. P&G's Lafley put it this way: "We have to open our minds, open our doors, open our ears, and open our hearts to good ideas that can come from anywhere."[10] Playing offense requires well-placed external feelers, a careful and unbiased ear to the ground, and a disciplined process that links opportunities and capabilities within your organization.

DO YOU LOOK FOR OPPORTUNITIES AS IF YOUR SURVIVAL DEPENDED ON IT?

A desire to innovate must come from the firm's top leadership and permeate every muscle and sinew of the organization. At Google every engineer is charged with investing 30 percent of his or her time on new products and ideas (split between related businesses and totally new initiatives). Sergey Brin, one of Google's co-founders, described the management practices as a 70/20/10 rule: "We spend 70 percent on core search and ads, 20 percent on adjacent businesses, and then at least 10 percent of our time on things that are truly new."[11] Of course, the portion of time a company devotes to innovation will vary by industry and the stage of business development it's in.

> The organization needs to be continually on the offensive.

Peter advocated that innovation be explicit and supported by management. Google has an e-mail list devoted to new ideas, which is open to anyone in the company as well as to select third parties who want to post or comment on a proposal. Marissa Mayer, vice president, search products and user experience and Google's champion of innovation, devotes regular office hours three times a week exclusively to brainstorming. She wants to ensure that new ideas rise to the surface when deciding which projects are ready for the review of Google's founders.

To gauge the orientation of your company to innovate, ask 100 people what fraction of their time they spend on innovation. Often, companies *say* innovation is important, but they don't *show* it's important. It gets pushed back and rarely receives the time executives think it does. "What is our company doing to innovate?" must be one of the top questions senior executives ask everybody in the organization, including the board of directors. And those who drive innovation must be rewarded.

ARE YOU LOOKING AT THE SEVEN KEY SOURCES OF OPPORTUNITIES?

Peter believed that academics should be immersed in the real world, and he practiced what he preached by testing ideas about where to find opportunities with the entrepreneurs and executives in his classes. Peter taught the first U.S. business course on innovation at New York University in 1956. In that class, he mapped out the seven key sources of opportunity noted below. Peter explained to me that when demand and supply do not fit as you expect them to, there is an opportunity. He added that new opportunities rarely mesh with the way an industry has traditionally approached existing business and that they require new thinking.

From that one extraordinary class, students started or transformed three businesses. Scott Lawn Care morphed from an outdated player to the leading lawn supply company in North America; *Psychology Today* became a leading middle-market publication; and many of the ideas behind investment bank Donaldson Lufkin & Jenrette were largely driven by the kind of thinking Peter inspired. Fifty years later, Peter Drucker's innovation road map still guides entrepreneurs.

The Unexpected

Frequent unexpected occurrences signal that business expectations are out of sync with reality. Recognizing and understanding the

---

- **The unexpected**
  - Unexpected successes; galling to management, counterintuitive, rarely reported
  - Unexpected failures
  - Unexpected outside events (suppliers, customers, complementors, competitors)

- **Industry and market disparities over time or geography**
  - Customers and expectations (e.g., developing countries)
  - Industry economics
  - Customer value proposition
  - Technologies and operations

- **Incongruities**
  - Internal misperceptions
  - Conflicting internal realities
  - Customer expectation gaps
  - Dysfunction or anxiety at a critical point in a business process

- **Process vulnerabilities**
  - Weak link in process
  - Technological vulnerability

- **Demographic changes**
  - Aging
  - Shifts in wealth
  - Urbanization, globalization
  - Culture and labor force change

- **Perception and priority changes that shift buying habits**

- **New knowledge**
  - Expensive innovation with long lead times and risks
  - Application of knowledge and information in new areas

Figure 3.1 Where to Look for Opportunities

reason for this mismatch is a powerful tool for innovation. These occurrences include unforeseen successes and failures within the organization, and unexpected activities at suppliers, competitors, customers, and complementors (partners whose products complement yours and thereby create a combined product or customer experience).

At my father-in-law's 80th birthday party, I learned a little more about how Sandy Weill, the former chairman and chief executive of Citigroup, had managed to move his firm, Smith-Barney, into the institutional equity market so rapidly. He did this in 1989, prior to the acquisitions of Salomon Brothers and Citicorp.

"The entrepreneur always searches for change, responds to it, and exploits it as an opportunity."

Weill always expected what others didn't. He viewed Drexel Burnham Lambert's unexpected bankruptcy in 1989 as an opportunity for him to pick up whole departments and capabilities of very qualified people with solid relationships in an area he wanted to pursue. Within 12 hours of the bankruptcy announcement, he had written notes by hand and had them placed on the doorsteps of key Drexel employees, including my father-in-law. Weill had described his approach in a very Druckerian mode: "The entrepreneur always searches for change, responds to it, and exploits it as an opportunity."[12]

On a recent visit to the Druckerian Club outside of Tokyo, I heard another story of a CEO who jumped on a surprise opportunity. In 2003 one of Japan's largest construction companies was concerned that demand in its core business, building bridges and tunnels, was declining. The CEO made the rounds, asking employees, "What do customers want that we do not supply, or that surprised you?" The key answer came not from a vice president, but from a receptionist who said she got two to five calls a week asking whether the company built parks and gardens. Several others in the organization confirmed that story. Today 20 percent of the company's work is on major gardens.

Rather than being constrained by history and expectations, the Tokyo firm identified the unpredictable—the unmet need. The company ultimately implemented a system for tracking every inquiry for services it did not provide, so that it could identify patterns and customer needs that represented new opportunities and then redirect resources to promising areas.[13]

Industry Disparities across Time or Geography

The second set of circumstances in which a mismatch between supply and demand becomes an opportunity is when a company has stayed constant while its industry structure or market has changed.

For instance, the increased availability of information can undermine the conventions of an industry. The Internet turned the travel industry on its head. Leisure travel and then business travel became self-managed by highly price-sensitive customers. Travel agents, who had relied on steady margins, had to appeal to luxury markets or find other specialties—or go out of business. At the same time, these shifts created opportunities for new online services such as Orbitz.com and Priceline.com. And they flourished.

India, for example, on the surface appears to be a terrible market for prosthetics. Most Indian consumers cannot afford $12,000 for an artificial limb, and health care is much more heavily regulated in India than it is in the United States. But Jaipur Foot made a radically cheaper prosthetic that was perfectly suited to the Indian market. The prosthetic can be used without shoes and is flexible enough to be worn in a cross-legged sitting position on the floor. It is priced at only $25.[14]

Incongruities

Incongruities in market behavior and expectations also signal opportunity. A customer value incongruity is a discrepancy between what the customer wants and what the company *thinks* the customer wants. JetBlue is a good example of a company that exploited such an incongruity. The airline industry had long focused on getting customers to their destinations. But JetBlue focused on upgrading and redesigning the experience of flying, from selling fresh food and providing wireless Internet service in waiting areas to fitting each passenger seat with television screens that feature many channels. JetBlue also made flying more family-friendly by offering snacks and TV programs that kids love. JetBlue exploited a discrepancy between what the customer wanted—a better flying experience—and what most airlines thought the customer wanted—a no-nonsense trip to a destination.

The company's management built a profitable $1.3 billion airline in five years by providing customers with what they really value: easy-to-understand low fares, convenient flights, friendly service, easy online booking and check-in, and the highest on-time performance of any airline. In the meantime, in 2004, five airlines, representing a quarter of U.S. capacity, were operating under bankruptcy protection.[15] The other airlines clearly had legacy costs that limited their competitive agility. But as Drucker maintained, when a high-volume industry is not profitable, opportunity lurks.

Process Vulnerabilities

A process vulnerability refers to some piece of the workflow or operation that is missing, difficult, or not working, ultimately preventing users from embracing the product. The critical innovation that morphed Scott Lawn Care into a successful company was the spreader to distribute seed on the lawn. Without it, grass seed was too difficult to plant, so there was a process vulnerability. TiVo built its success on a process vulnerability it perceived at the consumer level, namely, the limiting and sometimes frustrating process of taping a television program.

In our new world, smart small companies have profited mightily by finding new ways to deal in information and reduce vulnerabilities. It's possible to imagine many opportunities for creating value by connecting specific types of information with people who can benefit from that knowledge. In the real estate market, for example, buyers historically committed large sums of money on the basis of imperfect data. Today, 80 percent of buyers visit the Internet before they see their first house. Multiple services have taken off: realtor.com is the number one site that advertises real estate. Its advertising revenue today is four times greater than that of any single U.S. newspaper. Luxuryhomes.com and Zillow.com each play new and unique roles in this information-imperfect marketplace as well.

Demographic Changes

Broad shifts in demographics, such as a rapid growth in the population over 65 and their attendant income, asset-base, and longevity, create shifts in demand and mismatches with historical supplies of services.

Ikea has mined demographic changes to transform the global home furnishings retail market. The company recognized that young families with newborns no longer wanted to furnish their first homes with hand-me-downs from the older generation. To cater to this large but lower-income market, Ikea offered a self-service store filled with well-designed, assemble-it-yourself furniture at extremely affordable low prices. It then took this idea around the world, where many people, not just the young, had the same need for affordable yet attractive furniture. By 2005, Ikea had become a global cult brand with sales of $18 billion, driven by the mission to "create a better everyday life for the majority of people."

Perception and Priority Changes That Shift Buying Habits

Emory Ayers, retired chairman of Intercontinental Bakeries and one of the students in Peter's early class on innovation, recalled, "Peter emphasized that changes in perception don't change the facts, they just change customers' interpretation of the facts—and that creates opportunities." Demand and supply no longer square. For example, is Wal-Mart a hero or a villain, and how does that public perception create opportunities? It is hard to compete with a hero, but there are opportunities to partner with one. Many companies have grown with Wal-Mart, from Bell Helmet to Ol' Roy's dog food. There are opportunities to create a unique market position when the competitor is a villain. The articles contrasting the employee benefits at Target with the benefits at Wal-Mart have prompted both job defections and customer loyalty.

Perception is represented by both vulnerability and customer receptivity. Online banking and bill payment, a very useful service that eliminates almost all the hassle of paying bills, floundered until customers became more receptive to the idea of paying their bills online. Founded in 1981, CheckFree Corp. has built a business providing more than 1,700 financial institutions across the globe with software that enables millions of consumers to have the convenience of securely paying their bills online. The company struggled for 20 years. Founder Pete Knight estimates that in early 2000 there was a tipping point when people were no longer afraid of online transactions. Perception had changed; because the service had become established and secure, reputable businesses were using it, and enough nontech people were talking about it. By June 2005, more than 40 million U.S. households paid at least one bill online,[16] and the availability of online banking and bill payment now ranks among the top three considerations when selecting a bank for personal accounts.

New Knowledge

The most obvious source of innovative ideas is scientific breakthroughs. These innovations tend to have long lead times and are often both high risk and high impact. A good example of scientific innovation is Procter & Gamble's Crest, which defined the toothpaste market. People had been using various substances for several thousand years to clean their teeth (with some early formulas calling for everything from urine to dragon's blood[17]). In 1955, after years of intense research, P&G achieved a scientific breakthrough[18] and introduced the first fluoride toothpaste, clinically proven effective in preventing cavities. Crest was the first toothpaste to receive an endorsement from the American Dental Association, which effectively changed buyers' attitudes and created the market for therapeutic toothpaste. P&G brought Crest to the schools, where kids were taught to brush their teeth with the new toothpaste, helping P&G wrest U.S. market leadership from Colgate and keep it for the next 30 years. In addition, providing fluoride in the water became a community responsibility and created new market opportunities.

In 1997, however, Colgate[19] announced its own scientific, market-changing breakthrough. The FDA had approved the use of Triclosan (a soluble antibiotic) to combat gingivitis, and a groundbreaking oral hygiene pharmaceutical was born. Colgate's breakthrough product was Total, a compound that kept Triclosan on the teeth for over five hours so that plaque could not build up. One Colgate executive confided in me that he had not been to the dentist for five years. He was certain that Total had made that possible. Capitalizing on the fears of aging baby boomers that they risked losing their teeth to gum disease, Colgate Total regained the U.S. market leader position from P&G.

Unilever quickly imitated these two first movers, but in a new geography. It created its own versions of anticavity and gum-health toothpaste, which it sold in India and other developing markets in tiny packages costing a few cents each.[20] The toothpaste wars soon moved on to the next battlefield—whiteners. Current research efforts include leveraging marine biology to improve gum health and exploring, with pharmaceutical companies, alternative means for delivering medications.

The global toothpaste war is still in full force to determine who can best provide the whitest, tartar-free teeth and the healthiest, best-smelling gums in two distinct markets: to the aging population in developed countries and the poor in developing countries.

Collectively, the seven sources of opportunity—the unexpected, industry and market disparities, incongruities, process vulnerabilities, demographic changes, perception and priority changes, and new knowledge—account for the great majority of all innovation opportunities.

Peter Drucker first wrote in the 1950s about the need for disciplined processes to convert opportunities into real values. His ideas are still remarkably timely. In 2006, the American Management Association conducted a survey of 2,000 companies and found that the biggest challenge is creating disciplined processes for innovation, from defining an opportunity or creating an idea to implementing it with the customer.

DO YOU USE A DISCIPLINED PROCESS FOR CONVERTING IDEAS INTO PRACTICAL SOLUTIONS?

1. Do you brainstorm effectively? Do ideas and opportunities get put on the table for consideration?

2. Do you match up ideas with the opportunity?

3. Do you test and refine ideas—by fine-tuning them based on the market response?

4. Do you deliver the results by allocating the right resources, creating customers one by one, and monitoring progress with external barometers?

DO YOU BRAINSTORM EFFECTIVELY?

Once we have identified opportunities, it takes a real effort to capture them, put them in place, and actually deliver better value to customers. One way to do this is to conduct action-oriented brainstorming sessions that encourage employees to openly participate in developing new opportunities into viable products and services.

Listening is one of the hardest jobs, and at a brainstorming session it is critical.

To be effective, these sessions need to bring together people from different areas of the business—people with different perspectives. The meetings also need to strike a balance. On one hand they must be open: participants must be free to speak their minds and to propose ideas that may seem far afield of the topic being discussed. On the other hand, the sessions must focus on results and value. To achieve this balance, set ground rules that encourage constructive conversation which leads to action and that discourages never-ending debates about things that don't matter. These rules may be as simple as requiring the group to report back with a plan after a defined period of time.

To focus the discussions, ask questions Peter would have asked, such as:

1. Customer by customer, where are there possible problems and solutions that can create value?
2. What would it take for us to seriously consider this idea?

This type of brainstorming was used at Nokia, where senior management involved hundreds of employees in answering three questions: What new needs can we serve? How can we use our competencies in different ways? How can we change the economics of this industry?

The real work of top management in brainstorming sessions is not to generate the new thinking but to consider all the ideas and try to find within them the themes that will give overall direction to the company's innovation efforts. When I spoke to a senior executive at Nokia, he confided that his challenge at a brainstorming session was to keep telling himself to listen, to make sure he understood what was being said, and to keep his opinions to himself. Listening is one of the hardest jobs, and at a brainstorming session it is critical.

DO YOU MATCH UP IDEAS WITH THE OPPORTUNITY?

Will the idea respond effectively to the real-world opportunity? Finding the answer to this question falls somewhere between science and intuition. An idea is a possible mechanism for serving a customer need, such as a pink cell phone. Opportunities are unmet customer needs, such as the customer's desire to be stylish. The challenge is to assess the scope of the need and the ability of the idea to meet that need. With the proper analysis—often utilizing targeted market research—you can predict in many cases which ideas will be successful.

> "Aiming high is aiming for something that will make the enterprise capable of genuine innovation and self-renewal."

Aim high! Minor modifications rarely address unmet needs. When I spoke to Peter about this, he leaned back in his chair and told me: "If an innovation does not aim at leadership from the beginning, it is unlikely to be innovative enough to change the customers' habits." He continued, "Aiming high is aiming for something that will make the enterprise capable of genuine innovation and self-renewal. That means inventing a new business and not just a product-line extension, reaching a new performance capacity and not just an incremental improvement, and delivering new, unimagined value, and not just satisfying existing expectations better."

But how do we know what's right? "Most good ideas will not generate enough wealth to replicate the business's historical success, and many more will fail," Peter explained. "Thus, the need to aim high is a practical reality; the one big success is needed to offset the nine failures."

At the same time, Peter always stressed the need to be practical. When it came to innovation, he felt that the most practical approach was to use the absolutely best people. In many ways this is the art of innovation: remaining practical while having the courage to aim high.

> In many ways this is the art of innovation: remaining practical while having the courage to aim high.

The criteria listed in the box on the next page help assess whether an idea matches an opportunity and whether you are aiming high enough while still taking market realities into account. The analysis must also address the risks of success, of near success, and of failure. For example, in 2004 the Riddell Company launched a new football helmet that was designed to reduce the incidence of concussions by 50 percent. High schools traditionally replace 20 percent of their helmets every year, and

Riddell has about a 50 percent market share. The company expected its volume to double and wanted to be able to cope with up to a tenfold increase. Riddell identified outside manufacturers that could help it meet demand without investing in any new in-house capacity. It aimed high. In fact, volume tripled for two years running. Riddell sourced all the components of the helmet and used its reconditioning facilities to assemble the units. President and CEO Bill Sherman commented that it forced Riddell to enter the twenty-first century, working with a network of partners to manage the sudden surge in demand and control the quality of their product.

Does the idea aim high enough?	Does the idea align with realities and practicalities?
• Creates new utility for customers • Relates price to value to customer, not cost to produce • Responds to unmet customer realities/needs and problems • Delivers attributes (valued by customer) not products • Obtains a leadership position in market or niche quickly—defines the "white space"	• Makes reasonable speed to market possible • Is simple and focused—does one thing, satisfies one need • Is not too clever for or too far ahead of the market • Is consistent with the organization's strengths

Figure 3.2 Criteria for Evaluating Practical Success of Innovative Ideas

DO YOU TEST AND REFINE IDEAS BASED ON THE MARKET RESPONSE?

To make sure that you are not getting overly excited about a new idea, you must corroborate, reality-check, and test your analysis. Drucker pushed consumer testing in almost every client meeting. One manager at Motorola recalled him exhorting a team, "Why don't you test it in three distinct markets, for example, a suburb of Chicago, a more rural area in Missouri, and an area with a older population in, say, Arizona . . . From that you will learn more than testing it in a lab or with customers in interviews for the next five years. Go out and try it."[21]

Testing is phenomenally powerful not only for determining an idea's potential but also for finding out what's needed to make it succeed. When I worked with Riddell, executives tested the helmet on five professional football teams and found ways to make it more comfortable. Testing also enabled the company to document the reduction in concussions before it offered the helmet to the full market.

DO YOU DELIVER THE RESULTS?

When going live with an innovation, a company has to find a way to be aggressive but not foolhardy. Management needs to put the right resources on the project, separate the new effort from old activities, devise a living plan for creating customers one by one, and monitor progress with clear milestones and external goals. The living plan begins with management committing adequate resources. As Peter stated, "The best plan is only good intentions"— until it is effectively put into action with the right resources.[22]

> "The best plan is only good intentions"—
> until it is effectively put into action
> with the right resources.

An innovative organization has the discipline to manage both its existing business and its innovation efforts, recognizing that the two enterprises need different sets of skills. The existing business has to meet established quantitative performance standards, according to Drucker. "Managing the future" requires the encouragement of ideas, no matter how unripe or crude. . . . It is management's job to ask, "What would this idea have to be for it to be taken seriously?" He added, "A top management [team] that believes its job is to sit in judgment will inevitably veto the new idea. It is always 'impractical.'"[23]

New innovation efforts need a different set of metrics. To put it simply, applying the conventional metrics of the ongoing business would spell death for innovation—the way a 100-pound pack would cripple a six-year-old on a hike, to use Drucker's memorable phrase.[24] Enlightened management appreciates the need for disciplined controls focused on opportunity, not profitability. This is where so many corporate innovation efforts derail—they can't find a balance between nurturing new projects and applying responsible controls to them.

Enlightened management appreciates the need for disciplined controls focused on opportunity, not profitability.

I have seen many large firms acquire entrepreneurial ventures in what seem like brilliant moves. Soon, though, they became burdened with overhead and died. In many ways that's what Lucent Technologies did to Bell Laboratories. As one former research director told me, "At Bell we were independent, with independent financial accountability. At Lucent, we bore the burden of the whole and had more than 100 percent increase in overhead, which killed most of what we were doing."

However, even in an innovation project, accountability is essential. The success of the project must be continually measured and evaluated. One example is Allergan's approach to evaluating its drug development efforts. The drug discovery process is lengthy and high risk: Only 15 percent of new drugs entering development are expected to reach the market, and development cost per drug is estimated at $800 million.[25] Allergan uses an extensive decision tree to determine whether to continue, modify, or abandon a development project. After completing chemical, biological, and toxicological research, the company performs a cost-benefit analysis of bringing the potential drug to market. In the United States, before any clinical testing can start, the Food and Drug Administration (FDA) has to approve both the clinical trials and the new drug application, often calling for design changes in the clinical trials and causing Allergan to revisit its decision to continue versus abandon.

After the innovation is successfully commercialized and becomes an established business, it must essentially be put on trial along with the rest of the existing business. If it's not good enough, if it doesn't fit in as part of the future, it must be abandoned—bringing the innovation management process full circle, back to the initial step of making room for innovation through systematic abandonment of the old. Figure 3.3 is a flowchart of the first three questions that form Drucker's map for disciplined and continuous innovative processes.

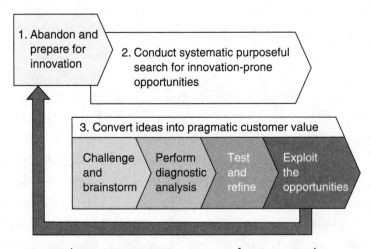

Figure 3.3 Drucker's Continuous Process Map for Organized Management of Innovation

---

**DOES YOUR INNOVATION STRATEGY WORK
WITH YOUR BUSINESS STRATEGY?**

1. What is your company's target role or influence in defining the new markets? What is the scope of your offering to this market?

2. How does your portfolio of opportunities fit with your business strategy?

3. Are you allocating resources where you should be making bets?

Suppose you have a number of opportunities to consider. What is your strategy? Do the opportunities fit together to define where you want to be and where you want to take the market—your tomorrow? An effective business strategy embraces external realties and opportunities and provides the context to help ensure that every decision, priority, and allocation of resources is geared to value creation. Innovation strategy is where the rubber meets the road, the program of change that will create the company of the future.

WHAT IS YOUR COMPANY'S TARGET ROLE IN DEFINING NEW MARKETS?

When Peter said, "The only way to predict the future is to create it," he was highlighting innovation as a tool for giving the enterprise a degree of control over the future, through removing some amount of uncertainty. To gain this control, you need an innovation strategy that explicitly articulates each opportunity in terms of your company's target role or *influence* in defining new markets and the target *scope* of your offerings for playing in the defined white space (see Figure 3.4).

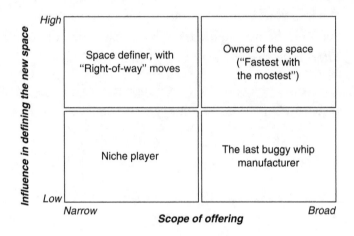

Figure 3.4 What Is Your Target Role and What Is the Scope of Opportunities?

The company that populates the new market first with the most integrated solution becomes the *first owner of the space*. The success of this type of innovation strategy is temporary, because its high visibility is a magnet for imitators who may bring more advantageous economics to the product, service, or industry. Federal Express pioneered the express package delivery market in the mid-1970s and held on to its market advantage for about two years. The U.S. Postal Service, UPS, and DHL all followed soon after, offering comparable services at lower prices and forcing Federal Express to reinvent itself multiple times over to survive.

In contrast, the *space definer* creates something that sets boundaries, defines the new space in some fashion, or executes an idea. A dramatic example of this type of strategy is Corning's invention of the ribbon machine to make filaments for high-speed lightbulb production, which in turn enabled the production and marketing of low-cost electric lightbulbs around the world. This innovation gave Corning a clear advantage because anyone who wanted to supply this new space had to buy Corning's ribbon machines to be able to make filaments cost-effectively. From the consumer's perspective, Corning did not own the space; GE and Westinghouse did. But it was Corning that absolutely defined the space.

Other enterprises purposefully let their competitors define the overall space and then become providers to these leaders with products, components, or solutions. I call these companies *niche players*. Electronic Arts (EA) carved out a very profitable niche in video games (such as Sims and Madden NFL Football) for PCs and for all major console systems, such as Microsoft Xbox, Sony PlayStation, and Nintendo. The video gaming industry is changing at a furious pace, going online, mobile, and global while new console technology is making high-end game development complex and costly. Given that the shelf life of some games may be only three months, EA has to continually reinvent itself and its products to remain the worldwide leader in video games. The hardware manufacturers define the game space. They determine the features and hardware capabilities available to game players and designers. EA provides an essential element—the game. It leverages new hardware capabilities as they become available but does not define how we play electronic games. This too is shifting, as more and more games are played live on the Internet.

Finally, there are those *last buggy whip manufacturers* who use innovation to incrementally enhance the economics of their existing businesses. However, even the most conscientious of organizations cannot secure its future solely by improving what it already has. While the ongoing business needs to be optimized, the innovation strategy must take care not to allocate scarce resources to existing businesses that are on the decline. These need to be abandoned, not given more resources. A successful innovation strategy has to focus on what will come next, not on what already is.

A successful innovation strategy has to focus on what will come next.

The strategies highlighted in Figure 3.4 are not necessarily mutually exclusive. Many companies play in multiple spaces simultaneously, but they use a different strategy for each space. Nor is any one strategy likely to be permanent in a given market space. As noted earlier, imitations by others dilute benefits to the original owner of the space. Other new realities such as a major innovation by a competitor, or social, economic, and demographic changes spur purposeful migration from one area to another—or sometimes force changes in strategy. Naturally, all these strategies depend on strong linkages to external partners: customers, complementors, even competitors, and other outside resources that assist in delivering value.

DO YOUR OPPORTUNITIES FIT WITH YOUR BUSINESS STRATEGY?

The effective innovation strategy builds a portfolio that creates tomorrow. It needs to balance:

- Innovation versus continuity.
- Core capabilities versus new skills developed for tomorrow.
- Defining new landscapes versus playing in existing ones.
- Focus versus reliance on multiple businesses.

A few years ago, I witnessed firsthand a flawed innovation strategy at Corning, when managers lost sight of core capabilities and failed to ask these questions, ushering in a brief period of trouble in the company's otherwise strong history. Even more than most companies, Corning is in the business of innovation. From the mid-nineteenth century until the 1990s, Corning introduced a long series of inventions and processes that became the foundations of sweeping changes. For example, it developed a process for making colored and unbreakable railroad signal lenses that effectively enabled railroad crossings. In the 1950s, Corning figured out how to make extremely low-cost CRTs (cathode-ray tubes)—leading the way to low-cost television. In the 1970s, it invented the core of the catalytic converter, which is the basis for most automotive pollution control systems and is credited with the marked improvement in urban air quality. At the same time, Corning pioneered the development of optical fiber capable of effective transmission of digitized data; the company had the foresight to predict the vast market in bandwidth telecommunications.

Despite these successes, Corning never viewed its accomplishments as the results of a systematic or intentional innovation strategy. It simply believed R&D and technological inventions were important. In the late 1990s, as the telecommunications industry boomed, the optical fiber business boomed with it. Corning did not question the overly optimistic demand projections provided by its telecom customers; instead it revved up production, spending more than $9 billion on acquisitions in fiber and photonics. In 2001, when the telecom bust occurred, Corning was caught by surprise. Thousands of people lost their jobs, and Corning found itself on the verge of extinction (in 2002 its stock plummeted to $1.70 per share from its September 2000 price of $113).

As Corning fought to recover, the senior team members asked themselves, "What are we really good at?" What they came back with is, "We're really good at certain kinds of invention and innovation in response to customer problems. We're not a marketing company, not a telecommunications company, not a systems company. What we are is a company capable of certain kinds of invention, and we need to focus on doing that well."

Corning's strengths are its extraordinary depth of understanding of certain kinds of materials and technologies, and its application of process expertise to that knowledge. The company knows more about glass and inorganic materials and glass ceramics than any other enterprise in the world. Consequently, in every product in which it has a significant business, Corning is a low-cost producer with greater knowledge and capabilities than its competitors. That is the card that it plays, opting not to compete where its technical materials knowledge is of little value, or where the game is only cost (e.g. window glass).

After acknowledging the company's strengths, senior managers realized that they had a recipe—and strategy—all along for innovating in concert with their strengths. They became the guardians of this strategy. Despite the memory of its telecom disaster, when Corning identifies a new arena or application that fits its strengths, it is still willing to invest huge amounts of money to take advantage of the opportunity.

However, Corning's management has also learned that if it wants to aim high and take big swings, the company has to rely on more than one product. In 2005, Corning devoted billions of dollars to LCD (liquid crystal display) applications, and it also invested heavily in pollution control devices for diesel vehicles. While its inventions come from inside the organization, in envisioning the future and seeking out opportunities, Corning routinely leverages the expertise and knowledge of outsiders (academics, industry experts, advisers, consultants), no longer relying on customers alone as its source for inspiration. Since redirecting its strategy to explicitly link internal strengths to external opportunities, Corning's performance has been on an upward trend—its stock reaching $19 per share and its profits moving from negative to over 12 percent.

ARE YOU ALLOCATING RESOURCES WHERE YOU WANT TO BE MAKING BETS?

Are you allocating resources where you want to be making bets? This is one of those "gotcha" questions that Drucker loved. Generally speaking, when Drucker pushed people to look at where they were allocating resources, they were surprised by the answer. Many of the people I interviewed remembered how shocked they were to find out that they weren't allocating resources for tomorrow. Marty Davidson, the former chairman of Southern Pipe, remembers, "When we saw how little time we were spending with our new branch managers and our new projects, our routine changed overnight. We now go back and check how we are spending time every six months to make sure that it fits with our priorities." He remembered another moment of truth with Peter: "When we saw how much of our resources were being spent in Texas and what it was going to take to build a position there, we realized it was not a wise bet."

HOW INNOVATION ENABLES GE'S LONGEVITY AND VALUATION

Along with DuPont and P&G, GE is one of only three companies that have made the Forbes 100 list every year since 1917. It is innovative to the core and has outperformed the overall market. GE adopted a Druckerian approach to innovation. Its competitor Siemens took a narrower view of innovation, with a very different result.

There are many similarities between the two companies. Both were founded on technological brilliance and have developed into huge global technology conglomerates. Both companies have relied on internally recruited executives and experienced very low turnover at the top. Yet there are fundamental differences, chiefly GE's agility and Siemens's inability to quickly reinvent itself. The result was that Siemens, despite its vast scientific capabilities, never achieved GE's success. From 1995 to 2005, GE grew twice as fast as did Siemens (7.9 percent per year for GE compared to 3.8 percent for Siemens) at almost three times the profit margins (10.2 percent average net profit margins for GE compared to 3.7 percent for Siemens).

GE, like Siemens, has innovation in its DNA. It evolved from the legacy of its founder, Thomas Edison—not only a brilliant inventor but also a truly customer-driven innovator. He sounded a lot like Drucker: "I never perfected an invention that I did not think about in terms of service it might give others."[26] Although other inventors had invented lightbulbs at the same time, Edison went on to create an industry by designing the infrastructure necessary to serve his customers—the wires and generators that made his light bulbs usable.

As GE found out early on, no company, however brilliant its founder or products, is immune to changes in the environment. The company was almost bankrupt a year after its founding, in the panic of 1893, when central power stations could no longer afford to purchase new materials. To survive this crisis, GE completely changed its strategy, shifting to an innovative focus on solving customer problems. Alas, Edison was not as good a manager as he was an inventor. He was asked to leave by J. P. Morgan, who replaced him with professional managers.

Despite the near disaster, the company remained focused on its products and on creating a culture that encouraged innovation. It is worth noting that Drucker worked with every GE CEO from

Swope through Welch, helping them create a culture of innovation that challenged the status quo. Gerald Swope was GE's president from 1922 to 1940 and again from 1942 to 1945. He said: "If we could fill this body of executives and leading men with the spirit of adventure to try even unheard-of things, the company would either make progress or go broke, and the older of us would try our best to keep from going broke."[27]

Jack Welch, GE's chief executive from 1981 to 2001, completely reinvented the organization's businesses and its corporate culture in order to stay ahead of global competitors. Central to Welch's strategy was the company-changing policy we discussed earlier of innovation through abandonment: GE had to be number one or number two in any business, and if not, the business had to be fixed, sold, or closed. This policy arose in response to two simple questions posed to Welch by Drucker: "If you weren't already in the business, would you enter it today? And, if the answer is no, what are you going to do about it?"[28] And so Welch set out to revamp GE's portfolio of businesses. (Drucker liked to say that Welch had "the courage of a lion."[29]) He quickly got out of low-growth businesses and used his high-valued shares as currency to buy companies in high-growth businesses, such as financial services and media. At the same time, Welch attacked bureaucracy, reducing management layers from nine to four. In the process, between 1981 and 1988, GE eliminated over 240,000 positions[30] from its workforce of 404,000, earning Welch the nickname "Neutron Jack."

At the end of the 1980s, GE was ready to push global growth and amended its number one or number two standard to mean its world market position. Taking the view that regions in crisis would provide the best risk-reward ratio, Welch invested heavily in Europe, Mexico, and Asia during their downturns, laying the foundation for double-digit international growth rates.

Employees were immersed in the Six Sigma quality program, the customer satisfaction dashboard feedback system, and the boundaryless entrepreneurial culture, which quickly became part of GE's operating system. Probably no other company is as well known as GE for its focus on developing its people. Welch built on this tradition and focused on differentiating the best employees and managers from the rest of the pack. Every year the bottom 10 percent, as well as anyone who did not share GE's values, was weeded out, while strong performers were rewarded with generous stock options and challenging assignments in other parts of the company—a practice Welch called the *vitality curve* (also known throughout the industry as *forced ranking*).

MAKING INNOVATION EVERYONE'S BUSINESS

Steeped in GE's corporate culture, Jeff Immelt was ready to follow Jack Welch's advice "Blow it up!"[31] as he replaced his mentor in 2001. Immelt inherited a business environment vastly different from the one Welch succeeded in. After the high-flying nineties, growth slowed, and the world became more volatile. Yet Immelt was committed to bringing GE's organic revenue growth rate from historic levels of 5 percent per year to 8 percent while increasing earnings by at least 10 percent and keeping growth in stock prices above the S&P 500.

For a company with revenues the size of Argentina's GNP, that meant building a new, profitable, $12 billion company every year. Immelt's thesis was that technical and market innovations are the key to building more service income and avoiding commoditization. There were no sacred cows. Immelt abandoned businesses favored by Welch, such as insurance, which turned out to be a poor fit with GE and a significant drag on operating profits. It is no surprise to me that Peter was already speculating in 1999 about how abandonment versus investment at GE would play out in the future. "My own guess is that the next CEO may split the company because they have grown apart. The next CEO will probably put as much effort into the nonfinancial businesses, which are now the businesses they really need."[32]

Immelt may not have agreed that GE should be split, but as of this writing he is making huge investments in fast-growth businesses such as health care, entertainment, infrastructure, energy, and "ecoimagination" (environmentally protective products). These businesses also fit the needs of developing economies, which are expected to account for 60 percent of the company's growth by 2015, versus about 20 percent in 1995–2005.[33] In 2003, Immelt declared that, "Ten years out, 90 percent of our company's earnings will have no competition from China. Eighty percent of our businesses will be selling to China."[34] The plan is to become a "general store for developing countries."[35] To this end, the organization was completely revamped and shaped around selling, building, and financing infrastructure products. The plan seems to be working, with revenues from developing countries growing at 20 percent per year.

Immelt is betting the farm on being able to transform a process orientation into a marketing-driven, innovative mindset. He is looking for leaders who are passionate about customers and innovation and willing to take risks. Managers will not be rotated around but are expected to stay put and become specialists in their own industries. A process for innovation, called *Imagination Breakthroughs*, has been launched, requiring each of GE's business leaders to submit at least three proposals per year that have the potential to take GE into new customer or geographical areas while generating incremental growth of at least $100 million. The hope is that the 80 innovation projects currently under way—a $5 billion investment—will generate $25 billion in revenue by 2007. Although the long-term success of Immelt's strategy remains to be seen, organic growth reached the targeted 8 percent in 2005.

What is clear, though, is what sets GE apart. At GE, change is viewed as an opportunity and is continuously pursued with a sense of urgency.

IN CONTRAST TO GE: SIEMENS AG

Werner von Siemens and Thomas Edison were described by Peter Drucker as "the first innovators" who, independently of each other, created the electrical industry and indeed our electrified world of today. "Siemens did not develop the electric railway because he had a generator; he developed the generator because he had visualized the electric railway."[36]

Subsequent members of the Siemens family were dedicated to research and technological innovations, capitalizing on emerging technologies from the telephone to electric power generation. The company had a history of firsts that includes Europe's first electric power transmission system, the world's first electrified railway and one of the first elevators, as well as the world's first X-ray tube.

The company developed a legendary ability to manage large, complex projects and prided itself on quality and durability. Siemens gradually developed into one of the largest electronics and engineering companies in the world, with 2005 revenues of $91 billion.

Different Cultures

Until 1971, Siemens was run and controlled by the Siemens family, probably making it tough to foster a culture of company reinvention and change. GE, by contrast, has a carefully orchestrated process by which a CEO picks a successor: gradually narrowing down a field of about 100 internal candidates identified many years before the actual transition.

Siemens didn't become a public company until 1966. Without pressure from external shareholders, the company could pursue long-term business activity while ignoring short-term profits. At

GE, to quote Jack Welch: "You can't grow long term if you can't eat short term. Anybody can manage short. Anybody can manage long. Balancing those two things is what management is."[37]

Siemens has a culture that evolved from serving primarily public-sector customers in regulated markets, thus fostering complacency and a civil-servant attitude. The sense of monopoly status with large customers such as Deutsche Telecom led to long delays in conversion from analog to digital telephone systems, which were introduced many years behind companies like ITT. Siemens's CEO also faced the challenge of navigating the decidedly unfriendly business climate in Germany, which is dominated by powerful labor unions aggressively defending their right to high wages, lavish benefits, and total job security. Siemens was thus ill prepared for the worldwide wave of deregulation and heightened global competition in the 1990s. Siemens CEO from 1992 to 2005, Heinrich von Pierer, acknowledged, "In Germany, competition was like a wind. Now it is a storm. And it will become a hurricane!"[38]

Differing Results

Whereas Welch approached his task of reinventing GE with an enormous sense of urgency, von Pierer tailored his approach to Germany's consensus-style corporate culture: "Good management is the art of making change painless."[39]

Siemens wanted to be number one or number two in every business, just like GE. It just seemed unable to deal with the second part of Drucker's question: If you are not, what are you going to do about it? While GE decided in 1970 that it would never become a leader in computers and sold the business, Siemens held on to its computer business for dear life despite decades of huge losses.

With the accession in 2005 of U.S.-educated CEO Klaus Kleinfeld, new winds began to blow within Siemens. Kleinfeld launched a cultural revolution of his own, with GE as his model.

123

Aggressive profitability targets were established, and Kleinfeld declared his intention to dispose of any business that didn't reach its targets by 2007 (then about half of Siemens's divisions).[40] True to that declaration, Siemens paid about $300 million to get out of its losing mobile telephone business while announcing layoffs in its troubled communications business.

By 2006, Kleinfeld was talking a different game and was quoted in *Fortune* as saying, "That is a fact of life. If I look at all our businesses, I see that only when we are in a leadership position are we able to sustainably make profits on a level that allows us to continue to invest heavily in innovation."[41]

CONCLUSION

Even the most brilliant research capability will not translate into superior profitability and shareholder returns unless the organization is capable of successful systematic organizational and business innovation. Reinventing the business to stay ahead of global shifts requires a sense of constant urgency and a willingness to embrace change.

In answering the forward-looking questions discussed in this chapter, it is critical to remember that:

1. The silent revolution has telescoped the timeline for innovation. Abandonment must occur frequently and rapidly; what needs to be considered for abandonment is everything about a business, not just products.
2. Each of the seven classes of opportunities has an information, geographic, and connection component, which may range from drawing on some far corner of the world to creating the unexpected to tapping into obscure confluences of information about consumer perceptions from multiple industries and sources.

3. The power of processes—to bring together key resources, foster disciplined decisions, and allocate resources—is exponentially more important in today's world than it was when Drucker first wrote about it.

4. Innovation strategy in the Lego world is about building relationships and inventing white space—not pushing products one more round.

One of Peter's biggest gifts to future generations is that he left a body of work that teaches managers and employees how to create the future. It is up to us to put those teachings into action. It's worth repeating: The entrepreneur creates new wealth-producing resources by four means:

1. Abandoning ongoing efforts to make room for innovation.
2. Continuously seeking opportunities.
3. Converting those opportunities into value for customers.
4. Strategically allocating resources.

That's how existing companies maximize their potential for creation. The next two chapters are about connecting with and orchestrating the best resources to collectively deliver innovations and create tomorrow.

FOUR | Collaboration and Orchestration

The "interdependence" of organizations is
different than anything we ever meant before
by this term.[1]

—Peter F. Drucker

I flew across the country to see the future in the form of the Myelin Repair Foundation (MRF)—a two-year-old research group that was redefining the way Americans did medical research. I had a hunch that this little-known nonprofit had invented a model of collaboration that exemplified Peter Drucker's most important ideas. I was convinced that the foundation offered valuable trail-blazing lessons that could help other nonprofits tackle social problems more effectively, and show businesses how to thrive and boost their profits. And after seeing the future, I would have a chance to share my observations with Peter, who would definitely challenge and perhaps confirm them.

Peter's vision of collaboration remains immensely relevant today. He believed that to give your customers what they need, you must follow two rules: first, you must do only what you do best, that is, play to your strengths; and second, to meet the full range of customer needs beyond your strongest capabilities, you must collaborate with other players, sometimes those you consider competitors, who can complement your strengths with what they do best. A tall order indeed.

127

THE POWER OF COLLABORATION

I arrived on a spring day in 2005 at a suburban office park in Saratoga, California, south of San Francisco. A small, discreet sign on the first-floor office door said Myelin Repair Foundation. Walking into the headquarters of this organization, which is devoted to scientific collaboration at the highest level, I expected to see Hollywood's version of a high-tech lab, where men and women with furrowed brows and long white coats use PDAs to beam code to each other amid giant plasma screens and LED displays. Instead, I stepped into a maze of cubicles—some of them piled high with papers. Scott Johnson, Myelin's founder and president, welcomed me and set about trying to find a spot where we could meet; the foundation was outgrowing its space and didn't have a conference room. I started to wonder if stepping into the future might be more like stepping back to my graduate school days at MIT in the 1970s, when we had to scramble for space in exciting places like Building 18 or Building E-52.

> To give your customers what they need,
> you must follow two rules:
> play to your strengths and collaborate
> with other players.

As Johnson and I sat with Rusty Bromley, the foundation's COO, in a cramped corner space, I felt that old sense of excitement return. Consumers don't yet know what myelin is, but it's likely to become a household world to the families of the 400,000 Americans with multiple sclerosis (MS).[2] MS attacks myelin, a fat and protein compound wrapped around axons, the fibers that sprout out of nerve cells and carry nerve signals. Think of myelin as insulation. When explaining MS to children, adults talk about electric wires in the body and how frayed wires often spark or sputter or fail completely. And as scar tissue forms in the place of myelin insulation, nerve signals are slowed, distorted, or halted. These sputters and failures are the symptoms of MS.[3]

Years ago, I had a neighbor with MS, a gentle teacher who loved word games. It was tragic to watch her steady decline, from walking awkwardly to hobbling with a cane to needing nursing care. I soon learned that Scott Johnson, who had been a senior executive at FMC Corporation, a chemical company, and then president of a start-up company, knew all too well how critical myelin was. He had been diagnosed with MS 30 years before. His own investigation of the state of the art in MS research was the catalyst for the Myelin Repair Foundation.

The untold secret of R&D, including publicly funded medical research, is that the very research centers that are supposed to work for the common good are often too internally focused. They don't want to cooperate with others, whom they perceive as competitors, because they fear losing their funding. Maddened by this inefficiency, Johnson set about creating the Myelin Repair Foundation, attracting top scientists with the enticement of pioneering a new model designed to harness their collective expertise to attack and solve complex medical problems that they couldn't solve on their own, and guaranteed funding. Experts kept telling Johnson that curing MS would take decades. Despite funding from the august National Institutes of Health, which boasted of investing $50 million a year in MS research, most scientists said it would still be 30 to 50 years before a cure would be available. Having heard the exact same estimate 30 years earlier, Johnson wanted to see results in his lifetime. He challenged everyone by setting an ambitious goal: to have a solution for repairing myelin in just five years.

To make sure the scientists kept their goal in mind, Johnson also invited a handful of people with MS to attend a session where MRF brought the scientists together for face-to-face meetings three times a year. The experts were no longer dealing with an abstract problem of axons; they were dealing with fellow human beings suffering from an implacable disease. The foundation connected research centers at five universities to collectively find a way to repair myelin.

From Saratoga I drove to Stanford and met with people in one of the member labs. Their excitement was palpable. The scientists were amazed at how effective their monthly phone conference calls were with team members at the other four labs and the MRF staff. These calls enabled them to share information and procedures and to get frequent, objective, expert feedback on their research design and interpretation of results rapidly instead of at annual scientific conferences and during the actual experiments long after. The benefits of collaboration were immediately obvious to them and to me. The model adopted by the Myelin Repair Foundation—putting together the best that different entities have to offer and abandoning the notion that a company has to do everything itself—seemed to reflect much of what Drucker had written in *The Post-Capitalist Society*.

My visit with Scott Johnson and Rusty Bromley, and later discussions with Peter, confirmed my hunch that the Myelin Repair Foundation is a truly excellent example of what collaboration can provide. The quality and commitment of this effort and the consequent multiplier and accelerator functions of highly focused collaboration among the principal investigators, outside contractors, and MRF staff dramatically increase the chance of a near-term breakthrough in a cure for MS.

COLLABORATION AND ORCHESTRATION: THREE DRUCKER QUESTIONS

The morning after my visit to the Myelin Repair Foundation, I was unusually nervous as I approached the Drucker house. I had visited a Starbucks in L.A. to clean up my notes on a laptop, and then I stopped at Kinkos to print out the notes and questions for Peter. As Peter read through my meeting notes with Johnson, he asked me a number of questions and uttered "magnificent" several times. Then we began discussing the critical questions that the Myelin Repair Foundation, as well as any organization that wants to tap into the power of collaboration, had to address. Peter asked three fundamental groups of questions:

1. What are the goals of your collaboration? What are the shortcomings of the traditional business model? What are the needs that it leaves unfulfilled? And what is the prize a collaborative business model could deliver?

2. How should the collaboration be structured? What will be your front room? What does your company do best? And what organizations or individuals are best at the other activities necessary to fulfill your customers' needs? Who best complements your front room?

3. How do you orchestrate and operate a successful collaboration? What is the best way to set up your enterprise to be agile and cost-effective and to work with your backroom partners as one well-orchestrated whole? Can you manage down the risk that the partnership will backfire or be derailed by competitive issues?

As you consider these three groups of questions for your company, imagine you are just now leaving college and setting up your company from scratch. That's Peter's way of looking at the viability of a corporation—if you weren't in this business, would you enter it today? And if so, what would it look like and where would you collaborate or draw on others' capabilities?

If you weren't in this business, would you enter it today? And if so, what would it look like?

Some unmet needs are simply not possible without collaboration. For example, what if you could connect any service or gadget the way you really wanted wirelessly and plug and play? Imagine the possibilities. There would be only one fiber system into your home with multiple lanes. The wavelengths would be split much like radio frequencies, and the telephone, cable, Internet, video services, etc., would all flow through that single cable. You would have one easy-to-use remote device, with no unnecessary functions, for six different brands of electronic equipment. If you lost your remote device, you could pick-up another one at Radio Shack for $10, rather than the $1000 charged today for the high-end programmable remotes by the specialty stores. The spaghetti of wires behind your desk would disappear. It would be doable if companies collaborated and a third party or collaborator had the vision to connect the pieces. This is very much like what the Eisenhower government did when building the U.S. Highway

---

WHAT ARE THE GOALS OF YOUR COLLABORATION?

1. What are the shortcomings of the traditional business model? What are the needs that it leaves unfulfilled?

2. What is the prize a collaborative business model could deliver?

---

system—states guaranteed companies that they would get their money back if they invested in the shared highway system and thereby created demand for automobiles.

I would like seamless wireless coverage while traveling on Interstate 95 around the New York City area. There are moments I wish I were in Siberia, where I expect the coverage is better—linking all those T-mobiles, Verizons, and Cingulars might be a beginning. My kids could pull out their laptops, send e-mail or play on-line games, download a movie, or access their homework while I drove. Google is testing this service model in San Francisco. If companies are willing to collaborate, as Peter constantly said, "it's a great opportunity." If they fail to do it together, they won't be able to do it on their own.

As we discuss Peter's three groups of questions, we begin by looking at how the Myelin Repair Foundation answered these three questions as it was set up initially, discuss Peter's comments, look at how other companies have addressed these questions, and then consider the lessons we can learn from their collaborations.

Thirty years after being diagnosed with MS, Scott Johnson discovered that, by their own admission, scientists were no closer to finding a cure than when the diagnosis was first made, so he got proactive. He began searching the literature to assess the state of MS research, Johnson's "aha" moment came when he read a *BusinessWeek* article that talked about a repair—not a cure—for MS. He liked the notion of repairing the damage or simply treating the symptoms, the way that insulin is a treatment but not a cure for diabetics. Such repairs could radically slow the progress of the disease. "I just called the scientist who was mentioned in that article," Johnson recalled. "He suggested that I talk to other scientists, and that led me on a trail."[4]

Johnson's outsider perspective and business background helped him quickly identify key barriers to the timely development of drug targets in the scientific community. He explained during our interview that the prevailing academic model was serving the wrong customer. Scientists and their universities were the immediate beneficiaries of their research. Success is measured in papers published, grant monies, and tenured research positions, not in enhancing the quality of life for those suffering from a disease. And the drive to be first in making a breakthrough discovery means that information is sequestered rather than shared—until it is time to "break the story" in a peer-reviewed journal. Not only is the academic model not geared to benefit patients, but it provides strong disincentives for the kind of collaborative knowledge-sharing needed to achieve medical breakthroughs. The search for the next grant is never-ending, and the publication of original research in the best journals is the primary criterion for awarding grants. Thus, to be able to continue his or her work, the researcher cannot work with colleagues or share ideas ahead of publication. Critical time is lost because of the delay in making intermediate findings available to others, findings that might well accelerate the progress of their independent lines of research. One of the Myelin Repair Foundation scientists I spoke to put it this way: "Let's face it; Tiger Woods doesn't help Phil Mickelson improve his swing. Well, the same thing is true in science because it's a competitive environment."

The academic model does little to break down the natural silos that form around specialties. Nor is the private-sector approach much help either. Johnson met with leadership teams at several pharmaceutical companies to propose a joint project to develop and validate drug targets for MS. These companies had their own set of constraints. Under pressure to keep down costs and worried about lawsuits, they were cautious about MS research. Johnson found a wide cultural gulf between the very academics and private-sector researchers who should have been drawing on each other's talents. He expressed it this way to me, "A large number of the Ph.D.'s have never been outside the academic world. I think a lot of them have a negative perception of the business world and really don't want anything to do with it. They often view people who went to the commercial world as individuals who compromised their intellectual integrity."

To Johnson, the need was the ability to connect labs with one another, as well as link the academic world to the pharmaceutical world. The prize was a treatment, not a cure. And the timeline for securing that prize—for finding and validating a myelin repair drug target—was 5 years, not the 15 to 20 years that the scientists estimated it would take under the current system. Recently at a meeting with Genetech, someone commented that "you have industrialized academic research." The Principal Investigator there thought about it and responded, "Yes, that is exactly what we are doing." Two years ago he would have gotten up and walked out.

Johnson and his team quickly set the target at five years. "I think they [the MRF scientists] are amazed at how rapidly results are coming out," he said. There are no guarantees that the foundation will find a treatment, but they believe they have a much better shot at it if they address the shortcomings of the business and academic research models, define the prize, and pursue it relentlessly.

Another example of inventing a better business model comes from one of the pioneers of collaboration, Dell. As mentioned earlier, Michael Dell and his team discovered that users were eager to put together computer components themselves. The problem was that each computer company preferred selling customers its own brand and fully assembled computers. Dell's initial prize was to get customers a PC, customized to their specifications within one week. Dell made its front room the ability to plan and configure customized PCs, taking advantage of the vast components and capabilities available from other sources. This focused discipline plus stellar inventory management made rapid customized service possible.

Many of Dell's 15,000 direct employees are also collaborating with the company's corporate customers. For example, there are the 30 Dell employees who rarely see the inside of the home office because they work full time at one of Dell's customers, Boeing. There they function, in the words of Michael Dell, not "like a supplier but more like Boeing's PC department. We become intimately involved in planning their PC needs and the configuration of their network."[5]

In developing countries, collaboration has helped subsistence farmers overcome the economic, political, logistical, and infrastructure limitations they face while also securing a high-quality, low-cost sustainable source of supply for their customers. Here is one example that will change and has changed millions of lives.

After almost 100 years of buying soy from local farmers in India, International Tobacco Company (ITC) is leading the eChoupal initiative—a radically different, collaborative approach to the purchasing relationship. Under the 100-year-old system, farmers sold soy in an ostensibly open auction process in local markets. But soy prices were artificially set by ITC by means of arrangements with certain local distributors. Farmers were so marginal that ITC's supply was never really secure. To move beyond the subsistence level, the farmers desperately needed better information. They could not maximize their crops or yields or get the best price for a particular commodity without information on weather, agricultural conditions, the effectiveness of tools, and prices. Initially, the prize of the initiative was seen as giving farmers access to information to compete on an equal footing in the marketplace and enhancing ITC's soy supply.

ITC gave every farmer access to the Chicago Board of Trade and to the outside world. Under the system, each village (or choupal) got a PC, an Internet connection, a power supply with solar backup, and a printer—all at a cost of under $4,000 per choupal. With this equipment, farmers could access the ITC-updated eChoupal site for information on weather, crops, markets, relevant news, and the ITC itself. The site's frequently asked questions (FAQ) feature enabled the farmers to ask questions of ITC experts. The local operators of the Internet kiosks, known as sanchalaks, were farmers themselves. In return for operating the kiosks, they received commissions on all soybeans from their area sold to the ITC and commissions on ITC farming products sold in their area. The host farmer took a public oath to serve the community. Their homes became not only e-commerce hubs but also social gathering places for farmers and their families.

The system is no longer grossly lopsided. By 2006, 3.5 million farmers had gained access to the Internet and the outside world. Their total costs went down by almost 50 percent, as a result of better purchasing practices, better agricultural practices, and reduced administration costs. The old system provided farmers with an annual income equivalent to some $440 from their 8 to 12 acres of farmland. The new system increased price per ton by 25 percent and their overall tonnage yields. Not surprisingly, this program is extremely popular and continues to expand both geographically and across crops. Peter had no direct relationship with the ITC. Yet he is frequently quoted in its internal reports and the press about ITC, because his ideas resonate so deeply with the company and his approach to collaboration has worked so well for them.

The first step in structuring a collaboration is to identify your company's "front room," which Peter defined as your strengths, or the activity that is most important for you to do—that which stirs your passion and shows off your excellence. Everything else is your backroom, and it can be almost everything. One of Peter's famous quotes is, "the only thing you have to do is marketing and innovation."

In the traditional model, a business would add to its front room an array of ancillary activities needed to meet its customers'

HOW SHOULD THE COLLABORATION BE STRUCTURED?

1. What is your level of integration with customers and your scope of offering?

2. How are outsiders measuring and sharing results about your products and services?

3. How do these relationships all work together in a portfolio that fits?

4. Are you allocating resources where you want to be investing in relationships?

needs. The quality of those activities might not be first rate, or the activities might be relatively high cost, but the company had to have them in place to meet customer needs. The level of communication and coordination needed to team up with another organization made any other approach impossible for most companies. In the new world, however, you can eliminate many of these ancillary activities and do a better job of meeting customer needs via collaboration. In the new world, collaboration is not just an option but an imperative. It is critical that you do only what you do best, that you eliminate or minimize your backroom by teaming up with another organization. With the greater transparency typical of the new world, the customer can see everything and knows your flaws and strengths. And you can connect to and use someone else's front room, thereby better meeting customer needs and streamlining your operations in the process.

The Myelin Repair Foundation defined its front room as orchestrating and coordinating multiple elements of medical research that had never before been operationally linked. The foundation was the connective tissue joining the principal scientific investigators, the experts in the broader scientific and commercial communities, and the pharmaceutical industry. For the foundation, orchestrating meant seeking funding, helping plan the research, operationally linking the labs, providing resources, anticipating needs, and providing a healthy environment for a new, collaborative approach to research.

Research is the heart of the foundation and its reason for being; it is also its backroom. Johnson and Bromley worked together to assemble the best research team possible for this start-up venture. They asked neurobiology experts whom they considered to be the five best scientists in the field with firsthand experience in myelin research, and the same five names popped up every time: Ben Barres of Stanford, David Coleman of McGill, Robert Miller of Case Western, Stephen Miller of Northwestern, and Brian Popko of the University of Chicago.

They approached each of these scientists with their unusual request: We would like you (and your university labs) to work collaboratively with us, rather than in the customary isolation; to work under firm and aggressive deadlines rather than in the customary open-ended world of grants; to work toward a goal of developing treatments for patients (who would be the customer) rather than publishing papers for your own academic advancement; to be part of a collective decision-making process with less individual freedom; and, ultimately, to work in concert with business for the eventual marketing of the drug. They became the foundation's principal investigators despite its highly unconventional operational model.

In retrospect, Johnson understood just how lucky he and Bromley were, and how demographics had helped their quest. Luckily, all of the five scientists were in their late 40s or early 50s, and felt that they didn't have anything to prove. Each had already been established as a success in the academic process. Each felt that this new model might provide a different kind of return or fulfillment—the possibility of more rapid progress, the opportunity to collaborate rather than compete with brilliant peers, the prospect of demonstrating an entirely new model of research with the potential to broadly transform critical research, and the rewards of being associated with actual treatment.

In the world of high technology, the classic example of collaboration is Linux, the open-source operating system. It has revolutionized the way software is made and has emerged as a powerful model of successful decentralized collaboration. Linus Torvalds wrote the beginning, or, as he called it, the "kernel," of an operating system in 1991. He made it available to everyone and invited others to improve on it. His front room is the original kernel and the decision authority built into the software to accept changes. The backroom is executing all the changes.

The Linux operating system that resulted from this collaboration includes code written by thousands of volunteer programmers all over the world, united in their desire to make Linux a constantly improving product and an unstoppable force in computing. The Linux organization is a true meritocracy based on transparency. Any person can look at every bit of code and is free to participate, but only the best fixes are picked by Torvalds and make their way into the next version, which, in turn, will be probed by thousands of people for flaws and more opportunities for improvement. Despite its tremendous growth—Linux software is on more than one-third of the world's servers—the operation has managed to remain both agile and effective. Torvalds remains the undisputed, highly respected leader of this virtual spider web of programmers, top tech companies, and Linux distributors.

As the collaboration has expanded, more of the review process has been delegated and automated, but the fundamental idea remains the same. Top tech competitors such as IBM and Hewlett-

Packard work together and with distributors such as Red Hat on setting development priorities, offering their programmers' time on projects, and protecting Linux from potential intellectual property claims. The tech companies, in turn, make money not from selling the operating system, which is available for free at linux.org, but from selling services and software around the system. Thus everyone (with the exception of Microsoft) benefits from this cooperative ecosystem of global technology talent.[6]

Electronics powerhouse Toshiba has also benefited from a collaborative business model. In 2004, Toshiba saw an opportunity to build customer loyalty in the highly competitive PC market by offering a significantly shortened turnaround time for laptop repairs—a clearly felt customer need. To do so, Toshiba had to recognize that making repairs was not its front room and to look outside its own walls for the capability to repair and return products rapidly.

It was not critical that Toshiba itself repair its customers' laptops, as long as it could guarantee quality service to its customers. So Toshiba entered into a relationship with UPS. Toshiba provided the laptops and customers. UPS provided packaging and convenient drop-off shipping of laptops through The UPS Store retail network; it also set up a Toshiba-certified repair center at the UPS Supply Chain Solutions campus in Louisville, Kentucky, adjacent to the UPS World port global air hub. This center could receive and repair a laptop and ship it back to its owner in one day, with delivery as early as 8:30 a.m. the next morning. Customers could use other shipping services and other repair services as well. The bottom line: Toshiba customers could have their computers up and running within one to four days of returning them for service.

The customer cares much more about hassle-free, fast, and reliable service than about who performs the service. By eliminating service and shipping from its backroom and using UPS's front room capabilities, Toshiba was able to meet this customer need far more effectively than it could have on its own.

HOW CAN YOU ORCHESTRATE YOUR COLLABORATION TO BE AGILE AND COST-EFFECTIVE AND TO WORK AS A COHERENT WHOLE?

1. What sort of *living business plan* is needed to delineate the path to the prize?

2. What *structured communications* will connect the players to the shared goals and plan and build agile *decision making* into daily operations?

3. What *tracking and feedback mechanisms* support your living plan and ensure continued attention to outside results?

As Peter described this challenge to me, he said it is about knowing what you know and what you don't know, acting and learning, and then updating what you know. Getting more than one company to do this simultaneously—organizations that have never worked together before—is management's challenge.

Once the collaboration has been structured—when participants and roles have been defined in pursuit of a collaborative prize—the management challenge begins: orchestrating the collaboration so that two or more different organizations can work together in unaccustomed ways in pursuit of that prize with ever-changing learning and shifting priorities. Like other effective collaborators, the Myelin Repair Foundation devised a living business plan, structured communications and decision making to connect the plan to daily operations, and designed tracking and feedback mechanisms to stay connected to outside results.

CREATE A LIVING BUSINESS PLAN

Scientists don't have business plans. Their objective is to increase knowledge. But the research collaboration orchestrated by the Myelin Repair Foundation did need a business plan to articulate the commitment of all the players to sharing information, getting results, and achieving targeted milestones, as well as to provide a constant reminder that the foundation was challenging the open-ended academic model. Scott Johnson recognized that the foundation needed a living business plan, one that could be updated, modified, and accelerated—not a static plan meant to impress stakeholders and analysts. That way, the scientists would have the flexibility to build on advances and quickly bring a treatment to MS patients. The plan specified tangible goals, clear accountability, and explicit timelines. By its very nature, the plan was made to be flexible and grow organically alongside the foundation.

One of the scientists commented, "Once I saw the research plan, you couldn't pry me out of this collaboration." He could see how powerful and how useful it could be at attaining results. This plan defines as many paths of inquiry as needed to find the answers, but each year the principal investigators propose pilot projects that determine what investments will be made in the next year, and how to refocus resources.

The foundation's living business plan delivered results. In the fourteenth month of the project, one of the principal investigators told the management team that he had a target ready for preclinical testing, but the foundation's five affiliated university labs lacked the testing capacity. In the traditional academic research model, coming up with this capability would have required writing another grant or waiting until capacity became available in one of the labs. As Bromley told me, "In the academic world, if the scientists get a grant, they perform all associated activities in their own lab. They wouldn't contract out for things outside their lab." The foundation, however, quickly dealt with that bottleneck.

While the business plan had anticipated preclinical testing, it assumed testing would start in the third year. Even though this need arose well ahead of schedule, management was prepared to handle the unexpected. The foundation's budget also allowed for research sponsored by other universities as well as commercial entities, and it was able to move ahead with preclinical testing in short order.

The designers of the Myelin Repair Foundation's business plan also carefully thought through the endgame for incorporating the pharmaceutical industry into the initiative, guaranteeing results to donors, and ensuring future financial independence.

STRUCTURE COMMUNICATIONS FOR AGILE DECISION MAKING

What makes collaboration tick day to day and move in step with shortened windows of opportunity?

1. Well-structured communications
2. Rapid and effective decision making

The foundation's communications challenge was much greater than how best to connect people from different locations. With the melding of business and research, foundation participants had varying backgrounds and different expectations about pace, reporting procedures, and basic professional practices. The foundation needed a common vocabulary that would ensure immediate and consistent understanding among people unaccustomed to a businesslike operation. Initially, its business syntax and vernacular were different from the language used in science. Management had to tread carefully so that the scientists understood what it was they were trying to accomplish, how they would achieve their goal, and why their experience base and language would be an integral part of the solution.

This new vocabulary has helped the scientists adopt a more businesslike, outcome-oriented mindset and create an environment that is open to new ideas and approaches. One of the greatest challenges is to get the scientists to either abandon or postpone projects—not because the projects are not worthwhile, but because they have to continually reprioritize to make sure they're going after the things that have the greatest chance of success.

To ensure strong and regular communications among the geographically dispersed scientists, conference calls are scheduled monthly, along with face-to-face meetings every four months. The general agenda for these conferences (both telephone and in person) is to discuss research, share findings to date, reiterate a commitment to the prize (a treatment for MS) and the customer (the MS patient) rather than individual's research priorities, and establish new directions and priorities for research.

To keep the customer foremost in the scientists' minds, at least one MS patient is present at almost all the foundation's meetings. To keep the scientists focused on their common research priorities, the Scientific Advisory Board (SAB) attends two of these triennial meetings each year. And in its oversight and peer-review capacity, the board helps ensure that no unnecessary or unpromising work is being done or planned. The principal investigators (PIs) view the triennial meetings as milestones and seek to move toward results that they can share with colleagues there. To keep the decision process on track, the management team's role is one of taking the principal investigators' information, putting that information in the context of what the other scientists are doing, how it contributes to developing a treatment, and feed it back to them. Rusty Bromley elaborated on that interaction, "What we are doing is listening to them talk from our outside-in vantage point . . . and when discussion centers on 'we really ought to be able to do this, but none of us really can,' we assess the criticality of the activity and find resources."

The PIs develop what they believe is the critical path. They then articulate the research priorities it implies and share their view with the SAB. This is also a dialogue, a real-time discussion, and the PIs go back and modify their plans based on that discussion. Ultimately, the SAB has to accept the plan and recommend to the board of directors that it be funded.

As a collaborative, rather than a solo, institute, the Myelin Repair Foundation is well positioned to ensure that its decisions are focused on the right issues. Johnson shared a story with me that very much illustrates this reality:

> One of the PIs has been taking sections of brain tissue and spinal cord tissue to look at how the key genes change over time in a particular animal model of a demyelinating disease. After his second report, the group said, "We think the sections [of tissue] are too gross [no pun intended] and, consequently, the other tissues are muddling the genetic expression information." So he's gone back to the drawing board and is now looking at some very advanced laser dissection techniques that would enable him to take out very small groups of cells specifically associated with the lesions that form in the disease model. Had he been functioning independently, it probably would have taken two years to recognize the dissection problem, as he would have been so busy generating data that he wouldn't have necessarily seen the forest for the trees. Not until he was getting ready to publish his findings would he have shared them with someone outside his lab, and maybe then the problem would have been raised, possibly as a critique from a reviewer at a medical journal.

So now, instead of spending two or more years working on an experiment before discovering its flaws, our PI was on track within three to six months. And the usefulness of his experiment was also expanded because of the Myelin Repair Foundation's collaborative mode. Although he started by looking at the expression of a small group of genes, the other members of the team continually fed him other genes that they wanted him to study. So, what began as gene expression of about 6 genes expanded to about 15, enabling him to rapidly confirm in an animal what they might be seeing in a cellular model of some sort.

TRACK PROGRESS AS MEASURED BY EXPECTED RESULTS

As Drucker said to me, whether you are a functional member or the orchestrator, the fastest way to undermine your collaboration is to mistake movement for progress. Because the collaboration brings together multiple parties to achieve a common goal, each party will have an explicit role, with explicit responsibilities and accountability—all of which is eminently trackable.

Because the collaboration is by definition a temporary relationship, you need a set of metrics for determining when its purpose has been achieved (whether by your organization or by some other entity), when its purpose needs to be adjusted in light of changing circumstances, or when it needs to be abandoned because it is no longer relevant to customer and market realities.

Once the foundation had been structured and launched, management tackled the issue of how best to measure progress and introduce accountability into the research process. The importance of accountability was underscored by the donors' need to know how their money was being used. That the Myelin Repair Foundation has a tracking and measurement process is yet another characteristic that sets this young organization apart from the conventional research institute.

To help ensure meaningful progress, the foundation constantly reevaluates its path and its goals, with the regularly scheduled conference calls and face-to-face meetings natural forums for such reevaluation. This review begins at the start of each year when the PIs, the SAB, and the management team sit down together to look at what has been accomplished to date and compare it to the Myelin Repair Foundation's road map. At that time, each principal investigator presents proposals for pilot projects to address as-yet-unsolved problems on that road map, with the objective of reaching consensus-based decisions on the best pilot investments for the new year and eliminating any pet projects that are less than relevant.

The foundation is also creating scorecards for evaluating work in progress. The foundation uses key metrics to evaluate progress, including results against plan, ability to react to and handle unexpected findings, benefits of the collaborative model (in terms of time saved/accelerated problem solving), and level of member enthusiasm for the effort. On all fronts, progress—not merely movement—is occurring.

Many of these practices resonate with us as customary business protocols. What is different for the Myelin Repair Foundation is its application of these protocols in a scientific/medical research context. What is different for those of us managing businesses is the fast-changing, collaborative world in which they are applied.

For the past 50 years, the prevalent business model has assumed clearly defined boundaries between a company and its suppliers, customers, and competitors. These walls are now constraints, not advantages. And outsourcing to reduce cost is only a small piece of the new business model. In fact, many younger companies were trailblazers in the area of collaboration, and several mature companies have already taken large steps in this direction—some out of necessity and others to go after opportunities.

LM Ericsson is another example of a company that has achieved great adaptation and orchestration. It effectively collaborates, and then its *collaborations* collaborate. Ericsson, the 130-year-old Swedish telecom manufacturer, has quietly gone about adapting to the Lego world.

Admittedly, Ericsson's collaborations were motivated out of necessity; they were survival tactics in the post-boom telecom industry, characterized by exceptionally rapid change and disappearing boundaries between media companies, consumer electronics competitors, Internet portals, fixed line and wireless telecoms, and cable companies. After the global telecom market collapsed in 2001, Ericsson had to recover from a near-death experience. For three years following the market collapse, Ericsson was swimming in red ink. (I can remember cruel market commentators saying that although the Ericsson logo resembled three little sausages, the downtrodden share value wouldn't buy one hot dog in Stockholm.) Ericsson shed half its workforce and emerged from this crisis even more successful.

Yet its reduction in workforce and the selling off of noncore assets that accompanied its downsizing are not what's significant about Ericsson's recovery. Those actions are typical of companies in crisis. Rather, it is how quickly Ericsson adjusted, fundamentally rewiring itself to deal with the often disruptive market impact of new, constantly evolving technology, much of which the company itself had developed.

Ericsson's management took a hard look at its industry, where technology advances, such as network architectures based on IP multimedia systems and turbo-charged 3G broadband, had enabled any player to become a one-stop shop for household communication essentially "bridging that last mile." This newly consumer-driven industry was faced with global demand for a Swiss army knife or a multifunction version of a handset capable of all types of communications and interactions—Internet, mobile communications, TV and video play, GPS, PDA, MP3 players, game consoles, camera and video recording, credit card transactions, and so on—all captured in a fresh-looking design.

Capitalizing on these changes by connecting the disparate pieces of the telecom industry, Ericsson began going after the prize: a world where 6.5 billion consumers can communicate regardless of their location and choice of technology. Guided by this vision, the company began rewiring itself. From its origins as a traditional developer and manufacturer of switches for fixed telephone land lines, Ericsson moved 180 degrees, emerging as a world leader in both manufacturing and service, making wireless telecom infrastructure equipment and managing operations for other telecom players.

Ericsson's strategy of being a one-stop shop offering a full range of telecom services is not new. What is absolutely new, however, is how that strategy is being executed. Ericsson is no longer trying to house all of its value delivery activities under a single management roof. Rather, it is availing itself of the consumer expertise of other players. It has taken a hard look at what roles it is uniquely positioned to play, what its front room should be, and what parts of the value chain should be another player's front room. Today, one-third of Ericsson's employees are in R&D, and another third work in global services. As Drucker and I discussed Ericsson, he talked about its changing front room and the need to think about it every day.

Handsets are a case in point. In early 2001, following several years of brutal competition and an industrywide slowdown in handset sales, Ericsson, then the third-largest supplier of mobile phones globally, announced that it would outsource all manufacturing of handsets to Flextronics but that it would continue its R&D and marketing activities in-house. Within a few months, it became clear to Ericsson that the handset was becoming more and more of a fashion accessory and that its own design and marketing capabilities paled next to those of competitors, including its next-door neighbor in Finland, the design genius and market leader Nokia. By October 2001, Ericsson had entered into a joint venture with Sony to develop and market handsets for both companies. With Sony responsible for style and design, Ericsson was free to focus on its core competency in advanced radio and infrastructure R&D and technology platform development, while benefiting from Sony's expertise in consumer products.

The Sony-Ericsson joint venture has proved to be a very successful collaboration. By 2006, its world market share had doubled to 15 percent, and it is aiming to recapture the number three spot. While not as profitable as Nokia, which has more than 30 percent of the market, the joint venture contributed $300 million to each of its owners in 2005—a sharp contrast to Ericsson's $1.5+ billion in handset losses in 2000 and to the $300 million that Siemens had to shell out last year to get rid of its handset business.

Part of the joint venture's success is its growing alliances with customers, content providers, and competitors. It outsources almost two-thirds of its manufacturing to lower-cost players. It has a music partnership with Orange (France Telecom's mobile phone network) for the new Walkman phones. It is working with Google to incorporate Google Blogger and Web search features into the handset. And perhaps most indicative of Ericsson's bold transition to the new world, the joint venture is working with archrival Nokia to develop mobile television.

Ericsson has also taken some bold steps on the service side, borrowing a page from its own playbook by helping customers shed activities that they are not the best at. The top 10 global operators are among Ericsson's customers, and 40 to 50 percent of the world's 2 billion mobile phone subscribers are connected via Ericsson networks. As consumers, we have come to expect seamless and speedy communications. However, most of us are probably unaware of the relentless pressure our service expectations place on operators. They have to upgrade constantly to next-generation networks and quickly devise low-cost packages of home phone, Internet access, cable, and wireless to fend off attacks from such nontraditional players as cable companies and Internet telephone companies—all the while protecting their legacy investments.

Ericsson saw the writing on the wall several years ago and knew that few if any operators could be experts at managing both the consumer end of the business and their own mobile and fixed networks; the divergent demands of the business increasingly necessitated different forms of unbundling and outsourcing. By 2005, Ericsson was managing networks for major national carriers in Europe, Asia, and Latin America, with two-thirds of its 18,000 global services employees working at customer sites in 140 different countries. U.S. operators continue to view network availability as a differentiator and have been reluctant as yet to turn their networks over to others. I suspect this attitude will change.

Meaningful collaboration goes far beyond simply outsourcing a particular function because someone else can do it more cheaply.

Those who have turned network management over to Ericsson have benefited in ways beyond being able to focus on what they do best. Specifically, Ericsson (and Nokia, which is never far behind) can provide operators with important weapons for penetrating developing markets, particularly India and China, which offer the most exciting growth potential for telecom players. For example, by offering "pay-as-you-grow" capacity and new antenna technology that provides better coverage with fewer sites,

Ericsson gives its global service customers much more cost-effective coverage in remote, low-subscriber areas.

The Ericsson lesson: meaningful collaboration goes far beyond simply outsourcing a particular function because someone else can do it more cheaply. By combining best-in-class capabilities from across the industry, a joint effort can better meet customer needs, including the need to jettison activities that are not the customer's strengths.

In one of our conversations, Bill Pollard, former CEO of ServiceMaster, recalled a trip he took to Japan. He and Peter were both speaking at a forum in Tokyo. Bill had invited ServiceMaster's Japanese business partner, from Osaka, to come to the forum, but the partner chose not to come. Bill commented that it was quite a large business and that ServiceMaster was having difficulty with it at the time. It was sending him a message that even though he had come to Japan, it really didn't want to see him, and he was irritated.

When Bill and Peter were catching up, Peter asked Bill if he was going to go down and see the partner in Osaka. Bill replied, "No, Peter. They didn't want to bother to come up here to Tokyo, I'm not going to go down and see them in Osaka." The evening the forum was over, Peter sat Bill down and gave him a lecture about interpersonal relationships. Bill recalled Peter telling him, "I should go the second mile, I should go down to Osaka, not only as a matter of just restoring a relationship with people that needed to be restored, but also to recognize the value, especially in that culture, of doing it in that particular way." Bill sat for over an hour while Peter helped him understand some of the nuances of the way the Japanese mind works. As always, Peter complemented his specific advice with some type of knowledge or historical reference.

The next day Bill was on the train down to Osaka. The advice was not only helpful in restoring the relationship, but it helped in negotiating a solution to the business problem and establishing a longer-term relationship.

CONCLUSION

To succeed in the Lego world, you must collaborate. You must tap resources outside your organization. Just as no one person can be an island, no business can isolate itself. The examples I have shared with you here are not exceptions; similar stories abound in every industry and sector. In our conversations, Peter identified the following characteristics of successful collaborative organizations:

1. A *reputation* as *the* place to work that attracts the best and the brightest.
2. A *flexible, easily adaptable infrastructure* and a *highly variable cost structure.*
3. *Pragmatic political and logistical solutions* that convert potential adversaries into allies.
4. *Influence* that flows from setting industry standards that shape the expectations of end consumers.
5. *Identification with their local communities* through holistic branding.

It's not just information that enables these alliances to be effective. For the past 100 years, the world has been building myriad international standards for both processes and products. Consequently, an engineering schematic created in France can be understood by engineers working in China and everywhere else around the world regardless of language. And a part built in Korea fits with a component built in Brazil and meets U.S. OSHA standards; standards that further international collaboration.

These confederations will facilitate the near-instant spread of and access to knowledge and will have the potential to move business ideas quickly across organizational boundaries.

Imagine yourself bringing together the best capabilities from across the globe to cost-effectively deliver maximum value to every customer. Envisioning the way to do it requires bringing unfettered creativity to the three basic collaboration questions: What is the unfulfilled customer need and the prize that collaboration seeks? What is your front room and what is your backroom? How do you structure and orchestrate the collaboration? Remember:

1. Defining the need is not bound by existing business practices. In fact, the most powerful collaborations target needs that cannot be met by traditional businesses.

2. Delineating your front room from your backroom. Decide what your company is best at and challenge whether you need to perform all other roles. You should be collaborating with someone else who can do those activities better.

3. Shared objectives and relationships of trust are often more important to a collaboration than is technology, and orchestration must be deliberate; it does not happen by itself.

Core to all of Drucker's work was an absolute respect for relationships. In one of our conversations, he went so far as to say that it doesn't matter what your discipline is or how sophisticated you are technically. If you can't learn how to respect people and how to develop and nurture relationships, you can't reach your potential as an individual or a company. Nobody works alone anymore at anything.

As usual, Peter hit the nail on the head. As he put it, "The corporation will survive—but not as we know it. Organizations are critically important as organizers, not as employers. Often the most productive and profitable way to organize is to disintegrate and partner."[7] The agile organization positions itself as a bundle of capabilities and resources. The next chapter focuses on people and knowledge—the resources that define your front room.

FIVE | People and Knowledge

Management is about human beings.
Its task is to make people capable of
joint performance, to make their strengths
effective and their weaknesses irrelevant.[1]

—Peter F. Drucker

Peter Drucker stressed, throughout his life and in all his work, that businesses, including nonprofits, always had to put people first—employees and customers, as well as shareholders and stakeholders. Because Peter viewed businesses as the critical engine of a thriving and sustainable democracy, he focused heavily on the people element both in his writings and in his own interactions. In a thriving democracy, people have opportunities to earn a living, to grow and contribute their skills as valued members of an organization, to have a purpose beyond subsistence. In a thriving democracy, the broader society is economically healthy, benefiting its individual members.

As I traveled around the country interviewing Drucker clients, I met many executives and grad students who to this day still feel a very personal affinity to Peter. In our impersonal age, where companies routinely lay off thousands of people, Peter knew and genuinely cared about his clients' children. Jim Collins, author of *Good to Great*, said it best when he recently described Peter as "infused with this humanity and, above all, I believe, a very, very deep compassion for the individual."[2]

Paul O'Neill, the former Treasury secretary, retired CEO and chairman of Alcoa, and Peter's former student, credits much of his business success to his former professor. When I asked Paul about his focus on individuals, he explained his philosophy of management. A test of an organization's potential for greatness, Paul told me, is whether every person in that organization can say yes to three questions every day without any reservation or hedging or stopping to think. Then he pulled out the yellowed, dog-eared notes he had taken 50 years earlier in Peter's class and read:

- Are you treated every day with dignity and respect by everyone you encounter?
- Are you given the things that you need—education and training and encouragement and support—so that you make a contribution?
- Do people notice that you did it?

ALCOA AND PEOPLE

At Alcoa, O'Neill put these ideas into practice by seeing to it that the company would become the first injury-free workplace in the world. He believed, "If we value individuals and our colleagues, we will work in such a way that people are never hurt at work. Not as a banner and not something you do as cheerleading, but something you set up and do using Drucker's ideas to create systems to help you realize your potential."[3]

When O'Neill first announced this policy, it was greeted with widespread skepticism both in the business community and inside the company.

Managers at Alcoa insisted that the company's performance in this area was already excellent. Alcoa's on-the-job injury level was running at one-third the U.S. average. Managers contended that it was simply impossible to achieve a zero-injury safety record given the fact that a certain level of risk was inherent in daily operations. Moreover, any attempt to achieve such a perfect record was likely to be undercut by the law of diminishing returns.

O'Neill rejected these contentions. He was intent on achieving something close to the theoretical limit of what was actually possible—a goal Peter aimed for in his own work and encouraged everyone to pursue. O'Neill believed that Alcoa could become the best at everything it did by committing itself to becoming what he called the world's first injury-free workplace.

For years, Wall Streeters failed to see the logic that connected human values, safety, and financial success. What Wall Street did not understand was that this focus on complete safety was the catalyst for improved productivity through human bonds and the commitment to understanding and improving processes by all of Alcoa's people. O'Neill knew that it is "people who produce value in any enterprise, and that people will respond to a set of values and proven ideas and principles to produce unbelievable increases in performance." Between 1987 and 2000, Alcoa's lost workday rate fell from 1.87 to 0.15 days per 100 workers, productivity went up by a factor of 3, and quality issues fell by a factor of 10. Financial success followed. Once a threatened company with 1986 sales of $4.6 billion and net income of $264 million, Alcoa had achieved record profits of $1.5 billion on sales of $22.9 billion, while increasing market value by 800 percent, when O'Neill retired at the end of 2000.

> People will respond to a set of values
> and proven ideas and principles to produce
> unbelievable increases in performance.

Progress at Alcoa has continued, and in 2005 the lost workday rate was down to 0.09—18 times better than the national average. O'Neill is now turning his attention to an urgent problem, the U.S. health-care system, first as CEO of the Pittsburgh

Regional Healthcare Initiative and later as founder of a hospital consulting company. No wonder. It's 27 times less dangerous to be one of the 129,000 people working at Alcoa in one of 30 countries around the world with 2,000-degree Fahrenheit metal-melting machinery than it is to work in the average hospital in the United States.

Peter always believed that, "Management is about human beings," that a company is really its people, specifically, their knowledge, capabilities, and relationships. And well before the Internet arrived—even before PCs—Peter anticipated a different breed of worker, motivated by pride, accomplishment, and professional association. In the late 1950s, Peter coined the term "knowledge worker." He used the term to mean a white-collar worker whose primary task was interpretation, translation, and problem solving—requiring the use of gray matter rather than muscles.

A company is really its people— their knowledge, capabilities, and relationships.

With his human orientation and ability to translate trends into social implications, Peter pointed out that the old ideas about employee loyalty and retention no longer apply. He saw that knowledge is portable, and its application is not confined to a narrow specialty in one company or industry. In a sense, knowledge workers are more like independent contractors than like employees. They don't leave their work at the office—they take it home with them. They work for a series of companies over time (and may work in a number of different functional positions within a company). They value their knowledge and competence, and the recognition and prestige that come with it, as much as, if not more than, their jobs. While they expect to be well compensated for their work, they also insist on a far greater degree of autonomy, self-management, and respect. They respond best to the standards of excellence associated with their expertise rather than to the discipline imposed by traditional management practices.

Peter believed this new type of worker required a different type of management. He articulated this difference as effectiveness versus efficiency. For manual work, *efficiency*, that is, the ability to get things done, is key to management. For knowledge workers, *effectiveness*, or the ability to get the right thing done, is paramount. So instead of just getting the job done, a knowledge worker has to decide which job to do. Peter was the first writer to pick up on this critical distinction, understand it, and translate it to management principles.

For knowledge workers, *effectiveness*,
the ability to get the right thing done,
is paramount.

Peter also noted the rise of the service worker whose tasks support customers or help with transactions, such as a UPS deliveryman or a waitress, but who does not need extensive knowledge or high-level, problem-solving skills. Management here is another unique challenge. Service workers need to feel good about themselves; they are representing the company to customers, and their feelings are often reflected in their interactions with customers.

Today, according to the U.S. Bureau of Labor Statistics, knowledge and service workers together constitute just over 75 percent of the U.S. workforce, with knowledge workers slightly outnumbering service workers.[4] In our conversations, Peter indicated the current need to approach these two types of workers differently from the traditional blue-collar worker. All workers need respect and pride, and to be set up to win. They need to feel they are making a difference. How management sets workers up to win varies to some degree for the different types of workers. Much has been written about managing and motivating the traditional, blue-collar workforce; our focus in this chapter is knowledge and service workers.

People are more important to an organization's success and thus more powerful than ever before. As Drucker put it, "The knowledge world begins to reverse the balance of power between organizations and individuals." Nevertheless, most individuals still need organizations—not so much for a paycheck, but to combine their expertise with other people's complementary skills, insight, and relationships. They need to work toward a mission that has an impact on the customer and thus the world. They need colleagues. They need to be able to measure their effectiveness. This is what management must offer the knowledge worker.

> "What differentiates organizations is whether they can make common people perform uncommon things."

In the rest of this chapter, we examine Peter's classic questions about people and knowledge tuned to the twenty-first century and study Electrolux. Then we'll look at how a focus on people and knowledge drives day-to-day corporate life and strategy at the financial firm Edward Jones.

INVESTING IN PEOPLE AND KNOWLEDGE: FIVE DRUCKER QUESTIONS

People are the business. They are your front room, your connections to others and to the customer; they are your knowledge and your access to changing opportunities and resources. Peter said that, "What differentiates organizations is whether they can make common people perform uncommon things—and that depends primarily on whether people are being placed where their strengths can perform"[5] or whether, as is all too common, they are being placed for the absence of weakness. Given this dynamic, it is critical to constantly ask and re-ask five Drucker questions:

1. Who are the right people for your organization?
2. Are you providing your people with the means to achieve their maximum effectiveness and contribute to the organization's success?
3. Do your structure and processes institutionalize respect for people and investment in human capital?
4. Is knowledge and access to knowledge built into your way of doing business?
5. What is your strategy for investing in people and knowledge?

Regardless of whether your organization taps into different sources and types of workers or it finds better, smarter ways to search for workers, the challenge of finding the best possible tal-

---

WHO ARE THE RIGHT PEOPLE FOR YOUR ORGANIZATION?

1. What is the task?

2. What knowledge and working style will help an individual win with the task?

3. Are you accessing the full diversity of the population to best tap the global customer base and shifting demographics?

163

ent is more important in the twenty-first-century knowledge economy than ever before. In one of our conversations, Peter repeated one of his basic statements: "The only thing that requires even more time (and even more work) than putting the right people into a job is unmaking a wrong people decision."[6]

WHAT IS THE TASK?

The standard approach to hiring someone is to ask the question, What skills are needed to do this job? Recently, the executive committee at a leading European consumer goods company sent me the target skills for its new head of sales and asked me to edit the list. Peter suggested that managers ask very different questions:

1. What is the task?
2. What is the knowledge base required to carry out the task?
3. What are the necessary working characteristics of the individual carrying out the task and the team dynamics (e.g., self-starter, problem-solver, connector)?

The more explicit the job definition and requirements, the greater the likelihood you will be able to identify what the position really requires and find the right candidate.

Whole Foods, the $3.9 billion natural food retail chain, has developed a highly successful method for finding the right people. The employees of each store are organized into self-managing teams responsible for the operations of the store, including merchandising, scheduling, and hiring. They are also charged with writing the job descriptions and tasks. Team leaders screen and recommend candidates for jobs with specific teams, but every hire must be approved by a two-thirds majority of the team after a 30-day trial period. The company's approach to hiring, managing, and rewarding its personnel has resulted in high morale, a lower employee turnover than the industry average, and a top ranking on Fortune's 100 Best Companies to Work For in both 2005 and 2006.

WHAT KNOWLEDGE AND WORKING STYLE WILL HELP AN INDIVIDUAL WIN?

Once the task is defined, attention turns not to what skills are required, but rather to what knowledge and working style will help the individual win in performing that task. Peter believed that, for knowledge workers especially, that simple shift in question is important for bringing the right worker to the task. With the rate of change in what and how so much is done, there is no one set of skills that will fit all the tasks going forward. However, an ability to access and use knowledge and work with a team will be critical.

One way to spot that ability is to look at the breadth of candidates' experience, particularly in leadership positions. For example, Lou Gerstner's highly successful tenure at IBM had a lot to do with the scope of his experience—his training as an engineer and top jobs at McKinsey & Company, American Express, and RJR Nabisco.

In its search for a CEO, The Conference Board surfaced over 20,000 candidates with private sector experience. When it added the requirement of public sector and academic experience, the list shrank to seven names. Richard Cavanagh got the job. The broad experience he brought with him at the Office of Management and Budget, McKinsey and Company, and Harvard's Kennedy School of Government helped him elevate The Conference Board's focus and broaden its membership.

Drucker listed five rules for making hiring decisions:

Look at a number of potentially qualified people.
Test your understanding of the position and its requirements by considering several qualified candidates. Envisioning each of several strong people operating within your organization may broaden your own understanding of the position's demands and potential impact.

Think hard about what each candidate brings to the position and the organization.

What are the strengths of each, and are these the right strengths for the assignment and the organization? Focusing on strengths is fundamental to making knowledge workers as productive as possible, and it starts with staffing decisions. Emphasize what each candidate can bring to the job and the organization, not skill gaps or weaknesses in their résumés. For example, in picking the members of their cabinets, both Franklin Roosevelt and Harry Truman said, in effect: "Never mind personal weaknesses. Tell me first what each of them can do." It may not be coincidence that these two presidents had what many consider the strongest cabinets of the twentieth century.

Have a variety of people get to know the candidate— as a person.

The personal qualities each candidate brings to the organization are as important as any other qualification. Ability to interact and work collaboratively with other professionals—peers and subordinates as well as the boss—is a key determinant of effectiveness, motivation, aspirations, and a feel for corporate context.

Discuss each of the candidates with several people who have worked with them.

One executive's judgment alone is worthless; several perspectives provide a more complete picture and also guard against bias or the overly rosy picture some references feel obligated to present.

After the hire, follow up to make sure the appointee understands the job.

It is much easier to evaluate a candidate who has been in the position for a while. Ask, "You have now been regional sales manager or whatever for three months. What do you have to do to be a success in your new job? Think it through and come back in a week or 10 days and show me in writing. But I can tell you one thing right away: The things you did to get the promotion or to land the job are almost certainly the wrong things to do now."[8]

ARE YOU ACCESSING THE FULL DIVERSITY OF THE POPULATION?

In our conversations, Peter emphasized the need today to recognize the globalization of markets and customers and the new demographics of potential contributors to an organization, and to think broadly about possible candidates.

A diverse global workforce is necessary, according to Peter. Educational elites in emerging nations bring knowledge and the ability to integrate that knowledge into a value proposition that has global appeal. The president of the Massachusetts Institute of Technology, Susan Hockfield, told a story that perfectly illustrates Peter's point. The executives of a money management firm described their target candidates to her as "smart, numerate people who were raised in cultures other than the U.S." When she asked about whether candidates needed specialized financial and economic education, the managers responded, "What we need is people who understand their culture and how one operates in the culture. We can teach them the financial analysis, the sensitivity to market flows, and negotiation management. We need to learn from them in turn how the culture operates."[9]

Given twenty-first-century demographics, management should also be asking, "Are we tapping into older, more experienced talent by offering employees more flexible work schedules? Are we open to high-talent telecommuters and temps?" In 1993, after reading *The Post-Capitalist Society*, Hewlett-Packard's management recognized that many talented people could devote only part of their time to work because of family responsibilities. HP pioneered "work-share" arrangements that enabled them to tap into this talent pool. Many firms followed suit, devising special working arrangements for parents, retirees, and people caring for aging parents as well as telecommuters and "flex-time" employees. It's

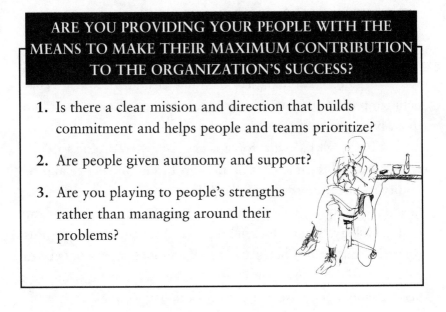

ARE YOU PROVIDING YOUR PEOPLE WITH THE MEANS TO MAKE THEIR MAXIMUM CONTRIBUTION TO THE ORGANIZATION'S SUCCESS?

1. Is there a clear mission and direction that builds commitment and helps people and teams prioritize?

2. Are people given autonomy and support?

3. Are you playing to people's strengths rather than managing around their problems?

another example of the shifting balance of power between organizations and those they employ.

It was a wet day in April of 2005 when Peter and I focused our discussion on people. I rarely take notice of weather, but I remember the rain hitting the cover of the Druckers' pool that day. I frequently needed to look outside to ground myself in the reality and importance of what Peter was saying. He began our conversation by contrasting what it takes to set people up to win today with what it took historically.

> What made the traditional workforce productive was the system, whether it was Frederick Winslow Taylor's "the best way," Henry Ford's assembly line, or W. Edward Deming's "total quality management." The system embodied the knowledge. The system was productive because it enabled individual workers to perform without much knowledge or skill. In a service-based organization,

you need a system that supports the worker, but the worker needs to support the customer individually. In a knowledge-based organization, it is the individual worker's productivity that makes the entire system successful. In a traditional workforce, the worker serves the system; in a knowledge-based or service-based workforce, the system must serve the worker.[10]

When Peter talked about the system serving the worker, he was talking about setting workers up to win with high stakes—the heart of management's most important impact on people. To set people up to win, he emphasized teams and missions, authority and independence, and playing to their strengths.

When Peter talked about the system serving
the worker, he was talking about
setting workers up to win with high stakes.

IS THERE A CLEAR MISSION AND DIRECTION THAT BUILDS COMMITMENT?

It has been proven time and again that individuals achieve their greatest successes when they work with others toward a common goal they are passionate about reaching. Drucker first saw this phenomenon in work teams at General Motors and over the years in many of the not-for-profit organizations he counseled.

Similarly, when I had the opportunity to consult with work teams or cells on the plant floor, their results were astonishing. At Clairol, these teams of batching chemists and packaging workers were managing everything from scheduling to the delivery of what was being made. They met the customers. They called Sally Beauty

Supply frequently, even daily, to make sure the stores had enough inventory on hand. They tracked their own performance. Beyond the reduced management burden, labor costs went down by over 30 percent, and customer satisfaction with service moved well past 99 percent for the first time in the company's history. The results showed that a committed team could set new performance benchmarks over and over again.

Crucial to such a team is a well-defined shared mission that sets the team up to win. At Clairol the mission was satisfying the customer every day in every way. And everyone on the plant floor understood how they impacted that mission. Without an effective mission there will be no performance, and knowledge workers may labor away unproductively without true focus or impact. "Every enterprise and team requires simple, clear, and unifying objectives. Its mission has to be clear enough and big enough to provide a common vision. Without a commitment to a common vision there is no enterprise; there is only a mob."[11] Drucker would often add, "A mission statement should fit on your T-shirt."[12]

> ## "A mission statement should fit on your T-shirt."

In our conversations, Peter referred to the team that created the first user-friendly computer at Palo Alto Research Center (PARC), set up by Xerox Corporation and led by Bob Taylor. Sadly, as a company, Xerox never really connected with this team or benefited from its work, but the team's formation and internal management exemplify setting knowledge workers up to win in their own sphere and not within the corporation. Taylor was credited with "creating the ideal environment for basic computer research, a setting so near perfect that it enabled four dozen peo-

ple to invent much of the computer technology we have today. [13]"
He had thought systematically about how to best manage research
and developed a model emphasizing recruitment, structure, communications, and tools. In recruitment, Taylor was looking for
people with rare intelligence and creativity who wanted nothing
less than to reinvent computer science. He was, however, willing
to forgo a disruptive genius in favor of someone who could work
collaboratively. The computer science lab had a flat structure,
with all 40-plus scientists reporting to Taylor. Scientists could
move from one project to another, and the best projects attracted
the best people, allowing the most valuable ideas to emerge from
the process. Communication and sharing of information were critical to the success of the group. In the mandatory weekly meeting,
every member of the group listened to the ideas and fragmentary
accomplishments of the others. That meeting was also an opportunity to allow tensions and disagreements to surface and be
worked out on the spot. Access to the right tools and cutting-edge
technology was of course critical, and Taylor was willing to risk
his career to provide this support to his group. He refused to use
an inferior computer developed by a newly acquired Xerox company, and PARC ended up making its own computer.

Most important, Taylor succeeded in making all the scientists
feel that they were members of an elite group, "Doing a thing that
they all thought was worthwhile and really thought would change
the world."[14] They were committed to the mission and connected
to the other members of the group. And although they failed to
provide a benefit to Xerox, they did develop technology that
changed the world. After "a walk in the PARC," Steve Jobs of
Apple and Bill Gates of Microsoft both became convinced that a
graphical user-interface-based operating system was the future. A
few years later, Apple launched Macintosh, and Microsoft
launched Windows.[15]

ARE PEOPLE GIVEN AUTONOMY AND SUPPORT?

Especially for knowledge workers, Drucker was a strong advocate of autonomy rather than control. Liberating knowledge workers entails giving them the guidance and perspective they need to assess and direct their own efforts and to take responsibility for the results. Employees who bring substantial intellectual capital need a large measure of autonomy—real freedom to pursue their mission *their* way. This means delegating responsibility and often decision-making authority *and* providing up-front direction when defining the task. Drucker once told me that when you delegate a task to other people and they do it inefficiently, you must let them learn how to do it their way as long as it is not unethical or illegal, unless they ask for help. There is risk in doing this, and a knowledge worker's autonomous behavior needs to be closely monitored. Yet the risk must be taken if people are to be allowed to define their own paths.

> Drucker was a strong advocate of autonomy rather than control.

Well aware that he was advocating a radical departure from the reigning hierarchical approach to management, Drucker warned that conventional bottom-line-focused managers would resist granting such autonomy. "They believe 'that there is one right way.' Well, there isn't." He went on, "If you're uncomfortable with the idea of vesting people with the power to fire their boss, then you are not ready for the task of leadership in the next century."[16]

Peter smiled and brought up Marvin Bower, the founder and former head of consulting giant McKinsey & Co. and the subject of my earlier book. "Marvin and I would frequently discuss how we could get CEOs to understand this idea as we rode the train together." In fact, Marvin had written, "It is part of our basic strategy to maintain the kind of working atmosphere that is attractive to the high-talent people we need to serve our clients well. Such an approach should include a philosophy of relying on autonomy and responsible self-government by the individual just as far as we can. Operationally, this means that the burden of proof should always rest with the proponent of centralized control and bureaucratic rules."[17] Is this a test you might use in your organization?

Jim Collins, who heads a management research lab, echoed Drucker's call for a new management paradigm when I met with him: "The whole key to the high-performance climate for our research team is our use of mechanisms of commitment and connection rooted in freedom of choice. We operate off a clear set of deadlines and project objectives, yet team members generally select their own deadlines, as people feel much more committed to a deadline they have a hand in setting. . . . We have weekly gatherings at the lab in which team members interact with each other, and we assess overall progress and discuss emerging ideas. The meeting serves as a glue, bonding the team members together. Most important, we design the work process so that team members must draw from each other's work as the project progresses.

"This 'commitment plus freedom' approach requires heavy up-front investment in selecting the right people. They don't need rules. You need to guide them; you need to teach them; you need to provide direction; you need clear objectives; you need mutually agreed deadlines; you need mechanisms of commitment and connection. But you don't need control."[18]

As big a step as it may be for some managers, Peter proclaimed, "Autonomy is not enough." Management must ensure that knowledge workers take responsibility for their own work and then provide them with guidance and oversight that is appropriate rather than intrusive. The term Peter would use to describe the manager's liberation of knowledge workers would decidedly not be "empowerment"—he despised this current buzzword. You don't "empower" people. You help them measure themselves by their contributions to the whole.[19]

> You don't "empower" people.
> You help them measure themselves
> by their contributions to the whole.

Ongoing management oversight, encouragement, and support are also essential to keep the team on track and to provide some adrenalin, guidance, and a broader perspective to the effort. The simplest way to approach this role is to ask, "What do I, as your manager, and what do we, as the company's management team, do that helps you in doing what you are being paid for? Is there anything we do—reporting requirements or purchasing or HR policies—that hinders your effort?" And listen closely. This is not only an issue of management style. Drucker's first business book, *Concept of the Corporation*, was about federal decentralization and the role of headquarters, setting up divisions as teams, and asking what headquarters could do to support the teams.

One of my favorite quotes from Peter that rainy day is, "You will achieve the greatest results in business if you drop the word 'achievement' from your vocabulary. Replace it with 'contribution.' Contribution puts the focus where it should be—on your customers, employees and shareholders." Helping people see that they have a unique contribution to make is central to setting them up to win.

ARE YOU PLAYING TO PEOPLE'S STRENGTHS RATHER THAN MANAGING AROUND THEIR PROBLEMS?

There is no better motivation for working hard than success. And if people work hard and play to their strengths, they can achieve success. This is a theme that runs through much of Peter's work, from the lessons he took from his favorite teachers to the advice he gave clients in the last year of his life. Identifying people's strengths can be difficult; often they don't even understand their own strengths or are stuck in positions where their strengths do

> You will attain the greatest results in business
> if you drop the word "achievement" from your
> vocabulary. Replace it with "contribution."

not matter. But some companies have started to focus explicitly on people's strengths. Bill Pollard, the retired chairman of ServiceMaster, described the approach: "Peter Drucker used to say . . . you gotta major in strengths and not in weaknesses. And I think the way we tried to implement that is through . . . our appraisal review process. When someone wasn't performing, we would first ask the question, 'Do we understand this person's strengths versus his or her weaknesses?' And is it the fact that we haven't majored in his strengths or her strengths . . . is that the reason why there isn't performance? And look for another position for that person. One can accomplish something only with his strengths. With his weaknesses, he cannot accomplish anything. Thankfully here lies an advantage of the organization. In an organization, we can bring an individual's strengths into play and make his weakness irrelevant."[20]

DO YOUR STRUCTURE AND PROCESSES INSTITUTIONALIZE RESPECT FOR AND INVESTMENT IN HUMAN CAPITAL?

1. Do you systematically match strengths with opportunities through assignments?

2. Do your structure and processes maximize the knowledge worker's contribution and productivity?

3. Do you systematically develop employees through assignments that play to their strengths and provide feedback that helps them grow?

The power of passionate teams is remarkable. Unfortunately, teams come and go, and all too often their cohesion is project-specific and not institutional.[21] If the larger organization is not geared toward supporting and sustaining teams, their successes may not advance the organization's mission and will almost certainly not be replicated. Bob Taylor's legendary computer science lab at Xerox PARC provided almost no benefit to Xerox because there was a complete disconnect between the research team and the Xerox organization. The downside of the elite team was its incredible arrogance; the PARC scientists were rude to and disdainful of Xerox officials, whom they referred to as *toner heads*.[22] Although the group changed the world by reinventing personal computing, its success was a Pyrrhic victory: Taylor and Xerox failed to align the group's mission with the corporate mission, and, consequently Xerox never commercialized any of the breakthrough technology developed at PARC.

In the knowledge economy, winning organizations are those that can deploy passionate, high-performing teams again and again—not just for what they accomplish for the corporation but for the satisfaction their members can derive from the experience.

DO YOU SYSTEMATICALLY MATCH STRENGTHS WITH OPPORTUNITIES?

If you ask someone, "What did you learn from Peter Drucker?" one of the most likely answers is, "That managers must match strength to opportunity." This requires allocating resources to tomorrow, rather than frittering them away on the problems of today. Putting the best people on the most promising projects seems straightforward, but as often as not, it doesn't happen.

Managers often make the mistake of diffusing first-rate resources rather than concentrating them: it is so much easier than confronting painful priority decisions. And the results can be fatal. Diffusion of resources killed Rubbermaid, a star of the 1980s. People who were phenomenal at designing unique plastic injection-molded toys were set to work designing products for multiple markets and found they could not focus on or "live in" those markets. As one engineer told me, "I don't get excited about the kitchen, and my creativity just doesn't turn on."

Similarly, in many companies, people are simply misallocated. Research departments, design staffs, market development efforts, even advertising efforts are allocated by transactions rather than by results, by what is difficult rather than by what is productive, by yesterday's problems rather than by today's and tomorrow's opportunities. Too often people are put on projects or task forces almost willy-nilly, to represent their departments, instead of to use their abilities and potential to greatest advantage.

Some organizational structures lend themselves to matching strengths with opportunities. A relatively flat, decentralized structure can minimize hierarchy and bureaucracy, and facilitate communication; it can also maintain the flexibility to allocate the strongest resources to critical tasks or projects at hand and to reallocate them as priorities shift. An organization without huge functional silos also has greater flexibility to field effective cross-functional teams.

The internal marketplace is another means of matching people to opportunities. It can range in form from an informal meeting to a database of staff résumés and projects in the works to the vast clearinghouse used at Electrolux. The internal marketplace makes it easy for managers to consider potential team members and for people to see the range of projects in which they might want to get involved. Jim Collins has used this approach to good effect with teams at his management research laboratory. "We break the research projects into discrete chunks and then have a draft in which individuals bid for the pieces they would most like to work on, a process that creates much greater commitment than preassigned responsibilities."[23]

DO YOUR STRUCTURE AND PROCESSES MAXIMIZE THE KNOWLEDGE WORKER'S CONTRIBUTION AND PRODUCTIVITY?

In the knowledge economy, management must maximize the use of each worker's focus and effort, because time is the capacity constraint. David Jones, retired chairman and CEO of Humana Inc., recalls Drucker's core lesson as, "Successful enterprises create the conditions to allow their employees to do their best work." Perhaps the most important rule—and the one to which few managers pay much attention—is to enable knowledge workers to do what they are being paid for. And the first step is simply to get out of the way, to eliminate unnecessary activities that eat up the day and disrupt the train of thought. One Microsoft staffer who became an independent contractor noted that her productivity soared the day she went off the payroll and was freed up from the revolving door of meetings that had dominated her working life. Many well-intended organizational mechanisms become nightmarish drains on productivity, such as nonessential e-mails and routine meetings that accomplish little. Management should make a practice of periodically reviewing how people's hours at work are spent and then eliminate nonessential elements that dilute focus and eat up time.

"Liberation and mobilization of human energies— rather than symmetry or harmony— are the purpose of organization."

Yet management must not confuse autonomy with isolation. Although connecting with a broader organization takes time, isolation can rob the knowledge worker of motivation and curtail opportunities for learning. As Drucker put it: "It is appalling in many ways how isolated and ineffectual knowledge workers can be when nobody understands their output." A flat organizational structure can help promote communication and avoid unproductive pockets of isolation, keeping the knowledge worker connected to the team and its mission. As Peter said, "The best structure will not guarantee results and performance. But the wrong structure is a guarantee of nonperformance. The right answer is whatever structure enables people to perform and to contribute. Liberation and mobilization of human energies—rather than symmetry or harmony—are the purpose of organization. Human performance is its goal and its test."[24]

A problem Drucker often cited is knowledge workers' productivity being far too low, with little improvement seen to date. While improving productivity of knowledge and service workers may not be an exact science, it is not rocket science either. Peter felt that many of the principles and techniques used to deliver operational excellence in the manufacturing world could also be used to improve efficiencies in the service and knowledge worlds, from reengineering to time management. By carefully nailing down the task or desired outcome, mapping out the process steps involved, identifying and sequentially reducing barriers, and, importantly, establishing key performance measurements and measuring results, companies in many different industries have been able to continually improve productivity.

Whole Foods has embraced the principle that you can manage only what you measure and uses feedback and visible results to fuel worker motivation and productivity. Its teams are continually measured and evaluated on operational metrics that are posted daily, such as previous day's sales by team, and product costs, aggregated salaries, and operating profits. All these measures are benchmarked against last year's results; other teams in a region; and occasionally industry best practices. Competition between teams in the same store and against other stores is encouraged, and the teams are pressured to set ambitious goals for themselves. Store employees are compensated based on performance metrics, and all compensation is publicly disclosed.

Even the U.S. health-care system has been addressing ways to increase productivity and quality. Studies have shown[25] that it is quite possible to reduce medical errors, medication errors, and central-line (i.e., catheter-associated bloodstream infections) infections (together estimated to cause as many as 167,000 deaths annually at U.S. hospitals) using processes adapted from the Toyota Production System. The Pittsburgh Regional Healthcare Initiative (PRHI) slashed the number of reported central-line infections by more than 50 percent between 2001 and 2004. I am amazed not that a systematic approach to quality and productivity enhancement achieves results, but that health care has been so much slower than other industries in organizing for continuous improvement. Paul O'Neill, who was the CEO of PRHI 2003-2005, and whose work at Alcoa created the inspiration for PRHI, is a perfect example of how a dedicated and passionate leader can help solve the interrelated problems of quality, safety, and cost in health care. From government agencies to the private sector, we are just starting to look in earnest for approaches to improve the productivity of knowledge workers. "It is an underlying most important challenge management faces in the twenty-first century."

DO YOU SYSTEMATICALLY DEVELOP EMPLOYEES?

Creating opportunities for people means helping them learn and develop. Peter often stated, "Every knowledge organization is a learning and teaching institution. Knowledge can't be taught, but it can be learned."

The best learning comes from a combination of experience, hands-on training, and mentoring, with explicit feedback loops. Development is still primarily experiential or "on the job," involving a series of progressively more challenging assignments, a structured rotation through various departments, organizational units, and geographies, or even a series of apprenticeships. Ideally, these are positions of substantial responsibility integrated into the day-to-day operation of the business, not separate programs. Home Depot, for example, keeps the learning curve steep for high performers: The average age at which managers get their first

P&L responsibility is 26. Unlike other retailers, the store managers have the freedom to hire their own people, order their own products, and set prices—the kind of autonomy that sets them up for learning.

A flat, decentralized organization provides an unusually broad range of opportunities for assignments of this type. Special projects are often good development opportunities. They usually require problem solving, cross-functional integration, the ability to persuade and influence, and a certain level of judgment, and many afford exposure to senior executives. Arrow Electronics frequently uses such projects to develop high-potential young managers.

Knowledge can't be taught, but it can be learned.

Formal training is another learning and development mechanism. Companies are increasingly organizing training efforts around application areas (e.g., benchmarking and continuous improvement teams) rather than subject disciplines or functions, thereby making it easier to apply new knowledge directly to rapidly changing tasks or opportunities. Moreover, training efforts are trying harder to accommodate diverse learning styles, moving beyond reading and presentations to incorporate firsthand experience, group problem solving, and the power of anecdotes.

Development is greatly enhanced by conversation, feedback, coaching, and mentoring—much of which happens informally. A tremendous amount of learning occurs through conversations and debate with colleagues and superiors. The feedback people receive on their performance is also a major source of learning, whether informal commentary from a team manager or peer, or a formal performance review. In many cases, the performance review is a missed opportunity; so many of them either politely gloss over opportunities for improvement or limit the discussion to shortfalls and mistakes.

Drucker's original blueprint for the performance review was management by objectives (MBO), which he designed as a way for workers to take responsibility for their contribution to the organization: The workers themselves define their objectives, thinking through their connection to the objectives of the company and the unit to which they belong, and discussing them in depth with their management. Then management and the workers agree on performance targets, which the workers make a commitment to achieve. The process demands that managers and workers communicate directly and honestly and encourages employees to be part of the decision-making process. Unfortunately, when it was widely adopted in the business world, MBO was often misused by management to dictate short-term goals to workers, and it lost a great deal of its effectiveness as a developmental tool. However, the original concept is still state-of-the-art when combined with the practice of 360-degree feedback from all the worker's colleagues, peers, and subordinates as well as the boss.

Much has been written about the learning organization, and at the core of it is the liberating quality of learning, which fosters the ability to challenge assumptions and abandon conventional wisdom. To build on this informed openness, the learning organization at every turn encourages open dialogue with colleagues and the dissent we cited as a key to innovation in Chapter 3. But the watchword for the knowledge organization is *strengths*—they are the avenue for the corporation to reinvent and thus sustain itself.

In many ways, Electrolux is the story of a company that recently sought and institutionalized a number of practices oriented toward building capabilities.

USING TALENT MANAGEMENT TO ACCELERATE STRATEGIC CHANGE

The Swedish company Electrolux is grappling with the challenges of managing its global pool of talent. I recently had the opportunity to talk with several of the company's senior executives— CEO Hans Stråberg; Harry de Vos, head of group staff human resources and organizational development; and Lilian Fossum, vice president for pricing appliances in Europe and de Vos's predecessor in human resources—about the company's experience in changing its approach to talent management. CEO Hans Stråberg told me, "At Electrolux, we aspire to be the world leader in each of our businesses. To do this, it's absolutely necessary that we retain, develop, excite, and attract highly talented people." But first, some background about the company.

BACKGROUND

Electrolux is the world's largest producer of white goods, an old-fashioned name for appliances derived from their white porcelain finish. The company's 2005 revenues were close to $18 billion.[26] It is a truly global company, with less than 4 percent of sales and only 9 percent of its 72,000 employees in Sweden. Founded in 1919, the company realized at the end of the 1960s that it was too small compared with its international competitors. It decided to diversify and gain global scale economies by undertaking an unprecedented international acquisition initiative: more than 450 companies to date. The company became very adept at turning around troubled appliance makers and also developed what became known as the "Lux culture," an engineering-driven but entrepreneurial climate based on quick decisions, cost efficiency, decentralized operations, and very little bureaucracy.

At the end of the 1990s, faced with higher interest rates, slowing appliance sales, and ongoing distributor consolidation,

Stråberg's predecessor, "Mike the Knife" Treschow, undertook a radical restructuring, spinning off noncore businesses, closing 27 plants and 50 warehouses, and eliminating 14,500 jobs—10 percent of the company's workforce.[27]

A CHANGING WORLD

In late 2000, Electrolux changed its strategy: A great engineering and industrial player, it sought to become a more customer-driven provider. Senior management knew that the strategy would require a new approach to managing the company's pool of talent. Stråberg said that the company needed new talent because it was becoming a consumer-driven marketing company that catered to global consumers and that it was in the process of reshaping its manufacturing base. "We found that we had good talent in the company but not for the positions that we needed. And we also had a number of people who would have been suited for those jobs leaving with entities that we sold off, or for other reasons. . . . As a result, external recruitment was substantial, and we had to bring in many of the new divisional leaders from the outside."

In 2000, Lilian Fossum was brought in as head of human resources and organizational development to spearhead the new talent management system and its mission. Ushering in a new era for Electrolux, she made "people" one of six companywide initiatives, instituted a coaching program, overhauled the evaluation system to identify strengths and development needs, and began posting almost all open jobs on the company's Web site (referred to as the open labor market or OLM) to encourage cross-divisional and geographical mobility.

Today, each of Electrolux's top 3,000 managers undergoes a rigorous talent review process that aims to identify areas for further development, to make employees better known to managers in other sectors of the company, and to identify and weed out underperformers. Managers are rated not only on their operational performance but, equally importantly, on their strategic orientation and people leadership and team-player attitude. In people leadership skills, coaching and effective communication are important. Group management spends two days together every year reviewing all direct reports to assign ratings and actions required for the person to reach his or her leadership potential. This process cascades down the organization, with sector management reviewing the next management layer, and so on.

Five years after this system was introduced, the performance reviews and open labor market, supported by significant investments in leadership and coaching training, are becoming part of Electrolux's culture. Some managers were resistant to losing their best employees, even to other parts of the same company. By making these internal transfers an essential part of talent development and by making talent development an essential part of the company's philosophy, Electrolux is changing its culture. Career development responsibility is shared between the individual employee and the manager. Stråberg explained this ongoing process, "We are actually creating a culture . . . in which managers talk with employees about their careers . . . In the annual appraisal talk or when people have an interest, they go to their boss and say, 'Hey, I've been in my job now for three years, I see this great opportunity, what do you think?' This atmosphere is an essential aspect of having employees think of their careers as 'Electrolux careers.'"

Stråberg also stressed the value of the increased transparency and insight developed about the talent pool: "After two or three years, people who were previously known only within their own divisions were known to other people in the organization as well. So that when a recruitment need came up, it was much easier because we had already reviewed people in the management group. It really helped that management could talk about these people, and they shared a common reference."[28]

IS KNOWLEDGE AND ACCESS TO KNOWLEDGE BUILT INTO YOUR WAY OF DOING BUSINESS?

1. Is knowledge built into your customer connection?

2. Is knowledge built into your innovation process?

3. Is knowledge built into your collaborations?

4. Is knowledge built into your people and knowledge management?

Still, the process is far from complete, and Electrolux recently hired Harry de Vos from GE to head its human resources and organizational development department when Lilian Fossum was rotated to a new leadership position. After just five years, some sections of the company are further along in incorporating these ideas than others. Moreover, as Electrolux's needs continue to change, the skills it seeks to develop in its employees continue to change as well. As Stråberg said, "We are trying to make the talent management process more proactive, to anticipate our needs so that we have people that know key account management, for example. We are operationalizing talent management to support our strategic direction."[29]

In Peter's writings, he did not separate knowledge from people. He wrote about the knowledge worker. He wrote about applying knowledge to what the knowledge worker does. He wrote about the real impact of information and how it changes knowledge and the knowledge worker. Yet he did separate information from people. And he talked about people's challenge in sorting through information and identifying the most critical elements. My assumption is that Peter viewed knowledge as people-dependent and information as a storage house that people can tap into.

Yes, knowledge is still power. Yet in this age of instant access and unlimited information, the power of knowledge in and of itself has been diluted. At an ever-accelerating rate, today's advanced knowledge is tomorrow's ignorance. The knowledge that matters—knowledge on which businesses and industries are constructed—is subject to rapid and abrupt shifts. For example, breakthrough technologies can create discontinuities that destroy or redefine whole industries. If, for example, the fuel cell, long under development, emerged as a feasible and economic electrical power device, 90 percent of the demand for oil would disappear, and the cornerstone of the world economy and geopolitical dynamics—never mind the oil industry and all that revolves around it—would shift radically. That shift would reflect the strategic harnessing of scientific and technical knowledge as well as business acumen.

Today's advanced knowledge is tomorrow's ignorance.

Along with the rapid emergence of new knowledge, the ability to interpret, integrate, and strategically apply that new knowledge has become immensely valuable—it can make or break a company. For example, confronted with the emergence of digital photography, Polaroid responded too late. It hesitated to embrace the new technology, because it was not consistent with its own differentiating heritage (instant photography) and knowledge base (chemistry). A late arrival to the digital arena, they could not compete effectively. Rather than continue to dominate its inevitably diminishing but still-profitable market or create a new white space for instant photography, Polaroid suffered a precipitous decline, which led to its 2001 bankruptcy and subsequent sale of the pieces of the company.[30] Peter would have found this "heritage" strategy abominable. Polaroid failed to abandon old assumptions. In contrast, Canon acted early. It embraced the anticipated shift to digital technology, set up an independent research group in Silicon Valley, and began testing new printing capabilities. It built on rather than bet on its heritage in technology, modified its allocation of resources, and invested in the future.

Every enterprise must build knowledge into its value proposition. Knowledge cannot be separated but needs to be an explicit part of everything about an enterprise.

Every enterprise must build knowledge into its value proposition, harnessing knowledge in every aspect of the way it does business—its customer perspective and interface; its efforts to abandon assumptions and reinvent itself through innovation; and its capabilities and focus, both in its own people and throughout the network it connects with in serving customers. Knowledge cannot be separated but needs to be an explicit part of everything about an enterprise.

IS KNOWLEDGE BUILT INTO YOUR CUSTOMER CONNECTION?

From the outside in, the business needs to ask, "How can the knowledge we have, or have access to, enhance our relationships and offering to our customers, and how might new knowledge change that?" With today's increased connectivity, information and knowledge can touch everything from answering the phone (with caller ID telling you it is Sheila calling) to fundamentally rebalancing the value of the bundle of services you provide. Peter emphasized that knowledge is not about doing what you do better; it facilitates your doing something new. By interpreting and translating the individualized customer knowledge that is often available, a company can significantly improve its customer relationships.

Sealy Mattress, in collaboration with Kittle's Furniture and other Sealy retailers, analyzed retailer- and customer-specific information from across its distribution network. When Sealy understood how its product moved on the Kittle's sales floor as compared to bedding retailer trends, it was able to help Kittle's move product more effectively, train salespeople to emphasize higher-priced mattresses, and put in place the right promotions and sales for each neighborhood.

Building knowledge into the product or service a company takes to market increasingly creates real value for customers. For example, an "intelligent" oil drill that bends its way to extract more oil from the pockets of underground oil formations commands more than twice the price of a standard drill. Self-diagnostic electronics have surfaced in an enormous range of equipment and consumer products, from photocopiers to automobiles. With information technology's capabilities and applications growing as fast as they are, knowledge-based improvements in product offerings and customer interface have, according to Peter, only just begun.

IS KNOWLEDGE BUILT INTO YOUR INNOVATION PROCESS?

One of the most direct ways knowledge creates value in a business is by fueling its innovation process. Simply to remain competitive, the organization must continually scan related fields for changes that could affect its competitive landscape. For example, a manufacturer of optical glass needs to monitor developments that might make plastic a more attractive alternative, such as scratch-resistant formulations or high-performance coatings. The scan must embrace not only key technology platforms but also substitute and enable technologies that will open the door for totally new approaches to technical problems.

As part of its scanning efforts, the R&D group at Corning frequently organizes workshops on new technological developments that have the potential to lead to new business opportunities, such as cell-based assays and cellular arrays, high-bandwidth applications, and photonic crystals. The company brings in world-class experts from academia or industry so Corning's scientists and business people are provided with a quick view into the state of the art. The workshops conclude with open brainstorming sessions about possible business ventures and their fit with Corning capabilities and business models. Corning has also been a leader in developing management processes to ensure that new knowledge and new ideas—even those completely unrelated to existing business units—are translated effectively into new ideas and developed rather than being left to languish in the laboratory. On this front, Peter was very curious about how Corning was listening to other companies. He commented, "Who would have guessed that prioritizing pursuit of new knowledge would be a management focal point?"

IS KNOWLEDGE BUILT INTO YOUR COLLABORATIONS?

Collaborations are often the product of shared objectives and knowledge. The Cochrane Collaboration is an international nonprofit organization providing a centralized online database with up-to-date, unbiased analyses of reliable and relevant health-care research studies. Its nearly 8,000 researchers and health-care professionals from a multitude of organizations around the world work together to help people make better-informed decisions about health care based on the best available research.

In this age of the Internet, collaboration is more important than ever. The Internet is the perfect medium for sharing information and for creating online communities, both of which enhance knowledge. Peter's grandson, Nova Spivack, takes his grandfather's work one step further and updates Peter's ideas for the online age. Spivack's point is that access alone has limited value. While individual interpretation and screening enhance the value of knowledge, exponential gains are evidenced from the collective interpretation of connected communities.

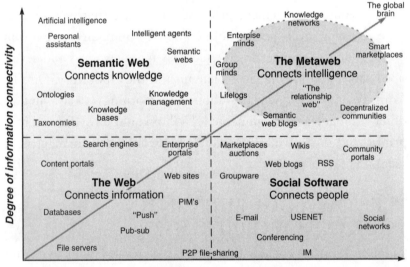

Figure 5.1 Knowledge and Connectivity of Information and People

IS KNOWLEDGE BUILT INTO YOUR PEOPLE AND KNOWLEDGE MANAGEMENT?

Perhaps the most direct use of knowledge within an organization is to build its own capabilities. From Peter's perspective, this ability to apply knowledge to knowledge will be the critical factor in productivity moving forward. The challenge is sorting through and prioritizing the knowledge. From where I sit, every one of my clients is struggling today to figure out how to prioritize the vast array of knowledge available to them and utilize it fully in their business, be it the retailer's data on consumer habits or access to every country's tax laws in deciding where to locate facilities.

Applying knowledge to knowledge will be the critical factor in productivity moving forward.

I recently connected with a friend who had returned to the management consulting firm Bain & Company after a two-year absence. He told me that Bain had become a different world. He had just started a piece of work at a major semiconductor company, looking at marketing spending and productivity. Before he visited the client, he got onto the Bain knowledge system and looked at the 10 most frequently used frameworks for analyzing and working with unnamed clients interested in enhancing and or reducing its marketing spending. He had access to every marketing effectiveness effort done by Bain over the last year, with commentary.

He then downloaded the most recent semiconductor industry knowledge and profile available at Bain. He commented that he was going into the study with understanding and capabilities far greater than anything he had ever had two years earlier.

I shot back that in five years everyone would have access to Bain's frameworks, and McKinsey's and BCG's, too. In fact, the information will be disseminated directly from clients and their partners. This access to high-level knowledge—as distinct from just information—will occur as experts and capabilities increasingly link and overlap across industries, and as the academic world becomes more collaborative. Bain's knowledge will become widely available and become information for the masses that aren't privy to the commentary, and so forth. Knowledge will be the ability to sort through the multiplicity of frameworks and apply critical questions to the problems at hand. He thought about my comment and said it will take 10 years. Whatever the time frame, knowledge and its availability are changing how business is and has to be done every day.

People, not policy, define a company's front room and move the company along the path it has delineated to deliver value to

WHAT IS YOUR STRATEGY FOR INVESTING IN PEOPLE AND KNOWLEDGE?

1. Given your overall business strategy and the scope of your product or service offerings, what core capabilities do you want to invest in?

2. What role does knowledge play in the value you offer customers and in your core capabilities?

3. How and to what extent are you investing in attracting and developing your people and knowledge base?

the customer. In so doing, people are informed by knowledge, the sources of which go beyond their own experience and education and training and include internal and external performance metrics, outside entities within the organization's extended network, research findings, and so on. Armed with knowledge, supported by an infrastructure (physical assets, intellectual property, information systems, material/component flows, etc.), and properly engaged and motivated (by means of a shared vision, a clear mission that contributes to that vision, and incentives that create accountability and reward results), people are the core of the organization's capabilities and agility.

> "The first sign of decline of a company
> is loss of appeal to qualified, able,
> and ambitious people."

In the new world of the knowledge worker, attracting and retaining high-talent people is at least as important as anything else a company does. Drucker said, "The first sign of decline of a company is loss of appeal to qualified, able, and ambitious people."[31] What attracts them is work that is truly interesting and the chance to make a contribution that is truly significant. But as highly skilled and independent professionals, knowledge workers are highly mobile. Despite their migratory nature, the knowledge organization invests in them and seeks to retain them by fostering an excellent working environment—a culture that respects and values them as knowledge professionals, and that sets them up to win.

However, a company's people and knowledge strategies depend heavily on the nature of its business and begin with the question: Given your overall business strategy and the scope of your product or service offerings, what core capabilities are needed to provide value to the customer? Which of these capabilities represents your unique strengths? Those are the core capabilities that define your front room. A key objective of the people and knowledge strategy is to ensure that you maintain and build your core capabilities while being strategically adaptable. This requires investing in people and knowledge—through your recruitment strategies, development and training strategies, knowledge management, and top-notch human resource management—not only in the Human Resource department but throughout your management team as an explicit part of your overall business strategy.

The next questions are: What role does knowledge play in the performance of these core capabilities, and what are the implications for your investment in people and/or knowledge? How large is the knowledge component of the value you deliver to customers? How important is knowledge to your value proposition? How much of this knowledge-based value do you provide through your core capabilities, and how much is provided by your "backroom"? How much are you investing in people and knowledge to maintain your capabilities?

The front room is the area of heaviest investment in people and knowledge; the backroom is where you cut costs by minimizing investment or farming out the activity entirely. For example, Morgan Stanley is moving the bulk of its information systems to India in an effort to reduce its backroom or support costs, but it is investing heavily in its front room by training and developing its traders. Apple, with its strong customer focus, has made working as a "genius" at the "genius bar" in its retail stores a prestigious and sought-after position, because serving customers is part of its front room. But Apple is outsourcing all its technical repairs, which are part of its backroom.

An organization may have more than one strategy, as Apple illustrates. An effective strategy is generally a function of the business's level of *investment* in people and knowledge, and the extent to which knowledge is a *component* of its product or service offering (see Figure 5.2). Peter and I discussed four general categories of strategies: the service provider, the knowledge provider, the commodity player, and the relationship-dependent connector.

Of the four types of knowledge strategy, the *knowledge provider* typically involves the highest investment in knowledge. The bulk of the knowledge provider's value proposition derives from people and knowledge, and it therefore invests heavily in them. As a management consultancy, McKinsey & Company, Inc. is all about people and knowledge: It has no physical product other than spiral-bound reports. What it brings to each client is pure expertise. McKinsey's staff plays the central role in its success. It pays them well and invests heavily in training programs around topics and problem-solving capabilities as well as knowledge sources and capabilities to support the staff's intellectual and professional growth. Fundamentally, McKinsey's people strategy is to create opportunity, provide growth, and foster a sense of

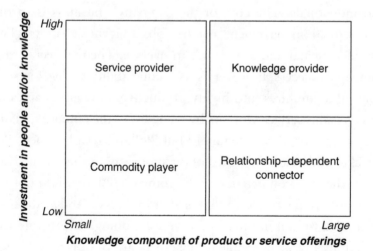

Figure 5.2 General Categories of People and Knowledge Strategies

belonging to "a special group" to attract and retain talent as well as to expand the firm. Its web site uses the word "opportunity" more than 20 times and makes the claim, "If you come here, we make the implicit promise that we're going to provide you with opportunities you cannot equal anywhere else." The development process—continuous mentoring, challenging experience, and collective learning—is at the heart of the firm's identity. McKinsey also offers these opportunities to its network of alumni and clients, who in turn provide support in the form of referrals and personal references.

The *service provider* has a smaller knowledge component in its offering; it is a purely service organization. It must therefore invest enough in its people (and, where relevant, in knowledge) to ensure that its service meets customer expectations for quality. A good example is ServiceMaster.

This organization has created a $3.8 billion business by making supporting functions (such as housekeeping, termite and pest control, and landscape maintenance) its front room and serving as a backroom for its customers—hospitals, schools, industrial firms, and individuals. The core of the company's business is to offer professional management of the jobs that most of its clients consider menial and a nuisance to oversee. The real secret to the company's success, however, is its unique ability to develop sometimes illiterate hires into highly productive, motivated, and quality-conscious service workers by recognizing the potential, dignity, and worth of the individual. Bill Pollard recalls when Peter Drucker addressed the board of directors after he had helped crystallize the core competency of the company: "He started out with a question to the board, 'What is your business?' And as the board responded to him in things that we were doing, he just told them something I was never able to tell our board of directors. He said, 'You are all wrong. Your business is simply the developing and growing of people. You can't deliver a good service without trained and committed people. You package it in different ways to meet the needs of your customers. And that is your basic business.'"[32] Today, ServiceMaster employs 38,000 people and manages an additional 200,000 people employed by others.

The *commodity player*, on the other hand, is all about low price; it carefully considers the return it will get from its people and knowledge investments and makes them judiciously. Wal-Mart, the world's largest retailer and one of its largest private employers with 1.7 million worldwide associates, has built its success on the ability to squeeze out cost at every step of its business system so as to offer consumers prices lower than anyone else's. Unlike a service provider, who typically needs to provide a fairly high level of service to meet customer expectations, Wal-Mart's value proposition is dominated by low cost, and its customers have lower expectations of service. Wal-Mart's effort to limit its investment in retail sales associates has made the company a lightning rod for criticism of its benefits and other employment practices, with local legislators putting in place statutes directed at Wal-Mart and advocacy groups mounting demonstrations and boycotts. Although Wal-Mart is always looking for sales associates with leadership potential and says, "We train at all levels, and everyone has an equal opportunity,"[33] the company notes that there is no difference in productivity between a sales associate of seven years' tenure and a one-year associate—the minimal training is not making a difference.[34] In logistics, however, Wal-Mart is the most efficient retail competitor and wants to maintain that position, so it has a different people/knowledge strategy in that function. Wal-Mart's logistics support functions have relatively high knowledge content, and it manages them more like a service provider, offering ample leadership and training programs.

Finally, there is the *relationship-dependent connector*, which has a high knowledge content within its offering and needs few people to operate, because its business is all about enabling others to interact. This approach is exemplified by eBay, the online auction house and the largest online market for the sale of goods and services by consumers and small businesses, which has created a virtual marketplace for people from around the world to buy and get rid of practically everything from old toys to fine antiques. eBay's value proposition is to make marketplaces more efficient by offering users an easy and inexpensive way to communicate, exchange information, and complete transactions for a huge variety and selection of goods. To this end, eBay has created an advanced, easy-to-use online trading platform, including software tools and services to make the search and trading process easy and efficient. eBay employs thousands of people[35] to serve and connect its community of over 200 million registered users. In 2006, Beth Axelrod, one of the authors of *The War for Talent* and coleader of McKinsey's global organizational practice, joined eBay as head of Human Resources. When we exchanged e-mails, she commented, "eBay recognizes that the key to building an enduring success story is focusing on our people and organization."[36]

Management thinking about the strategic application of people and knowledge is still in its infancy, although the best-performing, knowledge-driven companies clearly have built significant expertise in managing both their people and the knowledge base in which they have invested. People and their knowledge are at the heart of the enterprise's capabilities, both present and future—the ability to deliver today, with an outside-in perspective, and the ability to innovate and grow for tomorrow.

HOW PEOPLE MAKE THE DIFFERENCE AT EDWARD JONES

The investment firm Edward Jones was one of Peter Drucker's last clients, and he consulted with it as late as April 2005, at the age of 95. The relationship started in 1980, shortly after John Bachmann succeeded Ted Jones as managing partner. He and Jones had read Drucker's book *Management: Tasks, Responsibilities, Practices* and found it a useful set of instructions to define strategy and managing people. "We spent a year on it, every chapter. We would spend the time learning what the book had to say. And it—I would say the humaneness of it, respect for people—made it something we really related to. I mean, it was what we would aspire to do and be ourselves." In several letters, Bachmann told Drucker that his mark was all over Edward Jones and expressed an interest in establishing a consultant relationship. He told me that the company "aspires to build a great business, a great organization. And we come upon Peter and his writings, and said, this is the kind of company we want to be. We want to be a place that respects the individual. We want to be a place that's demanding and yet fair. We want to build on people's strengths."[37]

We want to be a place that respects the individual.

Over the years, Drucker met regularly with Edward Jones management groups to discuss questions raised by the team. Characteristically, Drucker did not provide straight answers to the questions. "He didn't come up with any answers. He doesn't give answers. He creates a framework; when you are thinking about mission, he doesn't tell you what the Jones mission is. He talks about what a mission is, how you go about determining your mission, and how you go about determining what strategies really are."[38]

Peter sometimes jokingly referred to himself as an *insultant* (who had the pleasure of "scolding clients and getting paid for it") rather than a consultant, based on his habit of challenging prevailing assumptions. Do you remember the Edward Jones, Wee Willie Keeler story from Chapter 2? Well, John Bachmann remembers it as the critical conversation that ultimately laid the groundwork for Edward Jones's future growth strategy

---

Peter sometimes jokingly referred to himself as an insultant.

Edward Jones has quietly built one of the largest, fastest-growing retail brokerage networks in the world, with over 9,000 offices, establishing, to quote Peter Drucker, "A confederation of highly autonomous entrepreneurial units bound together by a highly centralized core of values and services." Moreover, it has consistently generated returns on equity of around 30 percent,[39] exceeding those of every major competitor, including Morgan Stanley, Merrill Lynch, and A.G. Edwards. Jones is not your typical financial services company. For the past 50 years, the company has served individual investors with a strong focus on long-term, buy-and-hold, conservative investing policy, providing face-to-face service even to very small investors. To provide that personal service, Jones has built an innovative, decentralized organizational structure centered on a network of mostly single-broker offices staffed by entrepreneurially-minded investment representatives (IRs).

Central to the company's success is finding the right people for the organization. Jones "looks for people with passion, confidence, independence, and a belief in doing what's expected. We like to hire people who understand and can embrace our 'unfashionable' approach to investing. We try to recruit individuals who want to live in the community where they build a business." The company is quite selective. From the 15,000 job inquiries it receives each month, the firm hires only 200.[40]

In an organization that is built upon a far-flung network of independent offices, it is critical to instill a strong, well-defined, shared mission to make brokers and administrators alike feel part of a group with a common agenda. The challenge is to balance the freedom awarded the IRs to run their own businesses with the need to stick to the firm's strategy and principles. "We have canvas and we have paints," says Bachmann. "You're going to stay on the canvas, or you're not going to be here. And you'd better use our paints, or you're not going to be here. Which means that you don't get off into products that are highly speculative or dangerous. But as long as you use our canvas and our paints, then you paint your own masterpiece."[41]

As long as you use our canvas and our paints, then you paint your own masterpiece.

Consistent with these principles, the company does not offer penny stocks, options, commodities, or indeed any investment that is deemed speculative. Unlike other brokerage firms that live on the commissions generated by "churning," Jones frowns on frequent trading. Similarly, online trading is not offered (although bill payment and other services are offered online), since the company does not cater to the do-it-yourself segment of the market.

The organizational structure is very flat; in Bachmann's words: "Nobody reports to anybody around here, or they get their mouths washed out with soap!"[42] Every one of its more than 9,000 offices is its own profit center. The St. Louis head office is essentially a support function, providing a full range of operational and marketing services as well as research.

While it is hard to orchestrate frequent interactions between the company's employees, Jones uses several mechanisms to connect its network of brokers and encourage collaboration. Every office has its own satellite dish and is connected to a satellite network, which not only pipes trading information back to the St. Louis backoffice but also provides continuous learning opportunities, such as investment seminars and training modules, to the offices. The IRs get a 40 percent share of the gross commissions generated, but the bonus system kicks in if the firm is also profitable—the more profitable it is, the higher the bonus (provided that the office itself has reached a certain level of profitability). In the corporate culture, the emphasis is on growing the size of the whole pie rather than just getting a bigger piece for yourself.

Jones is the only major brokerage firm still organized as a partnership. Unlike other partnerships, in which only a select few become partners and share in the profits of the company, everyone from mailroom worker to broker at Jones has an opportunity to become a limited partner, which further serves to align employees' interests with those of the firm. There are 305 general partners and 4,636 limited partners.[43]

Jones's organizational structure is clearly an excellent way to grant autonomy and authority to IRs; they are given the freedom to decide how to run their businesses. There are, for example, no budgets or performance objectives (except for the requirement that new recruits personally make at least 25 calls per day). IRs literally set their own objectives, recognizing that they must become profitable. The company fully realizes that this very decentralized structure, coupled with the type of high-achieving, self-starting individuals attracted to Jones, could result in destructive behavior and competition, which are not uncommon in the brokerage industry. So there is no tolerance for "playing it close to the line," even if you are a star performer.

The company's advanced training program is recognized as one of the best in the industry. In January 2006, *Fortune* ranked Jones 16th in its 100 Best Companies to Work For. (This is Jones's seventh appearance on the list.) According to *Fortune*, what makes Jones great is that, "The education never ends at this brokerage firm, which spends 2.5 percent of payroll on training. A mentoring program pairs new brokers with veterans for a year, and lots of workers take subsidized business school classes."[44]

In many ways Edward Jones epitomizes the knowledge organization that liberates its people to pursue their mission. Solid IR knowledge and experience are central to both the service offering and successful client relationships, and this strongly decentralized organization gives its IRs extraordinarily high levels of autonomy, encouraging a highly entrepreneurial culture while inculcating clear ethical values and instituting a few clear and well-placed controls. Consequently, investment in people and knowledge has played a key role in the company's success.

GOOGLE'S 10 GOLDEN RULES FOR KNOWLEDGE WORKERS

In early 2005, Peter and I discussed Google. He commented on how powerful online communities were and would be and how managing these more autonomous workers to be productive and innovative is a challenge. Eric Schmidt, the CEO of Google, appears to have accepted this challenge with relish (see sidebar). In a conversation at a cocktail party, Schmidt commented that the team at Google has more in common with professional basketball players than with traditional workers. Most of them are free agents; they have specialized skills that they carry with them wherever they work; and their companies need them more than they need their companies. Nevertheless, the basketball player cannot be a star without a team to play on and a league to compete in.

In Eric Schmidt's view there are 10 golden rules:[45]

1. *Hire by committee.* Virtually every person who interviews at Google talks to at least half a dozen interviewers, drawn from both management and potential colleagues. Everyone's opinion counts.

2. *Cater to their every need.* As Drucker says, the goal is to "strip away everything that gets in their way."

3. *Pack them in.* Almost every project at Google is a team project, and teams have to communicate. The best way to make communication easy is to put team members within a few feet of each other. The result is that virtually everyone at Google shares an office.

4. *Make coordination easy.* Because all members of a team are within a few feet of one another, it is relatively easy to coordinate projects. In addition to physical proximity, all Googlers e-mail a snippet once a week to their work group describing what they have done in the last week. This gives everyone an easy way to track what everyone else is up to, making it much easier to monitor progress and synchronize workflow.

5. *Eat your own dog food.* Google workers use the company's tools intensively. "One of the reasons for Gmail's success is that we beta-tested it within the company for many months."

6. *Encourage creativity.* Google engineers can spend up to 20 percent of their time on a project of their choice. "One of our not-so-secret weapons is our ideas mailing list: a companywide suggestion box where people can post ideas ranging from parking procedures to the next killer application."

7. *Strive to reach consensus.* Modern corporate mythology has the unique decision maker as hero. "We adhere to the view that the 'many are smarter than the few' and solicit a broad base of views before reaching any decision." At Google, the role of the manager is that of an aggregator of viewpoints, not the dictator of decisions. Building a consensus sometimes takes longer but always produces a more committed team and better decisions.

8. *Don't be evil.* "Much has been written about Google's slogan, but we really try to live by it, particularly in the ranks of management."

9. *Data drives decisions.* At Google, almost every decision is based on quantitative analysis. "We've built systems to manage information, not only on the Internet at large, but also internally. We analyze performance metrics and plot trends to keep us as up to date as possible. We have a raft of online 'dashboards' for every business we work in that provide up-to-the minute snapshots of where we are."

10. *Communicate effectively.* Every Friday Google has an all-hands assembly, with announcements, introductions, and questions and answers. "This allows management to stay in touch with what our knowledge workers are thinking and vice versa."

CONCLUSION

At its core, according to Drucker, management is all about human beings and "the integration of people in a common venture. The test of a healthy business is not the beauty, clarity, or perfection of its organizational structure. It is the performance of people."[46] In a world where a company is its people, their capabilities, and their relationships, the importance of respecting employees and investing in them has never been greater:

1. People are much more than employees. They embody the knowledge, the capabilities, and the relationships that your company takes to the market. The organization is more dependent on its people than its people are on the organization. People *are* the most important investment a company makes.

2. Enabling people to live up to their potential, achieve their maximum effectiveness, and contribute to the organization's performance is what makes the difference between success and failure. That enabling is the role of management. In an organization of self-managing knowledge workers, "command and control" is obsolete. "Trust and support" is key.

3. Successful teams generally dissolve at the end of a project, but the knowledge organization must create and deploy them again and again.

4. Business survival requires applying and integrating knowledge continuously to create value all the time.

These realities and the corporation's need to operate effectively in the Lego world only underscore the importance of investing in and caring for people and relationships. Relatively few companies over time have done a consistently good job of managing knowledge workers, and this is a twenty-first-century challenge.

Connecting to the customer with innovation as the way of life, using the best resources anywhere in the world to deliver value, and by investing in people, an enterprise is set up to win—*if* it can coordinate its activities across different places and over time. That is the subject of the next chapter.

SIX | Decision Making: The Chassis That Holds the Whole Together

A decision is a judgment. It is a choice between alternatives. It is rarely a choice between right and wrong. It is often a choice between two courses of action, neither of which is provably more nearly right than the other.[1]

—Peter F. Drucker

I t takes smart decisions and execution to traverse the new landscape, even with a strategy or map. And by that I mean the right colleagues, and the right collaborators and strong customer connections—everything that helps spur innovative thinking. When Peter and I spoke, we referred to this as the *chassis*—the organization's ability to make well-informed decisions about what needs to be done and its resolve to get it done.

Peter was passionate about management effectiveness—setting priorities, managing time, and making effective decisions. His internationally bestselling book *The Effective Executive* is very much about getting the right things done. In the Lego world, with knowledge workers and a vast array of collaborators playing important roles in the enterprise, people cannot be closely supervised. They can only be helped and supported in their ability as managers to make effective decisions. The days of the gray-suited micromanager, hovering over his employees' desks, are over.

Managing in this amorphous environment is a delicate balancing act between preserving what makes the enterprise strong and channeling innovation to go beyond past successes. Peter used a circus analogy: The company must constantly be on a strategic tightrope toward the future, finding this balance even as the safety net below is shrinking.

Logic suggests that decision making and decision execution, which define this narrow and demanding path, are made easier by today's vast amounts of information and knowledge. This is not true. Rather, the broad base of accessible information is rendered somewhat dense, difficult, and shifting by both the blurred boundaries between parties in the value chain and the speed of change in the market—these distinguish today from earlier periods in business history. As Peter put it, today's manager faces a fast-moving barrage of apparent knowledge, some relevant and reliable, some not. Because events shift so quickly, a decision can be obsolete before it even gets put in motion.

> The company must constantly be
> on a strategic tightrope toward the future,
> finding this balance even as the safety net
> below is shrinking.

So, ironically, in the age of information, intuition and judgment play an even greater role in effective decision making and well-placed strategic bets than ever before. Don't get me wrong. There is no substitute for fact-based decision making, and no excuse for managing from the gut. But with unprecedented rates of change everywhere, getting the right assortment of reliable facts can be impossible within the time window available to take action. Sometimes we have to be able to see around the corners, and intuition and judgment play a valuable role in choosing which facts or feedback to trust. When store-based data began pouring in as Nivea for Men was introduced, the head of U.S. marketing had a gut feel that the large discrepancies between stores had something to do with the surrounding demographics and Latino concentration. He asked that the facts be checked store by store. As it happened, the stores selling the most Nivea to men were in neighborhoods with very high Latino populations. From there the company began a targeted marketing campaign.

In the age of information, intuition and judgment play an even greater role in effective decision making and well-placed strategic bets than ever before.

Although access to information was more limited in the past, the landscape was less volatile and managers could rely on certain assumptions or facts to inform decision making in a reasonable period of time. Today management's challenges are exacerbated by the increasingly bewildering transformation of the economic and social landscape. Forget predictability. Forget longevity. To make things happen, management has to step up and have the stomach to take risks. Beyond that, the culture of the organization has to support judicious risk taking.

DECISION MAKING: THE RIGHT RISKS

Certainly, risk taking has always been in the nature of business. Companies that took greater risks made it harder or riskier for their competitors to keep up with them. And they often have been the winners. Today's greater uncertainty along with the smaller room for error mean that decision makers confront even more risk. Managers need to move forward while taking the *right* risks, not necessarily the *least* risk. This involves making decisions at the right level of the organization, and having a disciplined, fact-based process for evaluating alternatives, making decisions, and acting upon those decisions.

Whether it has to do with customers, employees, corporate organization, innovation, or something else, decision making is uniquely and distinctly a management responsibility. Only management has the broad context needed to take into consideration factors inside the company and beyond—such as market conditions or energy costs. However, as Peter liked to say, senior executives should not spend the bulk of their time making decisions—on the contrary, they should spend very little time doing so. Their emphasis should be on making sure they have the time, information, and concentration to make the right decisions about the relatively few things that demand senior-level decision making and then making sure that the words are translated into action. That's not all. Management must stay on top of the results of the action, and know when to abandon a decision. Aside from this very focused decision making, they should encourage appropriate levels of the organization to make decisions. The amount of time spent in decision making is a much less meaningful metric than the effectiveness and relevance of the decisions themselves—the results. In fact, as Peter said, the more time spent, the more likely that the decision maker is "too busy with the little to take the time to see the big."[2]

The Linux Group is a twenty-first-century firm that keeps its "in-house" decision making focused on the big picture. Linus Torvalds established the group's purpose—to design and make a free operating system first for the PC and later on for powerful servers. At Linux, only a few people decide which of the many "outside-in" flows of suggested changes to include in new releases of the system. All other decisions are the responsibility of volunteer programmers, who choose which tasks to undertake, when and how to undertake them, and whether to work solo or in conjunction with someone else. Even this seemingly flexible and agile model is being challenged. Some long-term volunteers confided to me that Torvalds has become the bottleneck—too much is going on, and his control is limiting the ability of Linux to adapt as rapidly as users would like.

DECISION MAKING: FOUR DRUCKER QUESTIONS

Management has a stark challenge: It must create a climate with the best chance that everyone in the organization is making the right decisions about the right issues at the right time. There is no prescription for doing that, but there are questions that will bring clarity, guidance, and focus to this amorphous area:

1. Have you built in time to focus on the critical decisions—have you lightened your load?
2. Does your culture and organization support making the right decision, with ready contingency plans?
3. Is the organization willing to commit to the decision once it is made?
4. As decisions are made, are resources allocated to "degenerate into work?"

Successful decision making begins with the recognition that making good decisions is one of management's most critical responsibilities. The organization and your management team can offer invaluable support, but you need to take the time and set aside the mental space to engage in study and problem solving, to try different alternatives, to think about the issue on the exercise bike, or to sleep on it. Although the quality of your decision does not depend on the amount of time you spend arriving at it, it does

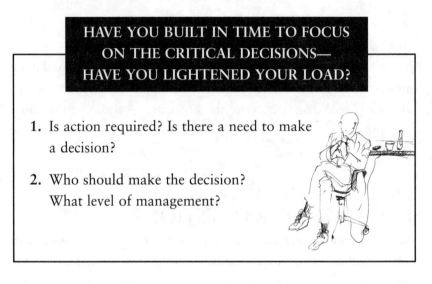

**HAVE YOU BUILT IN TIME TO FOCUS
ON THE CRITICAL DECISIONS—
HAVE YOU LIGHTENED YOUR LOAD?**

1. Is action required? Is there a need to make
   a decision?

2. Who should make the decision?
   What level of management?

require that decision making be a priority and a commitment to spending the time needed. To be able to do this while running an organization, you need to lighten your load—to cut through the fog in order to see clearly what situations really demand action and to find the appropriate decision maker. You can then concentrate on the relatively few important decisions that are yours to make.

IS ACTION REQUIRED?

For reasons that go beyond the obvious waste of precious time and resources, unnecessary decisions bring unjustifiable risk and repercussions. As Peter put it, no matter how innocuous the decision may seem, "Every decision is like surgery. It is an intervention into a system and therefore carries with it the risk of shock. One does not make unnecessary decisions any more than a good surgeon does unnecessary surgery."[3]

In judging whether a given situation or opportunity warrants action or not, several rules can be applied. These are shown in Figure 6.1.

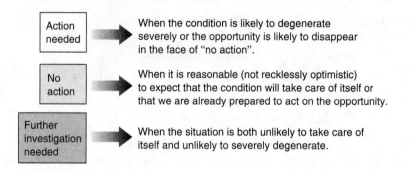

Figure 6.1 Decision Screen

Applying these guidelines helps draw a distinction between the truly important and the seemingly important situations that are, in fact, simply nuisances. The latter can correct themselves—they don't require major action. These rules will lighten the decision-making load by eliminating the situations that don't require intervention.

One does not make unnecessary decisions any more than a good surgeon does unnecessary surgery.

WHO SHOULD MAKE THE DECISION?

Top management's load can be further lightened by deciding early on which person within the management structure is the appropriate decision maker for a particular condition or opportunity. We all know senior managers who micromanage or frivolously reverse the decisions of their subordinates. Not only do they undermine the people who work for them, they distract themselves from the critical issues that require a senior-level perspective. The need for top management to be the decision maker is often informed by the following five criteria:

1. The time frame of the commitment.
2. The speed with which the decision could be reversed if necessary.
3. The number of people or areas affected.
4. The level of social considerations.
5. The extent to which precedent is being set. (Is the situation new and likely to be repeated?)

Peter strongly believed that where top-management involvement is not required, the organization is better served by pushing decision-making responsibility to the manager who is most knowledgeable and closest to the point of action. In such cases, senior management's role is to make an explicit and appropriate assignment of responsibility. The key consideration in delegating the decision authority is: How far down in the organization can the decision be made and still be effective? The answer is always: *low enough* that the decision maker has sufficient knowledge of and experience with the situation or affected function or area, yet *high enough* that the manager's authority covers the affected function or area. By ensuring that decisions are made at the right level, the organization faces an easier job of implementation and generally ends up with a better, more informed decision.

Although there is no such thing as a painless or risk-free decision, wrong decisions (i.e., the wrong solution to the right problem, the brilliant solution to the wrong problem, or the postponement of an urgently needed decision) are infinitely more painful than any properly timed, correct decision that responds to the right issues. The decision maker must commit to rigorous analysis—an integral part of fact-based decision making—and have the support of an organizational culture that is equally committed to making the right decision. Although it may seem natural that an organization would want to make good decisions, I have known many that could not. Some companies are biased in favor of what's fastest and easiest, others want the solution that doesn't rock the boat, and still others seek to avoid going head to head with tough competitors. There are many agendas that can derail good decision making.

Whether the decision maker is an executive or a purchasing clerk, his or her objective is to "get the equation right" before making any decision: As Peter would explain, "your fifth grade math teacher tried to teach you to spend time on setting up the equation. It's very easy to find a mistake in the manipulation and to correct it if the equation is right. If, however, you get the wrong equation and you do your figuring right, you can't really ever correct it."[4]

DOES YOUR CULTURE SUPPORT MAKING THE RIGHT DECISION WITH READY CONTINGENCY PLANS?

1. What's the real issue? What are you trying to accomplish?

2. What specifications must the solution meet? What are the minimum results required, and what organizational commitment is needed to achieve them? What are the risks?

3. Have you fully considered the entire range of alternatives in order to choose the best one? Do you have a contingency plan?

WHAT'S THE REAL ISSUE?

As I was listening to Peter, my mind was racing over my experiences as a consultant. One of the most useful tools we used to help clients define the real issue and break the problems into manageable pieces was the construction of an *issue tree*. The team would brainstorm the scope of the problem and agree on the key issue. They would then systematically identify the subissues underlying the key issue and then move on to breaking down the subissues into their component issues. The most eye-popping moments of insight always relate to issue trees.

At Pepperidge Farm, we were working with management on how to reduce waste in the manufacturing process using an issue tree. By carefully thinking about what the subcomponents of waste were, the company looked at its manufacturing process in a new way, ultimately saving the organization a lot of money. We defined waste as what it *didn't sell*; shop floor management defined waste as what it *threw away*. The foremen believed that they were caring for the customer, in accordance with the company philosophy, when they put a little extra batter into the cookies. In reality, the customer was on occasion getting fewer cookies per one-pound bag and Pepperidge Farm was spending extra money to boot. When we opened two bags of cookies that had 14 cookies in them, not the standard 15, and yet had passed the total weight test, it became obvious that waste is not just what you sell to the pig farmers; it's what you buy that you don't sell to the consumer. The consumer was buying 16 ounces and 15 cookies, not 18 ounces; 2 ounces were being wasted. The lightbulb quickly went on, and the shop floor changed its practices to provide exactly what is required and not deviate.

One of the decision maker's gravest and most common mistakes is to assume that his or her initial understanding of the issue is correct. As Peter maintained, only by taking the time to investigate what the decision really needs to be about can the decision maker distinguish between the symptom and the ailment, between the need for a topical or localized treatment and a systemic or surgical treatment: "You don't make a decision about symptoms when you have a fundamental, underlying, degenerative structure problem. Conversely, you don't fiddle around with the structure when all you have is an allergic rash."[5]

Only by taking the time to investigate what the decision really needs to be about can the decision maker distinguish between the symptom and the ailment.

To avoid focusing on the wrong issue and prepare for effective execution down the road, the successful decision maker invites and requires those who will be the implementers to participate in the study of the problem or opportunity. Not only will this make it easier to implement the eventual decision, but it will make for a better decision by drawing on the perspective and knowledge base of those who live with the problem every day. This group needs to be small enough to be functional, but ideally should include everyone with relevant experience and knowledge—including network partners and, if necessary, outside experts. Assembling this group is not, however, tantamount to abdicating decision-making authority. Rather, the purpose is to utilize the knowledge and perspective of those closest to the scene to define the issues and gain insight into their capabilities, while ensuring that the people who are going to have to carry out the decision are involved early in the process. What the decision maker asks from this group is a situation report, not recommendations. Such situation reports identify constraints and opportunities; their purpose is to inform, not to assume. Peter advised, "Don't go for a consensus, but insist on having enough disagreement in the group to get a little understanding. This is where we can learn from the Japanese. They take this group activity very seriously and don't allow anyone to have a recommendation at this stage."[6] My own experience suggests that the influential player is often the trouble maker. Engaging that individual to challenge the assumptions and be part of the solution goes a long way toward shifting the mindset of whole organizations.

WHAT SPECIFICATIONS MUST THE SOLUTION MEET?

Having worked toward understanding the true nature of the problem or opportunity, the decision maker is ready to begin defining solutions. It is surprisingly useful and very Peter-like at this point to articulate the organization's overall goals in devising these solutions through a series of questions, beginning with:

1. What is the prize you are going after?
2. What change are you trying to create—so as not to lose sight of the broader purpose of the decision?

The successful decision maker then specifies the boundary conditions that the action or solution must satisfy through the questions below. These specifications provide the framework for evaluating alternatives and for measuring the progress (or signaling the need for abandonment) of the ultimate solution:

1. Within the context of the overall business strategy and the particular situation, what are the priorities and minimum results required? Where is the need and/or opportunity greatest?

2. What are the minimum organizational commitments (people, time, and money) required? Are they realistically available, or will getting them require overcoming constraints?

3. What are the risks, including risks that the organization cannot afford *not* to take? As Andy Grove, the cofounder of Intel, noted, "Only the paranoid survive." Home Depot and Wal-Mart were paranoid ahead of Hurricane Katrina—a week before the storm hit the Gulf Coast, they had the logistics lined up to move people out and move goods in. Often, however, the paranoid can't afford to be risk-averse: The risk that you will miss an opportunity is every bit as serious as the risk of failure.

4. Given the rapidity of changes in the business environment, how long will it be until you get meaningful results? How long until you evaluate your success? How long until you revisit your decision?

The successful decision maker remains open to the full array of alternative solutions.

HAVE YOU FULLY CONSIDERED ALL THE ALTERNATIVE SOLUTIONS?

It is tempting at this point to push the easy button and opt for the solution that is the least disruptive, the least likely to meet with organizational resistance, and the most comfortable for the organization. But the successful decision maker remains open to the full array of alternative solutions. According to Peter, "This entails real brainstorming. What we want to know here are all the conceivable alternatives. And some should be weird. The function of the weird ones is to stimulate your thinking."[7]

And as usual, Peter practiced what he preached. Richard Ellsworth, professor of management at Claremont, described for me the first time he met Peter. He had just joined the faculty at Claremont. They were in a senior executive conference together. Richard presented his talk, and the room seemed in agreement. Peter stood up and said, "I don't agree," and proceeded to offer another view. And a discussion began. At the break, Peter went up to Richard and confided, "I really do agree, but I think we needed to discuss some alternatives."

Now is the time to take a sheet of paper and list all possible and seemingly impossible alternatives that might satisfy the specified boundary conditions. Then, for each alternative, ask:

- What would have to be done to make it viable?
- What are the risks, effort, and commitment required and the expected results if successful?
- How is this alternative better than others in satisfying the boundary conditions?

IS THE ORGANIZATION WILLING TO COMMIT TO THE DECISION ONCE IT IS MADE?

1. Are you willing to opt for the bold move to get the required results?

2. Can you marshal support for your decision within the organization and not rehash the decision?

3. Can you balance the visionary and the practical?

Here the decision maker strives for honest thinking about each alternative, guarding against stilted presentations or assumed solutions. Not only is this open-mindedness necessary to ensure the integrity of the decision, but it is an absolute requirement to guarantee that a safety net of contingencies is in place in the face of navigating through future unknowns. Peter put it this way, "The universe doesn't stand still and freeze the circumstances in which the decision was made. If you have no alternative to fall back on, you begin to drift if the decision doesn't work out."[8]

With the alternatives cut to a small number of serious ones, reality-checked intuition and informed judgment come into play. In *The Effective Executive*, Peter points out:

The important and relevant outside events are often qualitative and not capable of quantification. They are not yet "facts." For a fact is an event which somebody has defined, has classified and, above all, has endowed with relevance. To be able to quantify one first has to abstract from the infinite welter of phenomena a specific aspect which one can name and finally count. Man, while not particularly logical, is perceptive—and that is his strength. The danger is that executives will become contemptuous of information and stimulus that cannot be reduced to computer logic and computer language. Executives may become blind to everything that is perception (i.e., event) rather than fact (i.e., after the event).[9]

"If you have no alternative to fall back on, you begin to drift if the decision doesn't work out."

The effective decision maker chooses the alternative that best satisfies the specifications by providing a reasonable balance between:

- Risk and results.
- Time required and time available.
- Resources (people, capabilities, and investment) required and resources available. The best possible outcome and the minimum outcome required to move forward.

Striking this reasonable balance can be much less straightforward than it seems, and this is truly a test of the decision maker's mettle. Organizational support and culture aside, when the rubber hits the road, the decision makers who want to *change the world* must be willing to lead the organization out of its comfort zone—in contrast to the decision makers who want to do the best they can *in the world they know*. Ask yourself, of the last 100 decisions you made, how many carried real risk? How many were fundamentally strategic rather than tactical?

Until a decision has degenerated into work
and reaches the stage of actual execution,
for all intents and purposes there is no decision.

Striking the balance between the daring and the doable typically requires some concessions and adaptations to gain the necessary organizational commitment. Here is where decision makers must be courageous and have the conviction to stay true to the boundary conditions that will determine success, yet be pragmatic (half a loaf of bread is better than none). They must quickly come to some acceptable compromise. Otherwise, they stumble into a bad compromise (half a baby is worse than none) or risk a pro-

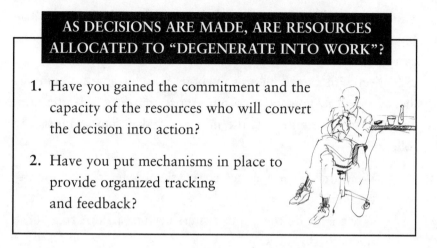

AS DECISIONS ARE MADE, ARE RESOURCES ALLOCATED TO "DEGENERATE INTO WORK"?

1. Have you gained the commitment and the capacity of the resources who will convert the decision into action?

2. Have you put mechanisms in place to provide organized tracking and feedback?

longed "selling time" so that when there are finally results, it's too late.

This final step takes the most effort. Until a decision has degenerated into work and reaches the stage of actual execution, for all intents and purposes there is no decision. To get any results, the organization needs to convert the decision into effective action, and support that action by tracking results and providing the feedback necessary to refine the action plan.

HAVE YOU GAINED COMMITMENT AND CAPACITY OF THE IMPLEMENTERS?

As Peter pointedly reminded me, decision makers in the United States and other Western countries can take a lesson from their Japanese counterparts, who put great emphasis on turning a decision into reality almost immediately. Japanese companies get a head start on making the decision effective by taking very seriously the early inclusion of those who will be part of the action. The decision maker who builds the implementers into the process has an ownership platform in place at the execution level of the organization and a good sense of the implementers' capabilities.

This enables a fast start in converting the decision to action. The Japanese are also well aware that people, not policy statements, carry out decisions. Until you have assigned responsibility for execution with a deadline to somebody who has made a commitment to action, you have nothing more than a good intention. To gain that commitment, the decision maker must address the following:

- What results are expected of the implementers and by when?
- What skills do the implementers need to acquire to achieve the desired results?
- How will they acquire these skills in time to be consistent with the time frame for the expected results?
- How do I/we communicate in language that resonates with each implementer so that each understands what is required of her or him and views the action as an opportunity, not a threat?
- How should incentives and performance measures be changed to support the implementer's commitment?
- What else do I and other members of management need to do to celebrate and support this commitment?

DO YOU HAVE MECHANISMS THAT PROVIDE TRACKING AND FEEDBACK?

Organized tracking of progress and results, accompanied by feedback, are nonnegotiable elements of any effective action program for many reasons. First and foremost, motion does not guarantee progress, and converting good intention into meaningful action requires accountability. The decision maker and the implementers have to be held accountable for the expected results within the determined time frame. Second, working hard to choose the right solution does not guarantee that the decision is correct, especially in a fast-changing world. Feedback is essential to alert management to the need for fine-tuning and to guide refinements. As Peter wrote, "Neither studies nor market research nor computer modeling is a substitute for the test of reality."[10] Third, decisions can quickly lose their relevance as circumstances change. If they are not monitored and periodically reviewed as part of an explicit process, action plans put in place will linger past their useful life, eating up precious resources and time along the way. Finally, tracking and feedback are essential for spotting unexpected successes, where actual results far exceed expected results. The organization that is unaware of or inattentive to such occurrences puts its opportunity at risk or loses it outright.

Organized tracking of progress, results, and feedback are nonnegotiable elements of any effective action program.

In 1993, when Clairol relaunched its Herbal Essences shampoo, it viewed itself as a hair-color company with some hair-care products, not as a hair-care company. With management focused on color, Clairol did not pay sufficient attention to the performance of the relaunched shampoo. In fact, the first indication of trouble came during a golf outing, where a key buyer complained to a Clairol salesman that the product was moving off the shelf much faster than the shelf was being replenished. Steve Sadove, president of Clairol at the time, recognized that this inventory "trouble" was actually evidence of an unexpected success. He delayed the international launch of the product so that the North American market could be better serviced, and he called in an outside consultant and asked, "If this product sells in the volume of Pantene (the number one shampoo at the time), where can I find capacity to make it?" The answer was, "Abandon your hair-color business assumption that outsourcing of a critical chemical balancing process is never viable. Put on your hair-care business glasses and look for third-party capacity to get you over the hump while you plan for longer-term capacity to handle this unexpected success." Sadove called the head of R&D and said, "Test the stability and tolerance of these formulas, and have the Quality Assurance process revised to support a third-party manufacturer."[11] At the same time, he created a plan to triple Clairol's in-house capacity. The Herbal Essences relaunch was an opportunity that could not wait. Over time, it virtually doubled the value of Clairol as the unexpected success exploded into a broad spectrum of other Herbal Essences hair-care products.

THE DECISION PROCESS

Disciplined management knows how to negotiate the tightrope the organization will walk while moving ahead in the amorphous future. As Peter said:

Effective executives make effective decisions as a systematic process with clearly defined elements and in a distinct sequence of steps. They do not make a great many decisions. They concentrate on the important ones. They are not overly impressed by speed in decision-making. They want to know what the decision is all about and what the underlying realities are which it has to satisfy. They want impact rather than technique; they want to be sound rather than clever. They are not content with doctoring the symptom alone. They know when a decision has to be based on principle and when it should be made on the merits of the case and pragmatically. They know that the trickiest decision is that between the right and the wrong compromises and have learned how to tell one from the other. They know that the most time-consuming step in the process is not making the decision but putting it into effect.[12]

When Peter commented that he believed one major reason for Toyota's success is its strong decision-making sense, I took a closer look at the Toyota way, the rigorous and systematic decision-making process that has made Toyota the world's second-largest auto company.

HOW TOYOTA GETS ITS EDGE

Toyota is one of the world's great companies. Since the early 1990s, business magazines have been trumpeting its rise, and, under the leadership of Hiroshi Okuda, it has overcome a brief period of stagnation and is now making its mark as a leader. In 2003, Toyota passed Ford to become the second largest car manufacturer in the world, and with its own predictions of a 10 percent increase in vehicles manufactured in 2006, it is expected to pass GM shortly.[13] Even as number two, Toyota posted 2004 and 2005 profits greater than its three most profitable competitors combined. It has been the highest-ranked non-American company on the Fortune Global Most Admired Companies list for three years running.[14]

With success comes scrutiny. Certainly much attention has been paid to Toyota's production efficiency, and rightly so. The Toyota Production System (TPS) has been the focus of countless books and articles, and several of its key elements, like "just-in-time" and "lean manufacturing," are now common business terms and methods. Toyota's efficiency on the factory floor is part of its overall approach to business, known inside the company as the "Toyota Way."

What has received far less attention is the effectiveness of the Toyota Way. Contributing to Toyota's indisputable effectiveness is its ability to make and successfully execute the right decisions and "bets" that have moved it up the ranks in the troubled automobile industry. What underlies this decision-making effectiveness is a disciplined process; well worthy of closer investigation by other organizations seeking to learn from the very best.

THE ORIGINS OF THE TOYOTA WAY

Much of the way Toyota operates can be traced back to the business climate in which it was born—a climate that had some things in common with the globalized business world of today. Founded as the Toyoda Automatic Loom Works in 1926, the company originally manufactured a type of automatic loom that was invented by its founder, Sakichi Toyoda. In 1930, Toyoda sold the rights to his looms to a British manufacturer and invested the proceeds in starting the Toyota Motor Company. ("Toyoda" was changed to "Toyota" because in Japanese "t" has one fewer stroke than "d"—thus saving time on printing signs and advertisements—an early indication of the ceaseless focus on efficiency that would come to characterize the organization.) It wasn't until after World War II, as Japan was trying to rebuild, that Toyota really began to grow.

The car market in Japan at that time was small, since capital for investment in anything not an absolute necessity was scarce. Moreover, countless new companies were opening every day, and with infrastructures completely destroyed, there was no advantage for old players over new. Because the competition was so stiff and capital so hard to accumulate, Toyota had to do everything possible to minimize the time between when it purchased parts and assembled vehicles and when it received payment—hence, the birth of the company's vaunted "just-in-time" production methods. At the same time, to offer a vehicle that no one would buy or to develop a plant that couldn't work properly would have been a catastrophic error, an inexcusable waste of money that had been painstakingly accumulated. Any business decision had to be reached carefully and through group discussion and consideration with all parties involved, to allow for quick and problem-free implementation.

HOW TOYOTA MAKES DECISIONS

Japanese companies are long-time, avid students of Drucker (who was himself an avid student and onetime professor of Japanese art and culture). Consequently, the overlap between the Toyota Way and the Drucker Way is not surprising, and Toyota's decision-making process is no exception to this shared mindset. Toyota believes that it can and must always do better; that change is an opportunity, not a threat; and that its strategic bets must be well informed by an outside perspective. Its decision-making process is fully in sync with this culture.

Do the Homework First

Whether the issue at hand is a problem, an opportunity, or both, Toyota takes the time and effort to do the homework necessary to see the full landscape and past the obvious, so that its decisions distinguish between the root causes or the root enablers and the symptoms. Accordingly, Toyota emphasizes always going to see for itself, and then asking "why" five times.

Going and seeing for yourself means that managers at all levels have to be willing to "get their hands dirty." This firsthand involvement is important to keep a growing company true to its roots, but even more so if it is going to extend its global reach and create and act on opportunities to market products in cultures other than its own. In 2003, when Toyota was redesigning its Sienna minivan to compete with the then-dominant Honda Odyssey import in the North American market, Yuji Yokoya, the chief engineer of the project, took time off and drove through every U.S. state and Canadian province, and through much of

Mexico. The new Sienna included features that made it more appropriate for: Canadian roads (which have a higher crown than Japanese, American, or Mexican roads), American trip lengths (Americans cities are farther apart, so American drivers are more likely to eat and drink while driving), American storage needs (Yokoya spent a day outside a Home Depot in Ann Arbor, Michigan, watching customers load their cars and trucks), and countless other small differences that no Japanese engineer could have discovered without visiting North America and no North American manager could have focused on without an outsider's perspective. The redesigned 2004 Toyota Sienna was voted best minivan of 2004 by *Car and Driver*.

Going and seeing for yourself helps managers understand how problems and/or opportunities manifest themselves. However, Toyota's homework is not completed until the Toyota managers, as I noted before, ask "why" five times to get to the root causes of the problem or the root enablers of the opportunity. As Taiichi Ohno, the originator of the Toyota production system, explained, "To tell the truth, the Toyota production system has been built on the practice and evolution of this scientific approach. By asking why five times and answering it each time, we can get to the real cause of the problem, which is often hidden behind more obvious symptoms."[15]

There is a puddle of oil on the factory floor. Why? The machine is leaking oil. Why? It has a broken gasket. Why? Because we bought gaskets made from a cheap material. Why? Because we got better pricing on them. Why? Because purchasing agents are rewarded and evaluated based on short-term savings rather than on long-term performance. So what is the real issue and hence the specifications that the solution must satisfy? Is it the puddle of oil on the floor that could easily be swept away in less than two minutes and escape management's notice? Or is it the purchasing agents' incentives, which have resulted in buying faulty equipment and must therefore be changed? Sweeping away the oil will address surface issues but won't prevent the problem from recurring, whereas a new purchasing rule will.

Look at All Solutions, Build Consensus among Stakeholders, and Set Sights High

Once it is clear "what this is all about," a round of meetings is held so that all possible solutions, no matter how implausible, can be discussed. In the case of the Prius, the first hybrid-powered car to be developed commercially, exploring all possible alternatives initially included analysis of over 80 hybrid engines. The list was eventually narrowed down to ten, then four. After that, tests were run on the four, and one engine was finally selected. By giving each of the 80 possible engines equal consideration in the beginning, Toyota engineers were able to see the problem from a variety of angles, and the final engine included modifications that reflected the best features of the original 80, modifications that engineers would never have incorporated without first examining such a wide range of options.

At Toyota, every worker who might be affected by the process must be consulted. This inclusionary approach not only enriches the perspective of the original developers, but also enhances the likelihood of a smooth and rapid implementation by anticipating problems, creating early buy-in of those participating in the development and production processes, and providing clear signals that Toyota cares what the stakeholders and executers think.

Toyota also purposefully sets its goals or expected results high, so high as to seem unattainable. By setting goals of 50 or 60 percent improvement rather than 5 or 10 percent, Toyota guarantees that its solutions will not simply address superficial issues but will generate real structural change. In 2000, when Toyota's North American Parts Organization (NAPO) branch wanted to eliminate the waste that had built up during its rapid growth, it set goals that seemed almost laughable. In three years: improve customer service by 50 percent, save $100 million in distribution costs, and cut $100 million of inventory out of the supply chain—all this for a business that was turning a steady profit, albeit in the face of rising costs. But by constantly pushing employees in groups to work toward those goals, NAPO achieved or came very close to achieving each of them in the allotted time. By 2003, NAPO had become a much leaner and more efficient business than anyone in 2000 believed possible.

Toyota also ups the ante by outlining goals in contradictory pairs. The first Lexus, for example, was expected to deliver increased fuel efficiency, but also a fast smooth ride; decreased noise, as well as a light body; elegant styling, and great aerodynamics, among other criteria.

Implement Rapidly

Having made a decision, Toyota is a robust planner and a rapid but effective implementer—in stark contrast to those organizations that mistakenly believe a fast launch equals a successful implementation. To elaborate on this difference, given a 12-month time period to implement changes, many companies will spend 6 months planning and then implement the program ahead of schedule. Once the final product is in the field, however, questions and concerns that might have been anticipated and addressed prior to implementation have to be handled in a triage situation. By arbitrarily reducing the time allocated for the planning activity, management is likely to delay the expected results from the new program or, even worse, to render the program obsolete before it can come to fruition. At Toyota, however, the planning process takes 11 of the 12 months. Actual implementation is then carried out very quickly and effectively—with the support of the entire organization and with many possible problems thought out in advance.

Perhaps the greatest testament to how rapidly Toyota can implement its plans is its product development: Toyota has managed to shrink the time from conception to production to just 12 months—half that of most automobile companies. Even the Prius, the first commercial hybrid-powered car, which required the development of a new engine, body, production process, and marketing strategy, was (at the prodding of Okuda) taken from clay model to production in just 15 months. The benefits of this kind of agility cannot be overstated. Being so effective in its decisions allows Toyota to anticipate and respond quickly to customer demands and to constantly innovate to meet customer requirements, and the impact of the few inevitable failures is minimized when just one year later a new version can be released.

As former Toyota president Fujio Cho described the Toyota decision-making process, "We place the highest value on actual implementation and taking action. . . . You can realize how little you know and you face your own failures and you can simply correct those failures and redo it again and at the second trial you realize another mistake or another thing you didn't like so you can redo it once again. So by constant improvement, or should I say, the improvement based upon action, one can rise to the higher level of practice and knowledge."[16]

DECISION MAKING BY ALFRED SLOAN

Many of Drucker's theories came from watching the work of those he admired, including GM's chairman Alfred P. Sloan during and following World War II. Sloan influenced many of Drucker's ideas, particularly that one of the most important responsibilities of a manager is to make assumptions given future uncertainty, test them for soundness, and revisit them in light of external and other changes, and to do so with rigor and discipline. In Sloan, Drucker saw this responsibility embraced and executed flawlessly:

As I sat in more GM meetings with Sloan, I began to notice . . . his way of making decisions. . . . I noticed it first in the heated discussions about the postwar capacity of GM's accessory divisions. One group in GM management argued stridently and with a lot of figures that accessory capacity should be expanded. Another group, equally strident, argued in favor of keeping it low. Sloan listened for a long time without saying anything. Then he turned off his hearing aid and said, "What is this decision really about? Is it about accessory capacity? Or is it about the future shape of the American automobile industry? It seems to me that you argue over the future of the automobile industry in this country and not about the accessory business, do you agree? Well then," said Sloan, "We all agree that we aren't likely to sell a lot of GM accessories to our big competitors, to Chrysler and Ford. Do we know whether to expect the independents— Studebaker, Hudson, Packard, Nash, Willys—to grow and why? I take it we are confident that they will give us their business if they have any to give."

"But Mr. Sloan," said the proponent of accessory expansion, "we assume that automobile demand will be growing, and then the independents will surely do well." "Sounds plausible to me," said Sloan, "but have we tested the assumption? If not, let's do so."

A month later the study came in, and to everybody's surprise it showed that small independents did poorly and were being gobbled up by the big companies in times of rapidly growing automobile demand and that they only did well in times of fairly stable replacement demand and slow market growth. "So now," Sloan said, "the question is really whether we can expect fast automobile growth, once we have supplied the deficiencies the war has created, or slow growth. Do we know what new automobile demand depends on?" "Yes, we do know, Mr. Sloan," someone said, "demand for new automobiles is a direct function of the number of young people who reach the age of the first driver's license, buy an old jalopy, and thereby create demand for new cars among the older and wealthier population." "And what do population figures look like five, ten, fifteen years out?" [Sloan asked] And when it turned out that they showed a fairly rapid growth of the teen-age population for some ten years ahead, Sloan said: "The facts have made the decision—and I was wrong." For then, and only then, did Sloan disclose that the proposal to increase accessory capacity had originally been his.

Sloan rarely made a decision by counting noses or by taking a vote. He made it by creating understanding.[17]

Though Sloan may not have seen himself as establishing a role model for leadership, Peter believed he did exactly that: "Sloan invented the professional manager. . . . [Sloan] was in many ways very narrow, with absolutely no understanding of this whole generation of anything outside the company. He didn't understand society. He didn't understand politics. . . . He never understood why the workers unionized. He was . . . focused on the business. But within that . . . he never asked who was right. He only asked what is right. He never, never was the star, although he was one. And yet it was absolutely clear that if he made a decision, it was the decision."

CONCLUSION

In today's world, every knowledge worker is responsible for a contribution that can materially affect the capacity of the organization to obtain results. The decision mechanisms and values of a corporation support or impair the right decision, be it the research chemist's choice of projects or the logistics manager's schedule of deliveries. Creating a healthy environment to support these decisions has become more critical, and the importance of intuition and judgment (human perception) has never been greater:

1. Very few decisions need to be the responsibility of top management. Taking the time to do justice to those that are cannot be understated.

2. Doing the right thing (even if not perfectly executed) is far superior to perfectly executing the wrong thing.

3. Decisions need commitment to become action. Without action, no progress is made.

4. A decision remains inert until resources are allocated for its implementation.

5. Decisions need to be viewed as a step on a path—moving two steps forward and one step back, learning, and adapting as appropriate—moving forward.

With all the elements in place to successfully traverse today's landscape, and a chassis holding the pieces together with solid decision mechanisms, the last requirement is to infuse vision and values into the whole through the actions of an effective CEO—the subject of our final chapter.

SEVEN | The Twenty-First-Century CEO

CEOs have work of their own.
It is work only CEOs can do,
but also work which CEOs must do. . . .
Each knowledge worker must think and behave
like a chief executive officer.[1]

—Peter F. Drucker

In the last years of his life, Peter Drucker focused like a laser on what had increasingly fascinated him—the role of the CEO. As corporations grew more unwieldy, worldwide competition sharpened, and customers and shareholders alike became more litigious, Peter rightly saw CEOs as more important than ever. They had to provide leadership—strategic leadership, moral leadership, human leadership—and balance. Today's rate and magnitude of change leave little room for leadership error. Peter believed that the CEO role was the next area of management research. Procter & Gamble's CEO, A.G. Lafley, called it "Peter's unfinished chapter."

Good or bad, the CEO sets the tone for an organization, its mission and culture, and its actions and results during his or her tenure if not thereafter as well. As a consultant and adviser, Peter worked with hundreds of CEOs and observed a remarkable diversity of leadership personalities in action, from Jack Welch at GE to Frances Hesselbein, head of the Girl Scouts of America; from President Eisenhower in 1950 to Mike Zafirovski, who ascended to the top spot of Nortel at the dawn of the twenty-first century—

almost seven decades after Drucker first worked with Alfred Sloan at General Motors.

For decades, Peter thought about how CEOs could be more effective. He mused about how they could change more than just corporations and foundations—how they could even shape the course of countries. And he worried about how they could harm all sorts of people if they were less than ethical. Once again, Peter offered us keen insight into the future. The reputation of CEOs has taken a pounding in recent years because of what I call the "Enron effect" (but one could also call it the "WorldCom wake").

With all the emphasis in the business press on the highest-level executives, it is easy to overlook the need for each knowledge worker to be his or her own CEO. The knowledge worker exists in a somewhat amorphous professional space. As Peter explained, "Knowledge workers are neither bosses nor workers, but rather something in between—resources who have responsibility for developing their most important resource, brainpower, and who also need to take more control of their own careers."[2]

The knowledge worker's professional life will typically span five or six or seven decades—far surpassing the life expectancy of most institutions and encompassing a variety of situations given the new mobility in space and time. It is both a great freedom and a responsibility to keep the bounce in our work and the spark of curiosity in our brain.

From my earliest days at McKinsey to my time with my own business, I have been a consultant to dozens of companies from the small, family-owned variety to the multinational Fortune 100, and I have been a CEO of a small firm. Yet I didn't truly appreciate Peter's near obsession with the CEO role until I spent a couple of years working with him. To distill into one word Peter's thoughts on what makes a truly great CEO, it would be *courage*. I have shared with many a client the four-word summary from the legendary CEO of Electrolux during the 1970s and 1980s,

Hans Werthen. When asked what it took for a small Swedish company to become the global leader in the white goods industry, Werthen responded: "Tigers don't eat grass."[3]

Whether one is at the helm of a company or a self-managing knowledge worker, it takes courage to do what is right, such as turning away from the temptation of quick short-term profits at the expense of investments for the long term. It takes courage to trailblaze change in an industry. It also takes courage to continuously redefine the business the company is in. It takes courage to face reality and get out of any product lines or businesses that "you wouldn't get into if you were not in the business today." Again, I stress what Jack Welch makes clear in his writings; he never hesitated when faced with the painful structural decisions or betting on the success of new ventures. Peter recognized that management's most important capability is to take uncertainty out of the future by helping organizations see and selectively move around corners and place courageous bets.

We are at a moment in time when there is often greater uncertainty in resisting or ignoring changes than in playing or placing bets. CEOs have the vision to place the bets for enterprises; they must have the guts to lead change.

In our conversations, Peter defined three characteristics unique to a CEO:

1. A broad field of vision and the ability to ask and answer what needs to be done.
2. His or her thumbprint on the organization's character and personality.
3. The influence he or she has on people—individually and collectively.

This chapter discusses each of these characteristics and illustrates them in action at a company Peter worked with closely: Donaldson, Lufkin & Jenrette, better known as DLJ. It also mentions other companies where I've seen the dramatic effect Peter described. The chapter concludes by translating these characteristics to individual knowledge workers as CEOs of their own careers.

FIELD OF VISION

Peter constantly exhorted his clients to produce good results by looking at the whole. Theory is not enough. Theory grasps the relatively thickest threads and ignores the rest, the nuances of real life. But theory without observation is meaningless. Observations of the whole and observations of how theories are applied to solve the challenge of the enterprise are the most important thing in Drucker's methodology.

> The most important thing in Drucker's methodology—looking at the whole.

No one has the ability to see the whole like the CEO. At many companies, engineers tinker away with a particularly knotty technical or design problem, but they don't look at 50-year trends in buying habits. Meanwhile, the vice president of marketing keeps close tabs on competitors but may have no idea how or at what expense his or her own company makes components. In any organization, the CEO links the inside—the organization—with the outside—society, the economy, technology, markets, customers, collaborators, the media, public opinion. Inside there are only costs. Outside there are results.

In looking at the whole, the CEO must ask, "What needs to be done?" To answer this question, the first task of the CEO is to define the outside of the organization, the outside where results are meaningful. Coming up with this definition obviously requires looking beyond the bricks and mortar (or sometimes virtual walls). But a truly honest and robust definition also means challenging assumptions, assessing what needs to be done and when, and selectively creating platforms for redefining and innovating the business, the organization, and even the industry. Through such courageous challenging and visioning, the CEO lays the foundation and boundaries for what needs to be done by asking essential questions (and not just assuming that the answers are obvious): What is our business? What should it be? What should it *not* be? The answers to these questions establish the boundaries of an institution. And they are the foundation for the work to be done by the CEO.

When CEOs fail to question long-standing assumptions or fail to listen to or see evidence that says, "These assumptions are no longer relevant to the opportunity that is our future," their companies are guaranteed to have short lives. The average life of a company on the Standards & Poors list is just under 10 years; of the original companies on the first Forbes 100 list, published in 1917, only 5 of those made the 2005 global top 100 list (DuPont, Ford, General Electric, General Motors, and Procter & Gamble). In 1999, at Drucker's ninetieth birthday celebration, he predicted that by his one-hundredth, in the year 2009, there would be five global automobile companies and that GM would not be one of them.

Experts summon all sorts of reasons why companies fail or are reconfigured into different pieces. Yet here's the simple truth: The inability to adapt to changing landscapes leads to the premature deaths of companies that were once vibrant. As Peter said, "Most business issues are not the result of things being done poorly or even the wrong things being done. Businesses fail because the CEO's assumptions about the outside provide decision frameworks for the institution which no longer fit reality."[4] These assumptions involve markets, customers, competitors, technology, and a company's own strengths and weaknesses. The best CEOs don't just ask what needs to be done; they also challenge assumptions along the way, and take off the table what doesn't need to be done.

I've touched on failure, so I should mention success. Six of *Business Week*'s top ten fastest-growing small American companies, and seven of the ten companies that have shown the greatest equity value gains over the last five years, didn't even exist twenty years ago. This dramatic performance highlights a key challenge to CEOs: to wrest the ability to challenge assumptions and redefine the way business is done from the financial markets. Up until now, the venture capital and equity markets have served as the primary vehicles for creating new ways of doing business and even innovation—closing companies and opening new ones. Sure, shareholders liked this power, but it flies in the face of the business's need to sustain itself. Ultimately this short-term obsession with results is closing down businesses, displacing employees, and ruining communities. It is the CEO's responsibility to use his or her uniquely broad field of vision to challenge the status quo when answering the question "What is needed?" so that companies and communities can remain viable. On top of everything else, CEOs must do an astounding balancing act: They must lead the enterprise for the customers and employees and accommodate, but not bow to, the harsh demands of the stock market.

Not long ago, Dan Lufkin, one of three founders and co-CEOs at DLJ, ushered me to a long table in his fairly simple conference room overlooking Fifth Avenue in New York City. It was a plain space with just a few pieces of art on the wall. I didn't even notice the astounding view until I was leaving because Lufkin was so engaging. He was reminiscing about the spectacular rise of Donaldson, Lufkin & Jenrette, from a minuscule company to a Wall Street heavy hitter. It was all because of a bold move that Peter encouraged. But first, as Lufkin noted, Peter helped the three leaders see things clearly. By 1961, Peter had helped them see that the future was not in brawn but in brains, through an *information* society.

Skipping ahead to 1969, DLJ had built a good reputation, but the three founders, Bill Donaldson, Dan Lufkin, and Dick Jenrette, were frustrated by how their own limited capital constrained their ambitions. While larger firms were copying their ideas and growing, Donaldson, Lufkin, and Jenrette didn't have the personal capital they needed to truly grow their brokerage business. With the growth of automated transactions and the ascendance of the institutional investor, serving the customer now required big blocks of capital.

Peter sat down with the three at the end of the turbulent 1960s. Rather than telling them what to do, he posed questions. Lufkin still remembers how the questions started: "How will you grow? What is the right thing to do for your clients, for your employees? What is the right thing for the New York Stock Exchange?" The questions got increasingly detailed: "Without some form of permanent capital infused into the structure of the New York Stock Exchange, can it exist in the future? How can it work with this growing community of institutional investors?"

Peter didn't stop there. He continued: "Would the strengthening of the greatest free market the world has ever known be enhanced by a more permanent growing base of capital? That being the case, tell me how would you do this if you didn't go public? What other tools are there available?" Lufkin smiled when remembering Peter's way of pushing his clients to think: "He would launch into some esoteric description of what happened in Germany during the 1930s that had little to do with the case." But Lufkin always came away from his interactions with Peter understanding that if he (Lufkin) were patient enough, Peter's ostensible "side stories" would ultimately lead to and help inform a broader field of vision. At a 1969 speech to the New York Stock Exchange (NYSE), Peter shared some of the same side stories.

Lufkin reflected on that crucial moment. "He forced us to think with the assumption that we could change the rules of the New York Stock Exchange. He forced us to think about the issues created by the lack of permanent capital against a growing base of business, and how to solve that problem. We honestly believed that this was in the best interest of the New York Stock Exchange itself. We needed more permanent capital and so did the whole Exchange. And that led to what was a very courageous act."

At this point, I should explain that in those days members of NYSE such as DLJ were not allowed to sell shares to the public and be traded on the New York Stock Exchange because of a long-standing tradition. The Exchange was set up in 1792 with 14 members and limited numbers of companies' shares traded. The Exchange had to approve every single shareholder of every member firm. Furthermore, the Exchange was a partnership—all members had joint and several liability for the solvency of the partnership. Members were also not allowed to trade their own shares because this was viewed as a conflict of interest.

Apparently customs had changed in the rest of the world—but not at the intersection of Wall Street and Broad Street. When DLJ announced it was going public, the Exchange went ballistic. Richard Jenrette has clear memories of that moment: "The Exchange was very comfortable approving every shareholder of every member. They were opposed to us going public because they said things like, 'The Mafia might take over Wall Street.'" Exchange officials were also worried that investors would see exactly how profitable Wall Street was. DLJ had a 50 percent pretax profit margin at the time. Jenrette added, "In reality, the member firms were afraid that institutional investors, their best customers, would gain access to the New York Stock Exchange. There was a fear of big, institutional customers like the banks." In fact, the fear of bank membership was realized many years later with the dilution, or weakening, of the Glass-Steagall Act in the 1990s, but the NYSE's worst fears were not. Securities laws and conflict of interest considerations precluded the bank trust departments from monopolizing the brokerage business through their own nonbank subsidiaries, and the growth of the institutional investor changed the balance. The pension funds and endowments became increasingly independent of the bank, and independent mutual funds began to expand rapidly.[5]

The printed prospectus of the original offering of DLJ contains a puzzling line. Essentially it says, "You are buying shares in a company that given the possibility that the offering will not be approved by the board of governors of the New York Stock Exchange," and, "If the rules of the New York Stock Exchange are not changed to allow this offering, DLJ will, at the stroke of the first share's sale, lose *70 percent* of its revenues." If you read that in 1970, you might have asked, "are they crazy?" Cut 70 percent out of any business that you know of, and tell me how it survives.

> The CEO sets the course for the
> company and commits to the goals
> that will define the company.

Finally, after DLJ threatened to resign from the Exchange and take its trades to a third market, officials caved. DLJ was allowed to go public and raise new equity capital, which it did in 1970, and became the first brokerage firm to trade on the New York Stock Exchange. As Donaldson remembers, "Institutions cheered when DLJ went public." With that move, DLJ changed Wall Street forever. In retrospect, DLJ and Drucker's insights were prescient. In the following 24 months, a period of extraordinarily high interest rates, many of the firms that hadn't followed DLJ's example of raising permanent new capital by going public failed to survive. The Exchange itself eventually altered its own legal status and today is publicly traded on the New York Stock Exchange. The permanent capital raised through public ownership is a major reason why Wall Street has remained the financial capital of the world. Donaldson, Lufkin, and Jenrette redefined their business, and in some ways their industry, with their vision.

The CEO's broad field of vision defines the business that the enterprise is in. The CEO sets the course for the company and commits to the goals that will both define and set external performance expectations for the company. This takes a keen scrutiny of the landscape, courage, and sometimes the ability to listen carefully, agree that there are potential and substantial risks—and still plunge ahead and make a tough decision.

On my first meeting with Frances Hesselbein, in her Manhattan office crammed with books, she described what she saw when she took over the Girl Scouts in 1976. She found a reliable—but not dynamic—organization that still prided itself on its history of awarding merit badges for sewing and cooking, as it had done since the 1950s.

Frances came in with a strong message: "We manage for the mission, we manage for innovation, we manage for diversity, we manage for results." She then asked Druckerian questions: What do we mean by great results defined by our mission? How do we know if we are actually impacting the lives of young girls and transforming them into capable women?" And it was there that Frances began to engineer a change in the Girl Scouts. She looked at the organization and said, "If we are going to deliver the results, not the input, the results of strong, capable women, then we must confront the fact that it's a different world than what people faced in the 1950s." She added, "That was all fine and good for a previous generation, but for the current generation, we need conversations around where's the accounting merit badge, where's the math merit badge, where's the fitness merit badge. Because what it means to be a capable woman in this era will be different. And we have to think not about our inputs, we have to think about our outputs. The outputs are the results defined by what happens to those girls. Results, results, results, results."

Frances's message permeated the total organization; it became a leadership benchmark—a simple but powerful way to describe the management and the focus of this great American institution. As Frances said, "Leadership is a matter of how to be, not how to do," and, "I learned that from Peter."

THE CEO BRAND

The CEO works to shape the company, define and create new opportunities and realities, and make the organization leaner and more competitive. Of course, he or she also keeps in mind the importance of creating a legacy. When we think of the early days of the Ford Motor Company and IBM, we inevitably think of Henry Ford and Thomas Watson—even those of us who can't recall their first products.

Every CEO, whether at a small family company or a multinational, leaves an imprint. As I visit clients and gain a sense of the company's history, I'm often struck by how a particular CEO shapes the future of the company. For example, at Campbell's Soup there is the Dr. John Dorrance era—when condensed soup was invented and introduced to the mass market—and condensed soup remains the identity of the company today. There are others as well. There's the James McGowan era, when Campbell's expanded into key ingredients—chickens, mushrooms, tomatoes— and the philosophy of caring about every ingredient is ingrained in the culture today. There's the William B. Murphy era, when the company expanded internationally; the Gordon McGovern era of acquisitions, growth, and low profits; the David Johnson era of back to basics; the Dale Morrison era of revitalizing brands; and the Doug Conant era of revitalizing the business.

As the CEO nurtures and forms an organization's personality, inevitably his or her own personality, or brand, rubs off on the place. Peter saw this thumbprint as being of the utmost importance to the next generation's leading organizations. He wrote, "In the next society, the biggest challenge for the large company— especially for the multinational—may be its social legitimacy: its values, its mission, its vision."[6]

The cofounders of DLJ had a dream. Fundamental to that dream was that each person in the organization could create or enhance an opportunity. The culture was that of letting a thousand flowers bloom. Donaldson and Lufkin believed in hiring people with passion whom they liked. And they were role models on what you can do with a passion. Donaldson and Lufkin had a passion for doing great research in smaller companies with strong management. Jenrette's fingerprint was institutionalizing the idea of letting each person soar, while the firm grew. The 2000 Wetfeet.com guide to DLJ quotes an insider describing the job: "I actually have some control over what kinds of deals I work on. I can tell VPs I really want to work on this deal or work in a specific industry, and they try to make it happen." The site quotes a recruiter's insight as, "A low enthusiasm level is the kiss of death at DLJ." Jenrette described the culture he worked to cultivate and institutionalize: "It was important that everyone took pride in what he/she did and understood that you didn't have to be the CEO to do well. We always had at least a half-dozen people that were paid more than the CEO. We never had any contracts telling you in writing that you could not leave at year end. Each DLJ'er was responsible for putting in writing what he or she had accomplished and their goals for the coming year.

The CEO nurtures and forms an organization's personality.

"In the 70s, when the market was down, we did not lay anyone off. And we did not distribute under-valued options to executives." Indeed Jenrette had to sell his townhouse during those down years. But he remembers the feeling of determination that carried the company through difficult times "We were all in this together. We never quit having fun and doing what we thought was right for our customer."[7] (Think for a minute. Would *our* colleagues use those phrases?)

The personal risks and people bets paid off. Under Jenrette's leadership, the firm grew to just under 10,000 people. In the 1980s and 1990s, it had the lowest staff turnover rate of any Wall Street firm.

After leaving DLJ, Donaldson put his fingerprint on a number of organizations: The New York Stock Exchange, where, as chairman, he changed the fundamental focus of the enterprise, lengthened trading hours and opened up the Global Exchange; the Yale School of Management, which he helped found and then shape as the school's first dean; and Aetna, where he stepped in as chairman and turned the company around. More recently, Donaldson served 26 months as head of the SEC. Thanks to his action orientation, the SEC made more changes during his tenure than at anytime since 1929, including imposing hefty fines on corporate wrongdoers and granting increased independence to boards of mutual-fund companies.

When Frank Weise became the CEO of Cott Beverage, the leading provider of private label sodas—including Sam's Choice—he needed to very rapidly change the personality of the business. Weise stepped into the role in 1998 after the founder, Harry Pencer, had died, and the company was failing. Despite great products, it wasn't delivering on commitments. The company's relationships with customers were deteriorating because of persistent stock-outs and unfulfilled commitments. Cott was regarded as a company with great products and impressive selling skills, but one that constantly failed to deliver on its promises.

Frank is one of the nicest people I know. When I met him at an airport outside of Philadelphia, he went out of his way to introduce me to his mother and to make sure I knew my way around his local airport. I started consulting with him after he stepped into the turnaround position. Initially, I wasn't sure if he had the stomach to do what would be required to turn things around at the company.

I watched in amazement as he put his name on the line and showed a firm resolve to do what needed to be done. The senior executives all had stock options that they could have exercised for 12 months after the company changed hands at a value of about $9.00 per share. Six months later, when Frank became CEO, the stock was trading at $3. Shortly after he arrived at Cott, we had a conversation about which executives he could not afford to lose. There were two whose departure I felt might jeopardize the company short term. There was a tear in his eye as he confided that he expected to lose one of them, but he was confident that this potential loss would not keep him from doing what he felt was necessary to put integrity back into the company. He told senior executives that they would keep their jobs only if they demonstrated their confidence in the company by not cashing in their stock options. He lost six of the top eight executives, including one of the two I had identified. Frank shared with every customer what he was doing to make the company live up to its potential and restore its good name. He invested in operations, brought in a head of quality with Six Sigma experience, and put in tracking mechanisms that provided a daily snapshot of what was happening at every plant and with every buyer. The stock rose as high as $35 and settled in at around $25 before Frank retired in 2005. The CEO is the brand, and Frank knew it from the day he took over.

When things go badly, the CEO is responsible. He or she cannot say, "I didn't know."

Peter maintained that the CEO sets the tone in all ways. That includes ethical standards. The CEO can take some credit when business surges, when profits rise, when analysts recommend the stock. When things go badly, the CEO is responsible. He or she cannot say, "I didn't know."

The story of Peter Drucker's life and work is one of optimism, a belief in tomorrow, and a passion to help businesses and non-profits survive and excel. But in the 1990s, Peter became disenchanted with several companies and CEOs that seemed to reward greed rather than performance. Drucker made bold statements regarding the excessive riches awarded to mediocre executives. He stood up to the greed, saying, "It is morally and socially unforgivable to reap massive earnings while firing thousands of their workers."[8] He emphasized that companies are not just about profit. Leaders forgot their missions when they became obsessed with raking in profits and ratcheting up the stock price. Drucker viewed the corporation as a human community built on trust and respect for the customer and the worker and not just a profit-making machine. And to counter what he saw as a culture of short-term gain, he stepped up consulting work with nonprofits as well as the CEOs he believed in.

At a company, someone must be in charge. That is why we have CEOs.

In the final years of his life, Drucker was distressed to note that some bad players tarnished the image of the CEO. He would shake his head as he read about scandals at Enron and Arthur Andersen, scandals at Adelphi, scandals at WorldCom. Drucker felt personally betrayed. Not only did these cases reek of duplicity and misdeeds and outright lies, but what made them worse was that the people at the top often proclaimed that they were innocent because they didn't know what was going on. To Peter, that was a sin. At a company, someone must be in charge, which requires that he or she be both fully informed on every significant aspect of the business and accountable for what happens. That is the role of the CEO.

INFLUENCE ON PEOPLE— COLLECTIVELY AND INDIVIDUALLY

The impact CEOs can have on people, their actions and their lives, is unmatched. As Peter wrote to Bob Buford, the CEO of a cable television network in 1990, "As I tried to stress, your first role . . . is the personal one. It is the relationship with people, the development of mutual confidence, the identification of people, the creation of a community. This is something only you can do." Peter went on: "It cannot be measured or easily defined. But it is not only a key function. It is one only you can perform."9

With Peter's encouragement, DLJ changed the game by embracing a people policy fundamentally different from that of any other Wall Street firm. Peter helped design this policy and helped ensure that it was woven into the fabric of the firm and its orientation around people.

As Bill Donaldson remembered, "If we were going to spend as much time as we were going to in the business, we felt that it ought to be fun. And for it to be fun, we had to have a measure of people around us and with us that were good people that were great fun to be with, intellectually smart. In other words, we didn't think we had to get some hard-nosed person that we couldn't stand being with just for intelligence. We thought we could find intelligence with people who shared our values, and shared the sense of fun and building something.

"DLJ worked hard to create a collegial atmosphere where colleagues also considered each other friends—certainly not the convention at the time. On Wall Street, up until that time, everybody was on a commission basis. They were building their own little businesses; they were fighting for accounts, etc. We didn't do any of that. Nobody was on commission. Nobody had an account. They were all firm accounts. We evaluated what people did at the end of the year both by them telling us what they thought they'd done during that year, as well as what we thought, as well as what our customers thought. Based on that, the compensation and rewards and so forth were allocated. It was sort of a total triangulation of evaluation. That made for teamwork. It allowed members of the firm to say that the fellow in the office next door really helped him, you know, and we rewarded that. And so we created an atmosphere, or DNA, if you will, at Donaldson, Lufkin & Jenrette that existed for over 40 years."[10]

Vision, organizational personality, and influence take uncertainty out of the future in the twenty-first century.

And Dick Jenrette noted, "Peter harped on how important people were and are. We had a number of organizational structures that played to the concept that the people were our most important asset. Peter also encouraged us to think of our employees as a volunteer organization would think of their volunteers."[11]

The human policy that DLJ had was built on themes only a CEO could define and make real—and in the case of DLJ it took three CEOs to turn the words into a thriving organizational personality.

Each of these characteristics—vision, organizational personality, and influence—needs to be understood, and nourished. None of them can be assumed. Field of vision requires listening and looking—not telling. It requires regular eye checkups and allocating

> The CEO's impact is also seen in how what he or she says or does is interpreted and translated into action, how it becomes part of the enterprise's personality. Soon after Richard Block became president of AGI (Album Graphics Incorporated, a media artwork company), he visited the company facility in Melrose Park, Illinois. It is the largest plant and houses a significant group of its management team. After touring the plant, he commented to the plant manager, "Why is there a window in the plant? Couldn't that harm some of the art work?" The next time he visited Melrose Park, about a month later, every window in the building, office and plant had been cemented over. He learned quickly the impact a CEO can have on actions. Understanding that power, Richard put it to good use, spending the next 20 years building an organization and culture that would challenge him and others to make the right decisions. AGI rose to become the number one media graphic supplier in the world, prior to its being sold to a venture capitalist.

time to step back and interpret what you are seeing, perhaps the hardest part for a CEO. Personality means looking in the mirror, checking translations and amplifications, and recognizing that you are always a role model. Influence requires respecting people and treating the organization as a living entity that needs care and feeding. Each of these characteristics—vision, organizational personality, and influence—takes uncertainty out of the future in the twenty-first century. That is what a CEO—and only a CEO—can do.

EACH OF US AS CEO

What can the self-managing knowledge worker learn from these three characteristics as CEO of his or her own career? Maintaining a broad field of vision requires having a sense of where you are going and what you are building. It is the same for individuals, or a company with one knowledge worker, as it is for a grand enterprise employing thousands. One of my clients

had a great analogy: "Have you ever been driving behind the eld-
erly lady who is looking three feet in front of her at a time? She
starts, and stops, and swerves. Compare that with a race-car
driver who is looking at the whole track as well as feeling the
immediate ground beneath her car." That is the difference in
vision in your career—are you going one step at a time, or being
the broader landscape. We have to place bets on ourselves, learn,
and bet again. To make the greatest contributions, we have to put
our heart and mind into it and be able to respond to the unexpected opportunities.

Peter maintained that this ability to see the whole and its
immediate challenges and opportunities simultaneously requires a
self-knowledge that most of us don't have. We need to know our
strengths, our values, and our passions, and we have to admit to
our arrogance. Knowing our true strengths requires a sometimes
painful level of consciousness. In Peter's world we must "ask,
check, and see." Here's one of his techniques for maintaining this
orientation only few of us have: Whenever you make a key decision or take action, write down what you expect will happen.
Then look back at it six to nine months later and compare what
happened to your expectations. Ask people to exercise this form
of self-discipline every day. Try to use your strengths in your work
and your connections. Get feedback concerning where and how
your strengths work and connect.

The second characteristic—organizational personality or
brand—is about knowing yourself and what gives you passion (or,
on the contrary, what puts you to sleep). As Peter so often
reminded former students, working in an organization whose
value system is unacceptable or incompatible with your own con-
demns you to frustration and to lackadaisical performance. He
told me the story of a woman who was the daughter of a promi-
nent banker, had majored in finance, and always assumed she

would be a financial adviser. When she began her career, she was miserable. Two years later, she was an administrator in a hospital having the time of her life. She had to learn what gave her passion to unlock her willingness to leave a thumbprint. At one point during that conversation, Peter commented that he thought finance never really interested David Rockefeller. As CEO of the Chase Manhattan Bank, Rockefeller was known for his people skills and unique ability to relate to customers. He could open doors to any company in any country. During a meeting at Chase, Rockefeller would inquire about the client's entire family (including pets) by name and birthday. But he did not seem to take an active interest in the day-to-day management of the bank. After retiring from Chase, he was free to stop doing what he was not interested in and could pursue his passion for serving and working with people through philanthropy.

Knowledge workers have to learn to ask a question that has not been asked before: What should I contribute?

As Peter wrote in 1999, "Throughout history, the great majority of people never had to ask the question, what should I contribute? They were told what to contribute, and their tasks were dictated either by the work itself—as it was for the peasant or artisan—or by a master or a mistress."[12] Knowledge workers have to learn to ask a question that has not been asked before: What should I contribute? And to answer that question they need to understand and meld their strengths and passions, and they repeatedly have to ask themselves the fundamental Drucker question: "If I were not in this career today, would I have gotten into it? If not, what am I going to do about it?"

Finally, the knowledge worker is both influenced by and influences others. We are influenced by the CEO—the premier role model who lives the purpose, values, and principles of the organization. That influence can and should be inspiring and transformative. Peter always said that if we are going to be passionate about our jobs, we must get the right signals from the top. We are also influenced by our individual passion and strengths. And, throughout our careers, we influence those many other knowledge workers with whom we connect.

The CEO has to live the purpose, the values, and the principles of the organization.

Successful careers are not planned; they are managed. And to manage them, we need to put on our CEO hat. The way we manage our careers—switch from company to company, or become consultants or contractors, or start our own business—will be the next revolution. Managing your own life and career takes courage. We have to take calculated risks as individuals if we are going to make the most out of the cards we've been given to play in life. These days, we are not simply salaried employees. We are collaborators, and we all need to think like a CEO.

Peter said it years ago: "Each of us is a CEO." As the CEO managing his own career, Peter Drucker was quite clear on what he wished his legacy to be. During one of our last conversations, he told me that he wanted to be remembered for one single accomplishment: "Enabling a few people to get the right things done. I mean that literally. I think the specific concepts for which most people know me, management by objectives, or what have you, are of very limited importance. My contribution, such as it is, is to create . . . no, not create . . . to highlight the concept of the responsible and effective executive of management as work and function and responsibility. The traditional definition of a manager is somebody who's got subordinates. My contribution is the definition of a manager as somebody who has results. That's very different. And it is not generally accepted. Most organizations staff their problems and starve their opportunities. And one of the things I'm good at is to counteract. And when people begin to start talking about problems, I say, 'No, wait a minute. Let's first look at the opportunities.' Those are my contributions. I try to make them look forward instead of backward. Opportunities have a habit of asserting themselves. As things collapse, you can't say, 'I'm busy.'"

> Peter said it years ago:
> "Each of us is a CEO."

Peter's last words to me were: "OK. I'm getting tired, and that's one thing I'm not allowed to do. Come back. I'll be here. I'm not going anyplace." He has left our physical world, but kept his promise to "be there"—his influence is embedded in our management past, our management present, and our management future.

ENDNOTES

Introduction

1. Jim Collins, dinner speech at The Drucker Legacy, Claremont, CA, May 2006.

2. Peter F. Drucker, *The End of the Economic Man* (New Brunswick, NJ, and London: Transaction Publishers, 2004), p. 59.

3. Peter F. Drucker, *The Future of Industrial Man* (New Brunswick, NJ, and London: Transaction Publishers, 2002).

4. Elizabeth Haas Edersheim, "What Industrial Policy," *Across the Board*, March/April 2005.

5. Peter F. Drucker, "Henry Ford: Success and Failure," *Harpers Magazine*, July 1947.

6. Frances Hesselbein, interview with author, 2004 and 2006.

7. Peter F. Drucker, interview with author, 2004.

8. Walter Wriston, interview with author, 2004.

9. Cornelius deKluyver, interview with author, 2005.

10. Peter F. Drucker, *The New Realities* (New York: Harper & Row, 1989).

11. Peter F. Drucker, "The New Society of Organizations," *Harvard Business Review*, September–October 1992, Reprint 92503.

12. Warren Bennis, interview with author, 2004; Warren Bennis, "The Invention of Management," *Directors & Boards*, Winter 1982.

Chapter 1

1. Peter F. Drucker, interview with author, 2004; Peter F. Drucker, "The Theory of Business," *Harvard Business Review*, September-October 1994, Reprint 94506

2. Lynda Obst, "We Lost It at the Movies," *New York Magazine*, May 1, 2006.

3. Anne Cushman, "Fifteen Weeks of Dharma Dating," *Tricycle: The Buddhist Review*, Summer 2006.

4. Stanley Reed, "Why You Should Worry about Big Oil," *BusinessWeek*, May 15, 2006, p. 68; Lola Naya, "India, China bid for oil firm," *The Times of India*, May 5, 2006. http://www.uofaweb.ualberta.ca/CMS/printpage.cfm?ID=45737.

5. Peter F. Drucker, interview with author, 2005.

6. Phillip E Ross, "Microsoft's Identity Crisis," *IEESpectrum*, October 2005, p. 45.

7. http://pages.stern.nyu.edu/~ADAMODAR/New.Home-Page/data.html.

Chapter 2

1. Peter F. Drucker, *The Practice of Management*, (New York: HarperCollins, 1986), p. 37; Peter F. Drucker, interview with author, 2004.

2. Peter F. Drucker, interview with author, 2004.

3. Robert E. Herzstein and Henry R. Luce, *A Political Portrait of the Man Who Created the American Century* (New York: Charles Scribner's Sons, 1994), p. 56.

4. Ibid., p. 61.

5. Peter F. Drucker, *Managing for Results* (New York: Harper & Row, 1964); Peter F. Drucker, interview with author, 2004.

6. Peter F. Drucker, interview with author, 2004.

7. Peter F. Drucker, *Managing for Results* (New York: Harper & Row, 1964), p. 123.

8. Mylene Mangalindan and Robert A. Guth, "eBay Talks to Microsoft, Yahoo about a Common Foe: Google," *Wall Street Journal*, April 21, 2006.

9. Bill Donaldson, interview with Ken Witty, 1999.

10. Colgate-Palmolive executive, interview with author, 2004.

11. Tom Krazit, "Intel Builds $400 Laptop for School Desks Worldwide," CNET News.com, May 3, 2006.62.

12. http://about.skype.com/2005/11/ebay—completes—acquisition—of.html.

13. *Wall Street Journal* staff reporter, "Skype Reports Subscriber Growth," *Wall Street Journal*, October 26, 2005, online edition.

14. AT&T 2004 10-K, October 21, 2005, transcript of third quarter 2005 AT&T earnings conference call.

15. In the 1940s, psychologist Abraham Maslow formulated a theory of a hierarchy of needs that motivate individuals, with the most basic needs for food and shelter at the bottom of the pyramid and psychological needs such as mastery, fulfillment, and security nearer the top. Abraham Maslow, "A Theory of Human Motivation," *Psychological Review* 50 (1943), pp. 370–396.

16. Nova Spivack, interview with author, 2006

17. "Forethought," Harvard Business Review, April 2006, p. 21; "Regional Economy," NY.frb.org, 7/1/06.

18. Colgate-Palmolive executive, interview with author, 2003.

19. Andrew M. Odlyzko, *Internet Traffic Growth: Sources and Implications*, (Minneapolis: University of Minnesota, 2003), pp. 4–5. http://www.dtc.umn.edu/~odlyzko/doc/itcom.internet.growth.pdf.

20. UPS.com/pressroom/US/press-releases/press-release.

21. A.G. Lafley, interview with author, 2005.

22. Durk Jager, P&G 1999 annual report.

23. Drucker at P&G, April 1999, transcription from tapes.

24. P&G 2000 annual report.

25. A.G. Lafley, interview with author, 2005.

26. Ibid.

27. Ibid.

28. John Anderson Miller, *Men and Volts at War* (New York: Whittlesey House, a division of the McGraw-Hill Book Company, Inc., 1947).

29. Patricia Sellers, "P&G: Teaching an Old Dog New Tricks," *Fortune*, May 17, 2004, online edition.

30. Katrina Brooker, "Procter & Gamble: The Un-CEO," *Fortune*, September 3, 2002, online edition.

31. A.G. Lafley, interview with author, 2005.

32. Gary Silverman, "How May I Help You?" *Financial Times*, February 4–5, 2006.

33. Indrajit Gupta, "Why P&G declared war," *Business World*, March 29, 2004, online edition, www.businessworldindia.com/mar2904/coverstory02.asp.

34. Arnold Corbin, Tony H. Bonaparte, and John E. Flaherty, eds., "The Impact of Drucker on Marketing," *Peter Drucker: Contributions to Business Enterprise* (New York: New York University Press, 1970), p. 147.

35. As quoted in, "Farewell, Peter Drucker: A Tribute to an Intellectual Giant, Strategic Management," from: http://knowledge.Wharton.upenn.edu/article/ 1326.cfm.

36. Ibid.

37. http://leadertoleader.com/leaderbooks/kotler/ondrucker.html.

Chapter 3

1. Peter F. Drucker, *The Age of Discontinuity* (New York: Harper & Row, 1968); interview with author, 2004.

2. Peter F. Drucker, *Adventures of a Bystander* (New Brunswick, NJ: Transaction Publishers, 1994).

3. William Bulkeley, "Boss Talk, Back from the Brink, Mulcahy Leads a Renaissance at Xerox by Emphasizing Color, Customers and Costs," *Wall Street Journal*, April 24, 2006.

4. Jim Collins, *Good to Great: Why Some Companies Make the Leap and Others Don't* (New York: Harper Business, 2001); Kimberly-Clark 2004 annual report.

5. Peter F. Drucker, interview with author, 2004.

6. Mark Henricks, "Letting Go," *Entrepreneur*, February 2000.

7. Peter F. Drucker, *The Effective Executive* (New York: HarperCollins, 2002), p. 108.

8. Peter Drucker, interview with John Goberman, *Live at Lincoln Center*. This interview was conducted in 1995 for an episode of "Backstage\Lincoln Center."

9. Peter F. Drucker, interview with Ken Witty, 1999.

10. A.G. Lafley, interview with author, 2005.

11. Wade Roush, "Google Pledges Transparency, Debuts New Gadgets," *Technology Review*, May 11, 2006, p. 1.

12. Peter F. Drucker, *Managing for Results* (New York: Harper & Row, 1964).

13. Hisato Doi of the Druckerian Society of Japan, interview with author, 2005.

14. P. K. Prahalad, Fortune Innovation Conference, November 2004.

15. David Neeleman, Chairman and CEO, and Dave Barger, President and COO, JetBlue Airways, "2004 Letter to Stockholders," http://64.106.229.11/jetblue2004/copy/letter.html JetBlue.com.

16. CheckFree Analytic Services, The Marketing Workshop, and Harris Interactive, "More Than Half of U.S. Online Households Pay at Least One Bill Online, According to CheckFree Survey," November 16, 2005. Checkfreecorp.com/pressreleases.

17. School of Dental Hygiene, University of Manitoba, Canada, "Interesting Facts and Trivia about Toothpaste,"www.umanitoba.ca/outreach/wisdomtooth/ toothpaste.htm.

18. "History of Crest," www.pg.com./company/who_we_are/crest_history.jhtml.

19. Linda Grant, "Out Marketing P&G," *Fortune—European Edition*, January 12, 1998, pp. 68-70.

20. Manjeet Kripalani and Pete Engardio, "Small Is Profitable," *BusinessWeek Online*, August 26, 2002, www.businessweek.com/print/magazine/content/02_ 34/b3796626.htm?chan=mz.

21. Peter F. Drucker, interview with author, 2004.

22. Peter F Drucker, interview with author, 2005.

23. Peter F. Drucker, *The Age of Discontinuity* (New Brunswick, NJ and London: Transaction Publishers, 2003), pp. 56, 57.

24. Peter F. Drucker, *Management: Tasks, Responsibilities, Practices,* (New York: HarperBusiness, 1993), p. 794; interview with author, 2005.

25. Armapreet Dhiman, "Pharmaceutical and Biotechnology Companies Adopt Outsourcing Practices to Combat Rising Costs," Frost & Sullivan Press Release, November 23, 2005.

26. Thomas Alva Edison as quoted on GE.com.

27. David Loth, *Swope of GE: The Story of Gerard Swope and General Electric in American Business* (New York: Simon & Schuster, 1958), p. 173.

28. Jack Welch with John A. Byrne, *Jack: Straight from the Gut* (New York: Warner Books, 2001); Jack Welch, interview with author, 2004.

29. Peter F. Drucker, interviews with author, 2004 and 2005.

30. Harvard Business School case 9-399-150, rev.: May 3, 2005.

31. Jerry Useem, "Another Boss, Another Revolution, Jeff Immelt is following a time-honored GE tradition: abandoning the most treasured ideas of his predecessor," *Fortune Online edition* April 5, 2004, http://money.cnn.com/magazines/fortune/fortune_archive/ 2004/04/05/366351/index.htm.

32. Drucker at P&G, April 1999, transcription from tapes.

33. Diane Brady, "The Immelt Revolution,"*Business Week online edition*, March 28, 2005, www.businessweek.com/magazine/ content/05_13/b3926088_mz056. htm?chart=search.

34. Brent Schlender, "The New Soul of a Wealth Machine," *Fortune Online edition*, April 5, 2004, http://money.cnn.com/magazines/ fortune/fortune_archive/ 2004/04/05/366370/index.htm.

35. Claudia H. Deutsch, "Instant Infrastructure," *New York Times,* July 16, 2005.

36. Peter F. Drucker, *Managing for Results* (New York: Harper & Row, 1964), p. 136.

37. John Byrne, "How Jack Welch Runs GE," *Business Week* (Archives*)*, June 8, 1998, www.businessweek.com/1998/23/b3581001.htm.

38. Harvard Business School case 9-602-061, rev.: March 18, 2002.

39. Gail E. Schares, Jonathan B. Levine, and Peter Coy, "The New Generation at Siemens," *Business Week online edition*, March 9, 1992, www.businessweek.com/archives/1992/b325545.arc.htm.

40. Dinah Deckstein, "Kulturschock in München," *Der Spiegel Online,*" November 7, 2005, http://www.spiegel.de/spiegel/o,1518,383428,00.html.

41. Abrahm Lustgarten, "Remaking a German Giant with American-Style Tactics," *Fortune Online edition*, August 1, 2006.

Chapter 4

1. Peter F. Drucker, *The Age of Discontinuity* (New Brunswick, NJ, and London: Transaction Publishers, 2003), pp. 178–179.

2. http://www.nationalmssociety.org/faq.asp.

3. Ibid.

4. Scott Johnson, interview with author, 2005 and 2006.

5. Gene J. Koprowski, "Dell Moves Beyond Its Computing Roots," *TechNewsWorld.com/story/32125.html,* 11/13/03.

6. Steve Hamm, "Linux Inc.," *BusinessWeek,* January 31, 2005; http://www.netfiles.uiuc.edu/rhasan/linux/.

7. Peter F. Drucker, interview with author, 2005.

Chapter 5

1. Peter F. Drucker, interview with author, 2004.

2. Jim Collins, dinner speech at The Drucker Legacy, May 2006.

3. Paul O'Neill, discussion with author, 2006; Paul O'Neill speech at The Drucker Legacy, May 2006.

4. U.S. Department of Labor Bureau of Labor Statistics Occupational Employment Statistics 2005, see http://data.bls.gov/ oes/areatype.

5. Peter F. Drucker, "The American CEO," *Wall Street Journal,* December 30, 2004, p. A8.

6. Peter F. Drucker, interview with author, 2004.

7. Harvard Business School case 9-705-476, June 9, 2005; Robert Levering, Geoff Colvin, "The 100 Best Companies to Work for 2006," *Fortune,* January 11, 2005, http://money.cnn.com/ magazines/fortune/fortune_archive/2006/01/23/ 8366990/index.htm.

8. Peter F. Drucker, "Getting Things Done: How to Make People Decisions," *Harvard Business Review,* July–August 1985, Reprint 85406.

9. MIT Alumni Meeting, New York, March, 2004, a discussion following the meeting.

10. Peter F. Drucker, "They're Not Employees, They're People," *Harvard Business Review,* February 2002, Reprint R0202E; Peter F. Drucker, interview with author, 2004.

11. Peter F. Drucker, *The Future of Industrial Man* (New Brunswick, NJ, and London: Transaction Publishers, 2002).

12. Francis Hesselbein, interview with author, 2005.

13. Warren Bennis and Patricia Ward Biederman, *Organizing Genius: The Secrets of Creative Collaboration* (Cambridge, MA: Perseus Books, 1997).

14. Ibid.

15. Frank Delany, "History of the Microcomputer Revolution, Segment 13—'A Walk in the PARC,'" *Raw Bytes Computer News*, National Public Radio, May 10, 1995.

16. Peter F. Drucker, *People and Performance*, (New York: Harper & Row, 1977); Peter Drucker, interview with author, 2005.

17. Marvin Bower, "Control and Conformity in the Firm," memo to McKinsey & Company U.S. consulting staff, April 7, 1966.

18. Jim Collins, interview with author, 2005; The Drucker Foundation, *Wisdom to Action Series* (San Francisco: Jossey-Bass, 1999).

19. Peter F. Drucker, interview with author, 2004.

20. Bill Pollard, interview with author, 2005.

21. Warren Bennis and Patricia Ward Biederman, *Organizing Genius: The Secrets of Creative Collaboration* (Cambridge, MA: Perseus Books, 1997), p. 78.

22. Ibid., p. 18.

23. Jim Collins, interview with author, 2005; Frances Hesselbein, Marshall Goldsmith, Iain Somerville, eds., *Leading beyond the Walls*, The Drucker Foundation, *Wisdom to Action Series*, (San Francisco: Jossey-Bass, 1999).

24. Peter F. Drucker, interview with author, 2004.

25. Steven J. Spear, "Fixing Health Care from the Inside, Today," *Harvard Business Review*, September 2005, Volume 83, Number 9, pp. 78-91.

26. Electrolux 2005 annual report.

27. Kerry Capell, Heidi Dawley, Ariane Sains, and William Echickson, "What Does a Knife Do When the Cutting's Done?" *BusinessWeek international online edition*, September 18, 2000.

28. Hans Stråberg, interview with author, 2006.

29. Ibid.

30. Lester Thurow, "Help Wanted: A Chief Knowledge Officer," *Fast Company*, January 2004, Issue 78, Page 91.

31. Peter F. Drucker, interview with author, 2005.

32. Bill Pollard, interview with author, 2005.

33. Charles Baldwin, "Training Leaders to Lead," by Marcus Luft, Honeycomb Worldwide Inc., May 20, 2004, quoting Charles Baldwin, VP Corp of people development at Wal-Mart.

34. "Reviewing and Revising Wal-Mart's Benefits Strategy," memorandum to the board of directors from Susan Chambers, *walmarttwatch.com*.

35. eBay 2004 Form 10-K (annual report required by the SEC), http://investor.ebay.com/downloads/2004AnnualReport/f06732h1e1

0vk.htm; Hani Durzy, director of corporate communications, eBay Inc., e-mails with author, 2006.

36. Beth Axelrod, interview with author, 2006.

37. John Bachmann, interview with author, 2004.

38. Ibid.

39. Measured as pretax return on equity since Jones is a partnership.

40. Peter Cohan, "Value from Values: Introducing the Concept of Value Leadership," *Babson Insight e-magazine,* www.Babsoninsight.com/contentmgr/ showdetails.php/id/611.

41. John Bachmann, interview with author, 2005.

42. John Bachmann, interview with author, 2005.

43. Edward Jones, March 2006, Form 10 K, Part I, p. 3, http:// premium.hoovers.com/subscribe/co/secdoc.xhtml?ID=40868& ipage=3372701&doc=1.

44. Edwardjones.com.

45. Eric Schmidt and Hal Varian, "Google: Ten Golden Rules," *Newsweek,* December 2, 2005.

46. Peter F. Drucker, *People and Performance* (New York: Harper & Row, 1977).

Chapter 6

1. Peter F. Drucker, *The Effective Executive* (New York: HarperCollins, 2002), p. 143; interview with author, 2005.

2. Peter F. Drucker, American Management Association interview, 1982.

3. Peter F. Drucker, *The Effective Executive* (New York: HarperCollins, 2002), p. 155.

4. Peter F. Drucker, American Management Association interview, 1982.

5. Ibid.

6. Ibid.

7. Ibid.

8. Peter F. Drucker, interview with author 2004.

9. Peter F. Drucker, *The Effective Executive* (New York: HarperCollins, 2002), extracted from pp. 16 and 17 and interview with author, 2004.

10. Peter F. Drucker, *Managing for Results* (New York: Harper & Row, 1964).

11. Joe Pereira, retired head of Quality Clairol, interview with author, 2004.

12. Peter F. Drucker, *The Effective Executive* (New York: HarperCollins, 2002), extracted from pp. 113–118.

13. Maynard, Michelle, and James Brooke, "Toyota Closes in on G.M.: Signs Point toward Japanese Maker Being the Top Seller Soon," *New York Times*, December 21, 2005, p. C1.

14. http://money.cnn.com/magazines/fortune/global500/2005/index.html.

15. Taiichi Ohno, *Toyota Production System: Beyond Large-Scale Production* (Portland, Oregon: Productivity Press, 1978), p. 17.

16. Jeffrey K. Liker, *The Toyota Way: 14 Management Principles from the World's Greatest Manufacturer* (New York: McGraw-Hill, 2004), p. 3.

17. Peter F. Drucker, *Adventurers of a Bystander* (New Brunswick, NJ: Transaction Publishers, 1994), pp. 286-287.

Chapter 7

1. Peter F. Drucker, "Managing Oneself," *Harvard Business Review*, March–April 1999, HBR OnPoint, product number 4444, pp. 65-74; Peter. F. Drucker, "The American CEO," *Wall Street Journal*, December 30, 2004; Peter F. Drucker, interview with author, 2005.

2. Peter F. Drucker, *The Age of Discontinuity* (New York: Harper & Row, 1968).

3. Louise Amell (Hans Werthen's daughter), interview with author, 2002.

4. Peter F. Drucker, "The Theory of the Business," *Harvard Business Review*, September–October 1994, Reprint 94506, pp. 95-104.

5. Robert Sobel, *A History of the New York Stock Exchange 1935-1975* (New York: Weybright and Talley, 1975).

6. Peter F. Drucker, *Managing in the Next Society* (New York: Truman Talley Books, St. Martin Press, 2002), p. 150.

7. Richard Jenrette, interview with author, 2006.

8. Donaldson, interview with Ken Witty, 2000; interview with author, 2006.

9. Bob Buford, interview with author, 2005.

10. Donaldson, interview with author, 2006.

11. Richard Jenrette, interview with author, 2006.

12. Peter F. Drucker, "Managing Oneself," *Harvard Business Review*, March–April 1999, HBR OnPoint, product number 444, pp. 65-74; interview with author, 2004.

BOOKS BY PETER F. DRUCKER
LISTED BY ORIGINAL PUBLICATION DATE

Germanicus, *Germany The Last Four Years** (Boston and New York: The Houghton Mifflin Company, 1937).

Peter F. Drucker, *The End of Economic Man: The Origins of Totalitarianism* (New York, London: The John Day Company, 1939).

Peter F. Drucker, *The Future of Industrial Man* (New York: The John Day Company, 1942).

Peter F. Drucker, *Concept of the Corporation* (New York: The John Day Company, 1946).

Peter F. Drucker, *The New Society: The Anatomy of Industrial Order* (New York: Harper & Brothers, 1950).

Peter F. Drucker, *The Practice of Management* (New York: Harper & Brothers, 1954).

Peter F. Drucker, *America's Next Twenty Years* (New York: Harper & Brothers, 1955).

Peter F. Drucker, *Landmarks of Tomorrow: A Report on the New "Post-Modern" World* (New York: Harper & Row, 1957).

Peter F. Drucker, *Technology, Management and Society* (New York and Evanston, IL: Harper & Row, 1958).

Peter F. Drucker, *Power and Democracy in America** (Notre Dame, IN: University of Notre Dame Press, 1961).

Peter F. Drucker, *Managing for Results* (New York: Harper & Row, 1964).

Peter F. Drucker, *The Effective Executive* (New York: Harper & Row, 1967).

Peter F. Drucker, *The Age of Discontinuity: Guidelines to Our Changing Society* (New York: Harper & Row, 1968).

Peter F. Drucker, ed., *Preparing Tomorrow's Business Leaders Today** (Englewood Cliffs, NJ: Prentice-Hall, 1969).

Peter F. Drucker, *Men, Ideas and Politics: Essays*, similar to *The New Markets . . . and Other Essays* (New York: Harper & Row, 1971).

Peter F. Drucker, *Drucker on Management* (London: Management Publications Limited, 1971).

Peter F. Drucker, *The New Markets . . . and Other Essays,* similar to *Men, Ideas and Politics: Essays* (London: William Heinemann Ltd., 1971).

Peter F. Drucker, *Management: Tasks, Responsibilities, Practices* (New York: Harper & Row, 1973).

Peter F. Drucker, *The Unseen Revolution—How Pension Fund Socialism Came to America* (New York: Harper & Row, 1976).

Peter F. Drucker, *An Introductory View of Management* (New York: Harper & Row, 1977).

Peter F. Drucker, *Management Cases** (New York: Harper's College Press, 1977).

Peter F. Drucker, *People and Performance: The Best of Peter Drucker on Management* (New York: Harper & Row, 1977).

Peter F. Drucker, *Adventures of a Bystander* (New York: John Wiley & Sons, Inc., 1978).

Essay by Peter F. Drucker, John M. Rosenfield, Ed., *Song of the Brush: Japanese Painting from the Sanso Collection,** An exhibition organized by Henry Trubner, William J. Rathburn, (Seattle: Seattle Art Museum, 1979).

Peter F. Drucker, *Managing in Turbulent Times* (New York: Harper & Row, 1980).

Peter F. Drucker, *Toward the Next Economics and Other Essays* (New York: Harper & Row, 1981).

Peter F. Drucker, *The Changing World of the Executive* (New York: Truman Talley Books–Times Books, 1982).

Peter F. Drucker, *The Last of All Possible Worlds*** (New York: Harper & Row, 1982).

Peter F. Drucker, *The Temptation to Do Good* (New York: Harper & Row, 1984).

Peter F. Drucker, *Innovation and Entrepreneurship* (New York: Harper & Row, 1985).

Peter F. Drucker, *The Frontiers of Management* (New York: Truman Talley Books/E. P. Dutton, 1986).

Peter F. Drucker, *The New Realities* (New York: Harper & Row, 1989).

Peter F. Drucker, *Managing the Non-Profit Organization* (New York: HarperCollins, 1990).

Peter F. Drucker, *Managing for the Future: The 1990s and Beyond* (New York: Truman Talley Books/E. P. Dutton, 1992).

Peter F. Drucker, *Post-Capitalist Society* (New York: HarperBusiness, 1993).

Peter F. Drucker, *The Ecological Vision* (New Brunswick, NJ, and London: Transaction Publishers, 1993).

Peter F. Drucker and Isao Nakauchi, *Drucker on Asia—A Dialogue between Peter Drucker and Isao Nakauchi (aka Chosen No Toki)* (Diamond Inc., 1995 in Japanese; Oxford: Elsevier Butterworth Heinemann, 1997 in English).

Peter F. Drucker, *Managing in a Time of Great Change* (New York: Truman Talley Books, 1995).

Peter F. Drucker, *The Executive in Action: Managing for Results, Innnovation and Entrepreneurship, the Effective Executive* (New York: HarperBusiness, 1996).

Peter F. Drucker, *Peter Drucker on the Profession of Management* (Boston: Harvard Business School Publishing, 1998).

Peter F. Drucker, *Management Challenges for the 21st Century* (New York: HarperBusiness, 1999).

Peter F. Drucker, *The Essential Drucker: In One Volume the Best of Sixty Years of Peter Drucker's Essential Writings on Management* (New York: HarperBusiness, 2001).

Peter F. Drucker, *Managing in the Next Society* (New York: Truman Talley Books/St. Martin's Press, 2002).

Peter F. Drucker, *A Functioning Society: Selections from Sixty-Five Years of Writing on Community, Society and Policy* (New Brunswick, NJ, and London: Transaction Publishers, 2003).

Peter F. Drucker with Joseph A. Maciariello, *The Daily Drucker* (New York: HarperBusiness, 2004).

Peter F. Drucker and Joseph A. Maciariello, *The Effective Executive in Action* (New York: HarperCollins, 2006).

Peter F. Drucker, *Classic Drucker: Wisdom from Peter Drucker from the Pages of Harvard Business Review* (Boston: Harvard Business Review Press, 2006).

*Peter Drucker edited or contributed chapters or essays to this book.
**Nonbusiness book.

ACKNOWLEDGMENTS

I am past, present, and future indebted to Peter Ferdinand Drucker for inviting me out to California in April 2004 for what would become the first of our many visits. Peter overlooked my initial ungainly attempts to distill his ideas for the twenty-first-century manager. Instead, he patiently, tactfully, and engagingly answered my questions, while helping to fact-check the manuscript. During the writing of this book, Peter had two pieces of advice, which I attempted to follow: First: "In synthesizing my ideas for the twenty-first century, you must do so as if you were the CEO of Drucker, Inc.—that is, question the whole of my work and let go of what has turned out to be misdirected, is no longer relevant, resultless, or just plain wrong"; second: "Don't get caught up in the theoretical, stay with the actual. There is a lot that has already happened."

Thank you, Peter, for liberating me, for allowing me to step out of my comfort zone, for helping me to challenge my assumptions, and to raise my expectations.

I also want to express heartfelt thanks . . .

To the many Drucker clients, friends, students, and coworkers who graciously shared their Peter stories with me. They breathed life into my interpretation of Peter's wide range of ideas. They provided perspectives of Peter the mentor, who changed each of their lives. He asked each of them to think, to play to their strengths, to do what is right. They taught me how he helped each of them clarify their ambition and embark on journeys to places and accomplishments they never thought they'd see.

To my friends Mark McClusky and Robin Esterson, who shared with me how simply reading Peter's ideas changed and enhanced their lives.

To my clients and partners over the years who educated me by being living examples of Drucker doctrines. To my friend and adviser, Arnoldo Hax, for helping me understand the business needs of today.

To the many colleagues and friends who helped me navigate through my emotions, insights, frustrations, and challenges: Joe Maciariello and Kerry Boyle, for helping me through the Claremont world, the Drucker archives, and just enjoying coffee in California; Nan Stone, for helping me understand the map and gain insight from her experiences as I was getting started, and repeatedly as I made my frantic phone calls to her office and home; Cecily Drucker, who in one call explained the inner workings of the Drucker household to me, and later took the time to be the "outsider" with inside blood reading a draft and offering suggestions; and Alice Martell, who quickly secured a contract with an excited team at McGraw-Hill.

To the team of editors, writers, researchers, and friends who read and contributed to countless versions of many of these chapters. Joan Wilson helped me get the words down the first time. Jeanne Glasser saw the potential of this project. Cheryl Hudson worked endlessly getting the pages ready for production. Jasmine Cresswell exhorted me during the revisions. Leah Spiro showed me how to rewrite. David Marcus, now at *Newsday*, made me write a story; every time I didn't, he called me on it. Paige Siempelkamp and Don Penny took photographs, designed pages, fixed computers, and read into the night. Jackie Barry, Mel Furman, Jim Wade, and Sara Roche never got tired of giving me feedback. Violet Edersheim said, "This is not bad, it just needs a little bit of translation," and then went to work translating. Ellen Harvey and David Meyer fact-checked, compiled, researched, drafted anecdotes, and proofed every detail. Herb Schaffner brought his verve to the project at McGraw-Hill.

I am especially indebted to Louise Amell, Atsuo Ueda, and T George Harris. This book would not exist without the significant contributions and global reminders of Louise, the challenges and Druckerian perspectives of Ueda-san, and the constant flow of encouragement and anecdotes from George.

To my father, Felix Haas, who shared the importance of a global perspective, allowed me to understand a Viennese critic's view of the world, and stressed the necessity of intellectual honesty since my childhood. And to my mother, Violet Haas, who showed me the power of not being afraid to tackle important challenges and who shared Peter's very fundamental belief that every person deserves respect.

And finally, to Alvin and Violet, who understood every time I said, "Just one more chapter," and then, "Just one more week," and even encouraged me to keep at it while we lived out of boxes waiting to be unpacked. I hope my generation leaves you a world with ethical, innovative companies that create opportunities while sharing your love of the environment and your sense of what's right.

Art credits

INDEX

Index

Index

Index

Index

Index

ABOUT THE AUTHOR

Elizabeth Haas Edersheim is a strategic consultant who works both with Fortune 500 companies and private equity investors. Prior to founding her own firm, New York Consulting Partners, Edersheim was one of the first female partners at McKinsey & Company. Her previous book, *McKinsey's Marvin Bower*, illustrates the business life and ideals of the founder of McKinsey, her mentor, who was a close friend and peer of Dr. Drucker. Aside from her numerous publications, Dr. Haas Edersheim has provided expert testimony to the U.S. Congress on Industrial Networking and Industrial Manufacturing policy. She holds a Ph.D. in Operations Research and Industrial Engineering from the Massachusetts Institute of Technology.

For more information visit www.definitivedrucker.com